D0554388

American River College Library
4700 College Oak Drive
Sacramento, CA 95841

SHOOTERS

SHOOTERS

Myths and Realities of America's Gun Cultures

Abigail A. Kohn

OXFORD
UNIVERSITY PRESS

2004

OXFORD

UNIVERSITY PRESS

Oxford   New York

Auckland   Bangkok   Buenos Aires   Cape Town   Chennai
Dar es Salaam   Delhi   Hong Kong   Istanbul   Karachi   Kolkata
Kuala Lumpur   Madrid   Melbourne   Mexico City   Mumbai   Nairobi
São Paulo   Shanghai   Taipei   Tokyo   Toronto

Copyright © 2004 by Oxford University Press, Inc.

Published by Oxford University Press, Inc.
198 Madison Avenue, New York, New York 10016

www.oup.com

Oxford is a registered trademark of Oxford University Press

All rights reserved. No part of this publication may be reproduced,
stored in a retrieval system, or transmitted, in any form or by any means,
electronic, mechanical, photocopying, recording, or otherwise,
without the prior permission of Oxford University Press.

Library of Congress Cataloging-in-Publication Data
Kohn, Abigail A.
Shooters : myths and realities of America's gun cultures / by Abigail A. Kohn.
   p. cm.
Includes bibliographical references.
ISBN 0-19-515051-1
1. Firearms ownership—United States.   2. Firearms owners—United States.
3. Firearms—Social aspects—United States.   4. Shooting—United States.
5. Subculture—United States.   I. Title.
HV8059 .K65 2004
306'.1—dc22   2003017928

9 8 7 6 5 4 3 2 1

Printed in the United States of America
on acid-free paper

For my family

Preface

AK: Do you consider yourself a handgun enthusiast?

Greg: Yes.

AK: And how do you define handgun enthusiast?

Greg: It's a term that I wouldn't normally use myself, but I would define it as somebody who enjoys and/or is interested in handguns. Either owning, possessing, collecting, firing, or fantasizing about it.

AK: What would be a more appropriate term, or what would be a term that has more resonance for you?

Greg: Shooter.

From the 1970s on, the American print media has carried on an all-out war against gun owners. They are labeled "gun nuts," "gun fanatics," "the lunatic fringe," "sickos," and "terrorists." Gun owners are laughable, contemptible, "a handful of middle-aged fat guys with popguns." Editorial after editorial calls for stronger gun control, ranging from licensing and registration of all guns to outright bans on handguns. The *New York Times* publishes "The Scourge of Guns" and "Addicted to Guns," straightforwardly indicting guns and gun owners for America's high rate of civil violence. Not to be outdone, the *Washington Post* publishes editorials entitled "Good Parents, Bad Kids: And Far Too Many Handguns" and "Illegal Guns and the District," arguing that "turning off the supply of handguns from around the nation" is the only effective way to reduce gun violence in the nation's capital and across the United States.[1]

On the other side of the country, a columnist in a major West Coast newspaper pens a piece about the Second Amendment Sisters, a pro-gun women's organization formed largely in response to the Million Mom March, which favored gun control. Entitled "Pistol-Packin' Polyester," the columnist describes the Second Amendment Sisters as "bored, under-educated, bitter, terrified, badly-dressed, pasty, hate-spewin' suburban white women from lost Midwestern towns with names like Frankenmuth all carrying firearms and somehow thinking they're aiding the species." Only moderately less inflammatory, another West Coast contributor argues that America's gun culture is responsible for the "tyranny of danger" and "omnipresent threat of death" in contemporary American society.[2]

The National Rifle Association (NRA) gets similar treatment. Social critics refer to it as a subversive "cult" with a dangerous creed. A high-profile newsman refers to the NRA as the "Negro Removal Association" because it opposes gun control laws that would supposedly prevent young black children from being murdered with guns. According to some of the top journalists in the country, gun enthusiasts and NRA members are racist, stupid, ignorant about history and politics, apathetic to violence, bellicose, and jingoistic. They are, quite simply, evil.[3]

It's difficult to imagine the media promoting these kinds of characterizations of particular ethnic or religious groups without a political firestorm. Yet these are routine characterizations of gun enthusiasts. Clearly, the American media has taken an active, vocal stance in the gun debate. The frequent editorials and op-eds size up the media's position fairly neatly: Guns kill people; therefore, gun owners are killers. Gun control is the best, if not the only, way to stop violence in the United States.[4]

Perhaps surprisingly, gun owners and the NRA don't fare much better in the world of academe. In the past fifteen years, health and medical journals have launched a rigorous campaign to promote gun control, lambasting gun owners and the NRA to give up their guns. The *Journal of the American Medical Association* (*JAMA*) and the *American Journal of Public Health* have published scores of articles and editorials arguing that guns are a "pathogen" that should be eradicated from American society, that gun-related violence is an epidemic, and that anyone who owns a gun stands a strong risk of becoming either a victim of suicide or a murderer.[5] The public health field clearly views gun ownership as a health risk and gun owners as inherently dangerous people who imperil both their own lives and the lives of people around them.

Other examples from the academy include a well-regarded sociologist who published an article in the *Chronicle of Higher Education* cautioning liberal scholars against researching guns and the Second Amendment. The scholarly endeavor should be informed by moral principles, he argues, and because supporting gun control is the right thing to do, good scholars shouldn't do research that could potentially undermine it. A Pulitzer

Prize-winning historian insists that the Second Amendment *does not* guarantee an individual right to bear arms, historically or contemporarily, and scholars who insist otherwise are guilty of rewriting history to suit their ideological inclinations. Law journals publish articles with intellectual rationales for why gun owners should be publicly excoriated. In the *Yale Law Review*, an eminent feminist legal scholar argues that all gun owners should be understood as potentially violent because gun ownership is prima facie evidence of apathy toward violence, particularly violence against women. Gun ownership and indeed the gun culture are straightforward examples of hegemonic masculinity and patriarchy. Another legal scholar writes in the *Boston University Law Review* that gun manufacturers and the NRA should all be labeled "necromerchants." In other words, the gun culture encourages murder.

These published examples are by no means unique. When I began my research into gun enthusiasm and gun ownership in the mid-1990s, I learned that a number of my academic colleagues held very similar views.[6] One colleague said (trying to sound positive) that I was committing a real social service by researching "such disgusting people." Another informed me that because neo-Nazis, white supremacists, and the Ku Klux Klan all obviously love their guns, until I recognized that the phenomenon of gun enthusiasm was intrinsically racist, I was an apologist for racist violence. A third colleague told me frequently that she found gun owners utterly repellant, and she was surprised (and more than a little suspicious) that I didn't find them repellant as well. She insisted that until I recognized and acknowledged the ugliness and inherent pathology of gun enthusiasm, my research was disrespectful to victims of gun violence.

If conventional wisdom suggests that gun owners are all criminals and troglodytes and supporting gun control is the right thing to do, then perhaps the negative reactions to the topic of guns in the United States are not surprising.[7] If the main source of information people have about the gun culture is media images of stockpiled weapons and angry sound bites from the NRA, small wonder that so many Americans are disgusted by gun owners. And quite frankly, some gun owners don't help their own case. One of America's most famous gun enthusiasts, former NRA president Charlton Heston, has articulated ideas that *do* in fact sound racist, particularly when he links gun ownership to being white. For Heston, guns signify the "white way." In a speech he made to the highly conservative Free Congress Foundation, he stated: "Heaven help the God-fearing, law-abiding, Caucasian, middle-class, Protestant or—even worse—admitted heterosexual, gun-owning or—even worse—NRA-card-carrying, average working stiff. . . . Why is 'Hispanic pride' or 'black pride' a good thing, while 'white pride' conjures shaved heads and white hoods?"[8]

Considering these words from Heston, arguably one of the best informed about how the NRA as an organization thinks and feels, I am sympathetic to those who distrust what they perceive as the true NRA ideology. As one *Washington Post* contributor put it, "The answer, of course [to Heston's question], is that people who proclaim 'white pride' often have shaved heads or wear white hoods."[9] To many critics of widespread gun ownership, Heston's speech sounds like the ravings of a racist, homophobic, and paranoid right-wing conservative, and thus the defining essence of the NRA.

The Heart of the Issue

Although ideologues tend to see these issues in black-and-white terms (and the gun debate has more than its fair share of ideologues), these issues are far more complex than they immediately appear. They are more complicated than Heston and the NRA seem to recognize, and unquestionably more complicated than critics will concede. In fact, in many respects, conventional wisdom regarding guns and gun owners is either overly simplified or simply wrong.[10] For example, a number of historians have argued that there *is* a legitimate historical basis for citizen gun ownership and that the Second Amendment does confer an individual right to own guns.[11] Criminologists have been pointing out for years that most gun owners can and do own guns safely and without criminal intent. Some citizens do use guns effectively to thwart crime.[12] Noted scholars have even suggested the ultimate of heresies—that gun control may not be quite the panacea that liberals insist it is.[13]

Needless to say, pro-gun advocates have employed these academic arguments and findings to promote their position and to further legitimize the NRA's stance against gun controls.[14] At this point, perhaps not surprisingly, no amount of persuasive rhetoric from either side does anything but speak to the already converted. Both sides in the gun debate have provided their mountains of "conclusive evidence," which generally consists of endless statistics that prove either the beneficial (or the detrimental) effects of widespread gun ownership.

But the question still remains: Why are so many Americans so attached to their guns? This is the heart of the issue, and *neither* side has addressed it effectively. Antigun advocates are mainly concerned with persuading gun owners to stop owning guns, not with understanding why gun owners are so attached to them. Pro-gun advocates have not explored this issue adequately either. The evidence they proffer about the benefits of gun ownership notwithstanding, most pro-gunners tend to say simply that guns keep Americans free. Although this symbolic association is indeed held by many gun enthusiasts, its basis is not entirely self-evident. If the historical roots of guns making us free are long gone, why do some Americans still believe in this idea so strongly? Can we really afford to assume that linking guns to freedom is simply an artifact of American history (real and imagined) and leave it at that? More to the point, what does the concept of freedom really *mean* in relation to guns?

If we assume that there's no mystery here, and guns equal freedom because Americans have always owned guns to keep themselves free (whatever that means), then there's really nothing to debate anymore. Guns are a part of American history, and no amount of contemporary naysaying will change that fact.[15] However, the sheer amount of rancor over these issues suggests that there is more going on than a difference of interpretation about our nation's history and what kind of bearing that history should have on contemporary American society.

Guns obviously have tremendous social meaning in American society. The different and complicated meanings that Americans do attach to guns is almost completely unexplored territory. Even conceptualizing the gun debate as a clash of political ideals, the difference between what conservatives value versus what liberals value, does not really address the core issues. At this point, both liberals and conservatives tend to treat the gun issue simply as more evidence of how ridiculous and "out of touch with reality" their political opponents are. As an explanation for why Americans find guns meaningful, this really doesn't cut it. None of these explanations or arguments really gets at the heart of the issue: *What does owning guns really mean for American gun enthusiasts?*

Acknowledgments

I am grateful to the following mentors, friends, colleagues, and family members for their generous support of me and this work.

This book began as a dissertation project. The following anthropologists and sociologists served on my dissertation committee and mentored me throughout my fieldwork and writing. At the University of California, San Francisco, Gay Becker was an outstanding dissertation chair who lent her considerable anthropological expertise, sharp eye, and boundless support throughout the process. She has brought out the best in my work. Judith Barker has been a long-standing and highly valued advisor, and I am very thankful to have worked with her. Her breadth of knowledge is extraordinary, and her penetrating and rigorous analysis has improved the text greatly. I have greatly enjoyed working with Jan Dizard at Amherst College. His patience, generosity of spirit, friendship, and scholarship in the field of firearms research have all been a boon. I have also been lucky to work with Lawrence Cohen at the University of California, Berkeley; his unique perspective has always proved fascinating and useful.

I would also like to thank Joan Ablon, Sharon Kaufman, Linda Mitteness, and Philippe Bourgois for their ideas and questions. I am gratified to have worked with all of these professionals.

The staff at Oxford University Press in New York has been consistently supportive and gracious, and I have benefited greatly from their knowledge and expertise. Thank you to Niko Pfund for responding so quickly and positively from the first, and Molly Barton for her assistance with the end stages. Thanks also to Jessica Ryan and her team for their extensive copyediting. My heartfelt and profound thanks to Dedi Felman for her fine editing skills, patience, willingness to talk me through each stage of the publishing process, and continued faith that we would bring out the strengths of the work together.

The following friends and colleagues have read and listened carefully to half-formed thoughts, discussed and argued with me, and generally provided much food for thought. Many thanks to Tessa Boyd-Caine, Ken Bowling, Janet Chappell, Robert Churchill, Chris Cunneen, Eric Davis, Norman Fineman, Gayle Green, Nortin and Carol Hadler, Robert Hicks, Liz Herskovits, Moira Killoran, Chris Lockhart, Julie Near, Fernando Ona, Linda Pitcher, Leslie Pollitt, Chris Simon, Julie Stubbs, Andrea Tisi, Meryle Weinstein, Bill Whitehead, Lara Wood, and Steve and Joanie Wynn. The following friends, family, and colleagues read chapters and shared their thoughts and comments—many warm thanks to Scott Anderson, Rye Barcott, Adam Byrne, Bev Davenport, Max Gulias, Rebecca Huntley, Cookie Kohn, Kate H. Kohn, Kristin Savell, and Philippa Strelitz. A special thanks to Jesse Dizard for getting me started down this road. Lynn Watts transcribed all the interviews with great skill and patience, and Karen Cantor formatted my entire dissertation: I owe them both beyond words. Karla Kruse in the Graduate Division of UCSF lent moral support and thoughtful advice about negotiating the UCSF system. I'd also like to thank several friends and colleagues who are also firearm researchers: Don B. Kates, C. B. Kates, and Mary Zeiss Stange have been especially helpful and supportive.

The following individuals assisted me by providing papers or information or speaking with me about their work: Deb Azrael, Paul Blackman, John W. Chambers, Phil Cook, Robert Cottrol, David Davis at DecisionQuest, David Hemenway, Don Higginbotham, Gary Kleck, Gary Mauser, Brian Anse Patrick, Carol Oyster, and Richard Slotkin. I also benefitted from the thoughful suggestions of Jack Katz and several anonymous reviewers. Thank you all again.

I also would like to thank the shooters of Northern California who so graciously agreed to speak with me, sharing their thoughts and feelings with such candor.

The Regents of California funded two years of this research with the Regents Fellowship and the Rosenberg Fellowship. I finished the writing and editing of this book while a Postdoctoral Research Fellow at the Institute of Criminology at the University of Sydney Law School in Sydney, Australia. I appreciate the generosity and professional support of these two institutions.

Finally, all my love and thanks to my entire family in Wisconsin, Illinois, Iowa, Florida, North Carolina, and beyond (I've got a lot of family). In particular, my love and thanks to my brother, Sam, and my parents, Lynne H. Kohn and Richard H. Kohn. I could not have done this work without you.

Contents

PART ◉ ONE

The Anthropology of Gun Enthusiasm

Introduction: Guns in America

In the fall of 1997, as a graduate student at the University of California, I set out to conduct an anthropological study of gun enthusiasm. To collect data, I used the traditional anthropological method of participant observation, which basically entails joining the designated group in question, making friends with its members, observing and participating in community events, and engaging in group activities with the community. For fourteen months, I spent time at shooting ranges, gun shops, and shooting competitions, all of which are open to the general public. I conducted in-depth interviews with thirty-seven male and female gun enthusiasts and spent hours hanging out and shooting with dozens more.[1] I asked the gun enthusiasts I interviewed how they were first introduced to guns, how long they had owned their guns, and what gun ownership meant to them. I asked them what guns symbolized for them. Their answers to these questions, as well as their beliefs and concerns, constitute the data discussed in this book.

I conducted this research largely in the San Francisco Bay Area. Because the Bay Area usually evokes images of the free-spirited bohemianism of Haight-Ashbury, the student-packed chaos of Berkeley's Telegraph Avenue, and the sprawling, misty beauty of the Northern California coastline, it is not a geographic locale that is usually associated with America's gun culture. And yet there is one. Northern California has an active, self-delineated community centered around guns and gun enthusiasm. When I conducted this research, there were between six and ten gun shops in the metropolitan area (depending on how the boundaries are drawn), six shooting ranges within a forty-five-minute radius of the inner city, traveling gun shows that stopped in the Bay Area several times a month (with local vendors in attendance), lo-cal chapters of national organizations like SASS (Single Action Shooting Soci-ety), IPSC (International Practical Shooting Confederation), and the NRA, and shooting competitions and events that occurred almost every weekend of the year.

These are but a few local examples of what constitutes a local manifesta-tion of America's gun culture. The term "gun culture" is often used but rarely defined. I define a gun culture as one that places enormous social, historical, and political *emphasis* on guns (both positive and negative and every shade of gray in between). A gun culture has structural manifestations pertaining to gun ownership in a variety of geographic locales. Even a place not strictly associated with guns can have a version of the gun culture if people in the area gather to talk about guns, buy and sell them, or recreate with them. A gun culture is one that uses a common language about guns and shares a set of signs and symbols pertaining to guns in everyday life.

In fact, academics have employed their own (more strict) definition of gun culture, suggesting that it denotes a geographic locale where gun own-ership is prevalent and where people are socialized into gun ownership and "pro-gun values."[2] As such, scholars have noted that gun prevalence is par-ticularly high in the South and then in descending order from the Rocky Mountains, the Midwest, the Pacific, and finally the Northeast.[3] Gun own-ership and socialization into gun use are strongly associated with rural areas as opposed to urban ones, and with conservative political values rather than liberal ones. Therefore, a site more likely to demonstrate "typical" gun owner-ship would be a rural area in the American South, where activities like hunt-ing and target shooting are common and politics are generally conservative.[4]

But attending a number of Bay Area ranges and shooting events on a fre-quent basis enabled me to see that there were plenty of regular participants, a loose-knit fellowship drawn together not by physical space but by shared interests, specifically an interest in guns. Members of the local gun culture love to talk about, shoot, and collect guns. The fact that this thriving exam-ple of gun culture coexists alongside everything that the gun culture sup-posedly is *not* (i.e., liberal, wealthy, multicultural, contemporary) made Northern California a fascinating place for this research. Clearly, some ver-sion of the gun culture can thrive in urban environs, even where guns are not supposed to be of much historical or material importance.

This research was also undertaken as an ethnography, or in-depth study of a particular community or small-scale society.[5] In the tradition of ethnog-raphy, the point was *not* to gather quantifiable data from a representative sample of gun owners. Rather, I sought to discover the "natives' point of view," or, in more contemporary terms, to learn which issues and concepts are most important to gun enthusiasts.[6] Ethnographic research is unique in its ability to provide an understanding of behavior and belief that is usually understood only in quantitative terms.[7] Academics actually do know a fair amount about American gun ownership in more statistical terms.[8] However, these quantitative methods yield data that are not particularly subtle or nuanced. Numbers don't present a window into how gun enthusiasts actually think or feel about their guns. Establishing a cohesive and inherently meaningful pattern of action, or worldview, is extraordinarily difficult when analyzing short answers from respondents, such as "Yes, I own two guns" and "I own my guns for self-defense." These short answers present only snapshots, images and pieces of a complex social world.

Ethnography, on the other hand, can combine and interpret these pieces into a richer and multifaceted whole.[9] Ethnography fills in the gaps and provides a window for the social world of any given group. These are the "warrants for ethnography" that provide the main reasons why ethnographic accounts have wider relevance than their small samples might suggest.[10] So while the thirty-seven shooters interviewed here are not "representative" in the sense that they can and should represent all gun owners or enthusiasts on a national scale, the concepts and issues they raise are broader than their own personal or phenomenological interests.[11] These shooters provide a window into the cultural concerns and issues that gun enthusiasts share more broadly, as evidenced by the similarities between the themes and concepts that these shooters raise and the themes and concepts discussed in such national publications as NRA magazines and gun debate articles published in national newspapers and magazines.[12]

Perhaps the most powerful reason for using ethnography to study gun enthusiasm, however, is simply that ethnography is uniquely capable of humanizing stereotypes.[13] Because policy is often formulated on the basis of what "those people" think and do,[14] discussing what gun enthusiasts *really* think and do, and what actually motivates their hostility to gun control, may be a valuable step toward advancing the gun debate.

Cultural Conflicts over Guns

The gun debate reflects not only cultural concerns but also cultural conflicts, which made studying gun enthusiasm in Northern California all the more compelling.[15] These cultural conflicts are most obviously articulated in the

Bay Area as sociopolitical differences. Guns and gun owners are viewed with wariness and even downright disgust by many Northern Californians, and local gun aficionados are well aware that their chosen lifestyle is disdained by local politicians, community organizations, and other non-gun-owning citizens. Local politicians have frequently sought to ban certain kinds of guns or limit the presence of guns on county property, and they have had a relatively high degree of success.[16] The area was home to the Million Mom March Foundation (formerly the Bell Campaign), a national, nonprofit gun control advocacy organization that provides a political voice to those victimized by gun-related violence.[17] The San Francisco/Oakland version of the Million Mom March in May 2000, drew up to five thousand supporters with little counterprotest.[18] These examples of organized antigun sentiment help foster an overall sociopolitical environment that throws the thoughts, feelings, and worldview of gun enthusiasts into sharp relief.[19]

These conditions provided a fascinating opportunity to investigate gun enthusiasm. Pro-gun and antigun worlds collided regularly in Northern California, as local politicians fought to ban the always crowded gun shows from public spaces and a Democratic governor passed several strict gun laws that banned a variety of long guns.[20] Insofar as Northern California maintains an "adversary culture" toward the gun-owning community, shooters in the Bay Area find themselves frequently defending their chosen lifestyle, whether at town meetings, to other parents in the neighborhood, or simply at parties or social gatherings with non-gun owners present.[21] As de facto members of Northern California's gun culture, they are frequently in a position to defend their interests, often to hostile audiences.

Although frustrating for them, this situation was helpful to me from a research perspective. The shooters interviewed here were well-placed to discuss and defend their views about guns and gun enthusiasm because they do so all the time, and they were often pleased and relieved to discuss these issues with a sympathetic, noncombative audience. Their discussions with me about how they feel about guns, and their struggle to justify their feelings about gun ownership to their friends and neighbors, brought home the extent to which the gun debate has become a true site of cultural conflict on a local and national level.

Shooters in the Study

I started interviewing people almost immediately after I started taking my first set of shooting lessons in the fall of 1997. I met people in coffee shops, restaurants, and their homes, which was usually their preferred setting. I conducted thirty-three interviews in total with thirty-seven people (four couples were interviewed together).[22]

The shooters I interviewed fell into three rather broad categories. They all share some basic characteristics: a love of guns, both handguns and long guns, a love of the gear associated with guns (gear for shooting, as for any middle-class sporting phenomenon, is an industry in itself), and an enjoyment of the activity of shooting, either competitively, for plinking (shooting outdoors at random targets such as tin cans or bottles), or for recreational target shooting. The basic underlying assumptions inherent in being a shooter are that you support private gun ownership and generally endorse pro-gun ideology. In other words, if you are a shooter, your political inclinations are (supposedly) self-evident.

The first group is composed of "general enthusiasts," which included thirteen people.[23] These shooters own guns for several reasons: because they like them, enjoy shooting them, engage in gun sports or hunting (but are enthused about guns and their sport, as opposed to simply enthused about sport), and/or own guns for self- and home defense. This category includes ten men and three women; one is Latino, another Asian, but the rest are white. All of these individuals are middle or lower-middle class, according to their income level and, in some cases, their self-proclaimed class status.

The second group of shooters are all involved with "cowboy action shooting," a shooting sport dedicated to Old West guns, outfits, and shooting scenarios. This category includes nineteen people, eleven men and eight women. I interviewed one black cowboy shooter; the rest are white.[24] This group is full of doctors, engineers, lawyers, and real estate brokers, many of whom are moderately wealthy. Three of these shooters work in the firearms industry and are apparently very successful at it. The few (four) that are not white-collar workers work as low- or mid-level administrators or artists; one was a retired law enforcement officer. There are in fact a good number of active or retired law enforcement officers who enjoy cowboy action shooting. I did not manage to interview more than one of them in this group, primarily because I lacked enough time.

The third group of shooters I call the "Generation X" shooters, not only because they are the youngest group overall (all were born after 1960), but because their thoughts, attitudes, and occupations fit the popular generational portrait drawn from media representations of Gen X. There are only five shooters in this category, all men, four whites and one Asian.[25] Several of these men organize shooting activities for themselves and their friends on public lands several hours outside of any urban center in Northern California. These shooting outings sometimes have a seasonal flavor. I attended a "Pumpkin Shoot" after Halloween, in which vegetables were destroyed with relish (no pun intended). Some of these shoots even make oblique social statements, as in the case of a shooting outing in which shooters fired at old computer equipment.[26] This event was called the "Hard Drive-Bye." It was intended to be social commentary: most of these shooters worked in the computer industry and enjoyed themselves immensely blasting away at computers and AOL disks for several hours. I usually shot with these guys in smaller groups at local shooting ranges or on public land.

Whether these shooters are demographically identical to the population of gun owners across the United States is difficult to say. Research by criminologists indicates that as a whole, gun owners in the United States are usually male, predominantly middle to upper-middle class, Protestant, married, and white. They generally own guns for hunting and sporting purposes, though handguns are owned primarily for defensive purposes.[27] This portrait does indeed fit most of those interviewed here.[28] However, the factors that make Northern California relatively unique should be kept in mind. The first is that gun ownership in the United States is filtered through a variety of factors, and regional differences (particularly the urban/rural divide) is an important one. The people interviewed here live in a primarily urban setting, and though some did grow up in rural areas, they are now urbanites or suburbanites. Urban dwellers generally own fewer guns overall than those in rural areas, where guns are used for such mundane activities as hunting, varmint control, and livestock management, activities obviously less relevant in urban settings.[29]

Also, although conservatives overall are more likely than liberals to own guns, the shooters here come from several political traditions.[30] About half asserted that they are conservative, and two stated that they are libertarians. About one quarter stated that they are politically liberal and usually vote Democrat.[31] There may have been even more interviewees with liberal leanings, but I counted only those who spoke openly about their liberal politics. Several liberal shooters expressed annoyance that they are continually assumed to be politically conservative because they own guns. Several shooters spoke eloquently about how their gun ownership is actually very much in keeping with their liberal inclinations, a point that is now counterintuitive because liberal politics are so closely identified with gun control.

A substantial number of the shooters interviewed had been victimized by crime and had used their guns to defend themselves during the incident.

Nine shooters in total, seven men and two women, said they had been physically threatened, almost mugged or robbed, or confronted in some way by someone apparently intending to hurt them. The degree of seriousness of each situation varied, as did the length of time that had passed since the event occurred. Several shooters reported incidents that occurred as long as twenty or even thirty years earlier, and others reported incidents that had occurred in the past several years.[32] Shooters mentioned these events spontaneously (I did not specifically ask if shooters had ever used a gun for defense, only if they kept guns for defensive purposes); they were asked to elaborate only if they mentioned that they had used a gun defensively, and/or if they felt comfortable talking about it.[33] Their descriptions of self-defense are discussed periodically throughout the book.

Finally, because so many Americans own guns, distinguishing between gun owners and gun enthusiasts is important. Not all gun owners are inherently enthusiastic about owning guns. I define gun enthusiasts as gun owners who met the following criteria: (1) have an interest in owning and using guns of any type, (2) legally own at least one gun, (3) take pleasure in talking about guns and shooting with other gun aficionados, and (4) organize regular (weekly, or in some cases monthly) activities around their gun interests. All of the individuals discussed here have no trouble fitting these criteria, and these characteristics do provide a useful starting point for understanding the basic mechanics of gun enthusiasm.

What Is Gun Enthusiasm?

At its most basic, gun enthusiasm is an enjoyment of and enthusiasm for firearms. Gun enthusiasts, like enthusiasts of any kind, take pleasure in the handling and use of the object of their pleasure. Pleasure and enjoyment are slightly different experiences. Pleasure is a subjective, individual sensation, an end in itself; consummation is the goal.[34] Enjoyment, on the other hand, is the integration of pleasure with a goal, a specific purpose that lies outside of the sensation of pleasure itself. Enjoyment "implies self-control, the development of skills in the pursuit of voluntary as opposed to spontaneous goals."[35] This differentiation is important because gun enthusiasts derive both pleasure and enjoyment from guns, as well as from the voluntary activity of shooting them. However, some gun enthusiasts make a distinction between feelings of handling the guns themselves, taking pleasure in them, and feelings derived from shooting guns with the accompanying skills, images, sensations, and other facets that are part of this activity. Other gun enthusiasts only collect guns and never shoot them. Guns can be highly valuable, and some collectors feel that shooting them even once immediately decreases their subjective worth. To a true collector (a gun collector is similar to a car, stamp, or coin collector in this regard), keeping the gun in pristine condition is obviously preferable, whereas a target shooter might find a gun that has been "field tested" to be of the greatest value.[36]

Shooters themselves are the most informed about what constitutes gun enthusiasm, and they produced fairly similar definitions. Gun enthusiasm can be broken down into three overlapping components: (1) an interest or pleasure in guns as collectors' items or historic relics, (2) an interest in guns as treasured pieces of sporting equipment (for target shooting, which has a wide variety of subcategories), and (3) using guns to attain or achieve certain feeling states or states of consciousness. This last component of gun enthusiasm could be defined as an enjoyment in the way a gun is used or a pleasure in the feelings derived from the activity of shooting.

Shooters who described their interest in guns as historic artifacts also volunteered that they were interested in different aspects of American history that they strongly identified with gun use. Jonathan, a white administrator in his early forties employed at a large university, explained: "Why do I like guns? To me it's just like—because I can shoot really well with them, I just have this affinity for them. I love to read about them. I like the history that goes with guns, like all the history of just . . . when I go out and shoot it relaxes me, very meditative and such." Jonathan is an avid reader, and he enjoys reading or watching documentaries about different periods of American history when guns featured prominently, at least as far as he is concerned. He consumes gun magazines and is particularly interested in nineteenth-century guns used on the American frontier. From his reading and self-educating, he is able to speak quite knowledgeably about what kinds of guns were developed when, how they were used, and the individual flaws and virtues of different guns in different eras of American history. For most of the shooters with whom I spoke, the most interesting periods in American history are colonial America and the movement west during the nineteenth century, the period popularly known as the "Old" or "Wild West."

Those shooters who mentioned their love of American history did not necessarily discuss this interest with me at length, as most perceived the interview to be about more modern and current issues relating to their gun enthusiasm. But their mention of history in relation to guns is important not simply because they discuss this history and "period guns" among themselves a great deal, but because history and its implications are an important way that shooters conceptualize their interest in guns now. Guns are rarely understood as objects outside of historical, cultural, and social contexts. They are almost always made meaningful through a discussion of the contexts in which they are owned and used. In other words, context often determines what a gun means to its owner. This is a crucial point for understanding what guns symbolize for shooters and is made more clear throughout the course of this book.

Savage Beauty

For many shooters, guns are beautiful objects. The intricate carvings on the frame or stock of a rifle or the smooth lines of a well-made revolver bring shooters a good deal of pleasure. Combining the excitement of shooting sports with the beauty of the equipment makes these activities highly enjoyable. For most of the shooters I met, shooting is a physically demanding activity that necessitates hand-eye coordination, concentration, and skill. Elliot, a white commercial artist in his midforties, describes the enjoyment of shooting this way:

> [The reason I like guns is] . . . well, first and foremost, I think because they're exciting. They're exciting to shoot. I like the bang, I like the flash, I like the smoke. And it was certainly—there's a sense of power that you cannot deny, that you can literally obliterate anything standing in front of you. And they're so precisely made, the good ones, and there's a kind of a savage beauty to them, I think. Part of it because they're just so beautifully crafted, with an eye to detail and an eye to the kind of an elegant sense of line. And partly because they're capable of such utter destruction. And there's kind of a delicate balance, which I think is kind of exciting. I like to handle them. I like to talk about 'em, I like to read about 'em.

Elliot's definition of gun enthusiasm conveys the relish that gun enthusiasts feel when shooting. Shooters often get highly technical in describing certain guns and how they work, and it's easy to get lost in the minute and intricate details of barrel rifling, powder measurements, and sight adjustments. Elliot also elaborated later on the inherently social aspects of shooting: showing a collection to interested friends and fellow shooters, talking with other people about a gun's history, and describing the experience of shooting each different gun. In fact, socializing is an important facet of shooting: gun enthusiasts are involved in gun-related social activities all the time.

Elliot also mentioned the inherent power of guns, their capability for destruction and violence. The fascination with such a powerful object is an important part of gun enthusiasm. Guns can be dangerous, and most shooters understand and respect that fact. Some shooters feel that sometimes, however, there is a lot of pleasure in simply destroying something: a paper bull's-eye, a glass bottle, even food (pumpkins, squash, etc.). Shooters spoke of the enormous excitement of these activities. Shooting guns that have been described as "bad" or "evil," such as high-powered assault weapons, can be enjoyable because the act itself is so transgressive. There is a perverse pleasure in doing something others find inherently repulsive. And the more those guns are considered innately repugnant and evil, the more some shooters dig in their heels and discuss among themselves the pleasure of actually shooting them.[37]

For some shooters, the thrill derived from shooting a gun borders on the sexual, and several spoke of their erotic pleasure in touching and handling guns. Though this point is not necessarily shared by all or even the majority of shooters I befriended, this point became apparent in some interviews. Morris, a white building inspector in his sixties, explained: "I'm content and I'm happy just to hold a gun in my hands. I can't describe it . . . it's . . . it's a work of art, a thing of beauty. . . . There's art, there's beauty, and then there's form and there's function. . . . Okay, for a man to tell you this . . . I would rather fondle a fine firearm than I would a naked woman. Now does that make sense?"

For some enthusiasts, the gun as a phallic symbol is obvious. Indeed, the metaphoric relationship between guns and penises has been a part of popular discourse on guns for some time.[38] But what is interesting about the eroticization of guns for some shooters here is that contrary to common stereotype, the gun was eroticized or fetishized as feminine rather than masculine. When shooters did eroticize guns, they characterized their guns as aesthetically pleasing in the ways women might be characterized by heterosexual men. This eroticization of guns as feminine runs counter to how guns would be conceptualized if they were extensions of literal and figurative manhood, as they are stereotyped in somewhat crude psychoanalytic interpretations.[39] Rather, guns are thought of as beautiful; they are aesthetically pleasing objects of figurative desire. Gendering a valued object as female is not uncommon; cars, boats, even musical instruments are likewise "feminized" (B. B. King's guitar Lucille comes to mind). Thus, for male gun enthusiasts, guns are gendered as female.[40]

In its most extreme form, this eroticization could be viewed as a form of misogynist pathology, as in "Trust a gun over a woman any time" or even

"Women and guns are dangerous and deadly."[41] But arguments suggesting that gun ownership is innately pathological (or, more precisely, pathologically psychosexual) would need to be supported with empirical evidence, and criminologists agree that no such evidence exists to support that characterization.[42]

The third aspect of gun enthusiasm voiced by a number of shooters recognizes the relationship between guns and their owners as more complex. This aspect of gun enthusiasm suggests that guns are enjoyed because they provide, in the words of one female shooter, an "avenue towards a feeling." The feelings that guns invoke are diverse, but the point is that guns are not enjoyed only for themselves but rather for the feelings they engender in the shooter. Andrew, a white journalist in his late twenties, talked about how he feels a sense of comfort derived from owning guns. He discussed growing up near Los Angeles and feeling vulnerable during the riots of the early 1990s: "How do I define a . . . gun enthusiast? I think somebody who enjoys shooting a gun because of—how can I say it without sounding . . . I think it gives you a sense of well-being in a way, gives you a comfort to know that you can use something as a weapon if there's ever an emergency. The understanding of something that can kill you. I think that's really . . . I think that it's important to be aware of what's around in your surroundings." Andrew believes that guns are a fact of life in certain geographic parts of the United States, and he feels more safe owning and knowing how to use guns. He wants to know and understand something that he feels he might eventually encounter, even if it is in a deadly situation.

Safety and Power

Other shooters talked about how owning and using guns is exciting or even sexy, and how guns incite feelings that the shooter doesn't necessarily associate with the more mundane or "average" aspects of his or her life. Thea, a white attorney in her late forties, elegant and articulate, said she enjoys the feeling of playing against type. She put it this way:

> So I think . . . it's a feeling. It's an avenue toward a feeling, toward safety, toward power, toward being part of the group, toward being kind of . . . having a new skill and an in-crowd kind of thing, toward being kind of a rebel, you know. The other thing, too . . . I think one of the things that this really does for me is, it makes me feel young and powerful instead of forty-eight and menopausal. . . . This is something that makes me kind of feel sexy and hot and like I've got something going on besides estrogen depletion.

Thea mentioned the social aspects of shooting, of being a part of a community that she enjoys and respects, as being an important part of the enjoyment of gun ownership and use. She takes pleasure in identifying with the shooting community, which has taken on a kind of rebel status in the more urban parts of the Bay Area. Politics in Northern California, particularly in the densely urban coastal areas, veers to the left, and as such, the area has experienced a certain politicized and institutional hostility toward gun ownership.[43] This hostility or distrust made analysis of gun enthusiasm all the more interesting, if somewhat uncomfortable for local gun enthusiasts.

Both Andrew and Thea mentioned feelings of safety associated with guns. Andrew feels safer knowing that he can have access to a gun in an emergency. Thea also mentioned safety; she meant that she feels physically safer because she has a working knowledge of guns and can use one if she needs to defend herself. Both shooters raise an interesting aspect of gun enthusiasm: most of the shooters interviewed felt that defending themselves with guns was an integral part of their gun ownership. Though most of the shooters I met use guns for sport or recreational purposes, all but two of the thirty-seven stated that they also keep guns in their home for self-defense purposes. Though keeping a gun for self-defense is not necessarily their primary reason for gun ownership, it is indeed a concern to them. In this sense, the shooters interviewed are similar to gun owners who report in nationwide surveys that home defense is not the primary reason for gun ownership, but it is an important one.[44]

Guns can thus be enjoyed for a variety of reasons that touch on enjoyment and interest in history, an aesthetic pleasure in a well-made machine, and because they engender certain kinds of feelings or emotions. In this last vein, guns can speak to the politics of pleasure for some shooters, the now oft-maligned sentiment that some things (e.g., eating fatty foods or smoking a cigarette), although not necessarily good for you, are undertaken because they give people pleasure.[45] As the question of whether or not guns are good for you is rancorously debated (to say the least), suffice it to say here that gun ownership is a valued and meaningful activity for *all* of the shooters I met. Gun ownership gives shooters both pleasure and enjoyment. They have little desire to give up this interest, regardless of the supposed inherent dangerousness of guns. In other words, trying to convince culturally motivated gun owners to give up their interest in guns would be "as difficult as convincing individuals to change religions."[46] Eradicating the gun culture, which has been the stated goal of a number of gun control advocates in the past several years, will be well-nigh impossible.[47]

Shooters: Good Guys or Bad Guys?

The gun culture is a vast and complex institution, and a variety of gun sub-cultures exist within the larger whole. Some of these subcultures include "sporting subcultures," such as competition and target shooters, "criminal subcultures" that use guns to commit crimes, and "rural hunting subcultures" that use guns for hunting and gun-related recreation. Guns are literally and symbolically important within certain gun-owning subcultures because they signify certain kinds of values, traditions, and/or ways of life that those gun owners see as part of their cultural heritage.

In that vein, some sociologists have astutely pointed out that gun ownership is a part of the American ethos.[48] Gun ownership is a way for some individuals to make a commitment to what they perceive as the "American Way."[49] This description aptly summarizes the worldview of the shooters with whom I worked, although they are also accurately characterized as part of a sporting subculture.[50] Though several grew up hunting and continue to hunt, most own guns for protection as well as recreation.[51] But all of these shooters stated that they own and use guns because guns give them pleasure in and of themselves, hence their self-identification as enthusiasts.

Shooters know and understand the ways that the gun debate has deeply politicized and stigmatized their interest in firearms. During the course of my fieldwork and interviews, shooters took great pains to dissociate themselves from popular culture's negative stereotypes of gun owners. Shooters employed "dignifying accounts" when they discussed their interest in guns, telling narratives designed to illustrate the inherent decency and dignity of their gun enthusiasm.[52] These kinds of dignifying accounts also tend to draw moral boundaries between self and other; in the context of stories about guns, dignifying accounts tend to make the shooter a hero of sorts, a moral actor who should be differentiated from the criminal other, despite the fact that both share the characteristic of gun ownership.[53] In this vein, gun enthusiasts perceive themselves to be the "good guys" who own guns, in contrast to the "bad guys," that is, criminals, neo-Nazis, militia members, white supremacists, and other undesirables who are more usually associated with the gun culture. These criminal others presumably share literal space (i.e., guns shows) and discursive space (i.e., pro-gun advocacy) with shooters, but are more likely than shooters to represent the public face of guns and shooting in American civic consciousness.

Shooters made these categorical distinctions to assure me that shooters were not those criminal others, and I shouldn't assume that they had anything in common with "the bad guys" per se. As far as shooters are concerned, they do not rob, cheat, steal, or hurt people with their guns. They are not interested in blowing up federal buildings or starting a so-called race war. Shooters wanted me to understand that they are not "the problem" and should not be confused with people who are violent with guns. Their discursive tactics served the classic sociological function of identifying deviance and criminality, helping to solidify the community by identifying points of in-group commonality and out-group difference.[54] In other words, shooters' self-delineated categories helped to affirm their own moral sensibilities while providing symbolic distance from the kinds of people shooters themselves consider deviant and immoral.

But the point is not that shooters are indeed the good guys and everyone else who owns guns are the bad guys. These are obviously ideological categories, meaningful mainly to the social actors who use them and usually for the reasons described. Questions about whether shooters are the good guys or the bad guys, or even whether guns are good or bad, do not yield objectively meaningful answers.[55] But critics of the gun culture have sometimes argued that whether or not most gun owners *actually* go out and shoot people is really besides the point. They *could*, and therein lies the problem. Critics of gun ownership tend to argue that access to guns straightforwardly increases gun violence.[56] Shooters firmly disagree with this point, but like their critics, they are profoundly concerned about these issues.

Thinking about all these issues and the ways that the gun debate structures discussions about them reveals the core difference in how pro- and antigun advocates conceptualize violence in society and what should be done about it. Shooters believe that society is a violent place, so they hone their skills and prepare for the possibility of doing violence themselves. They view this position to be the most responsible one they can take in relation to their own and their family's safety. Antigun critics also believe that society is a violent place, filled with guns and people willing to use them. They believe the most responsible position is to severely restrict access to guns for just about everybody, thereby reducing everyone's capacity for violence with guns. In contrast, shooters do not believe that forcible disarmament will reduce violent peoples' access to guns or the willingness to resort to violence. Shooters see gun control largely as a fantasy perpetuated by people who don't live under violent conditions and don't have to worry about being victimized by crime. All of these issues are explored fully in the following pages.

Guns and American Core Values

We usually talk about the gun debate as if it were simply about guns—whether or not Americans can legitimately own them, and whether widespread gun ownership positively or negatively affects American crime rates. But in many respects, the gun debate poses far more broad and fundamental questions. The gun debate has actually become the locus for arguments about three profoundly contentious concepts in contemporary American society: citizenship, public safety, and moral order. How Americans are thrashing out these concepts (in all their complexity and ambiguity) within the gun debate is more clearly revealed when we recognize what the debate is really asking of Americans. The gun debate is in effect posing a series of questions: What constitutes moral citizenship in the United States today? What does American history say about citizenship? Is that history still relevant today? How should individual citizens work to make themselves and their communities safer? And finally, how should Americans strive to maintain moral order within American society as a whole?

These are the issues and concerns that lie at the heart of the American gun debate. They all relate on some level to cultural formulations of citizenship and morality and have serious implications for public safety. But one of the reasons that the gun debate is so contentious and so seemingly unresolvable is that these questions have few inherent "right" answers. They engender responses that are as subjective as people's feelings about guns. Yet, many Americans now address these questions, and communicate their answers, through gun debate politics. Thus, at its most basic, the gun debate is about how Americans choose to define themselves as Americans and think about what being a good American actually means. Engaging with the gun debate, particularly by choosing to own guns and/or talking about guns publicly, means engaging with the notion of American identity in profound and complicated ways.

Through formal interviews, visits to shooting ranges, gun stores, and shooting competitions, and time spent simply sitting with people as they talked about their guns, I explored what it means to be a gun enthusiast. For shooters, guns signify American core values: freedom, independence, individualism, and equality. Thus, in essence, shooters believe that being a gun owner means being a good American. Through their own words and stories, I discovered that gun enthusiasts perceive the core values embodied in guns as both vibrantly alive and deeply threatened in the contemporary United States. Shooters in effect use their gun enthusiasm to infuse their core values into their day-to-day lives. For them, gun ownership is a central aspect of both individual and national identity, and for that reason, they hear attacks on guns as deeply personal attacks not only on themselves, but also on their family and community, even on their way of life.

Only by directly addressing what gun ownership really means to gun enthusiasts, and by recognizing and exploring the *attraction* that so many Americans have to guns, can we begin to have a constructive conversation about the role of guns in contemporary society. This is most effectively accomplished by considering what gun enthusiasts actually say about their gun enthusiasm and by carefully looking at and understanding the kinds of social activities with which gun owners are concerned. Much attention has been paid elsewhere to the values and principles of people who oppose gun ownership and support gun control, and how their values embody the best of American culture. But in fact, the principles that underlie gun enthusiasm are also intimately connected to larger, broader values and principles that run through American culture more generally. Only by understanding those connections and recognizing how and why guns are meaningful to their owners can we begin to understand why guns remain such an integral part of the United States today.

The World of Gun Enthusiasm

Despite the stereotype of the lone gunman, gun enthusiasm is actually a profoundly social practice.[1] Gun enthusiasts come together with friends to collect guns, discuss them, buy and sell them, and get down to the business of shooting them. In the following two chapters, I describe the world of gun enthusiasm and shooting sports in the Northern California area, discussing the places that people go to engage in these gun-related activities. I also introduce a number of people who have made guns integral to their lives, in a wide variety of ways, and what kinds of social practices are most meaningful to shooters in relation to guns. In doing so, I illustrate the ways gun enthusiasm as a social practice both reflects and constitutes some of the main issues and concerns that face Americans in their everyday lives and in everyday situations. Ironically, because gun enthusiasm has become seen as something profoundly ugly and pathological, it's very easy to forgot that in essence, the gun culture is a quintessential part of American culture. Shooters themselves help make this basic point more clear throughout the chapter.

Shooting Ranges and Shooting Classes

Shooting ranges are one of the most common places that shooters exercise their love of shooting, and where they gather to socialize with other shooters. I consequently spent most of my time on various ranges in the Bay Area, and those ranges became the primary places I met and got to know the movers and shakers in the community.

John and I met while I was signing up for an introductory shooting class for the first time. John runs a combination gun shop and indoor shooting range called Franklin Firearms, which he actually inherited from his father. John is friendly and sociable, a former military man in his early forties, muscular and fit with a deep, husky voice and a very firm handshake. Franklin advertises in the Yellow Pages as a good place for novices to be introduced to handguns and gun safety, so it seemed an ideal place to start learning more about the world of guns and shooting sports.

During our initial meeting and in the visits that followed, I got to know John and recognize the ways that his shop and range reflected his own views about guns and shooting more generally. John and his employees work hard to ensure that beginners find their first experience with guns safe, comfortable, and positive, all of which John believes are core aspects of gun ownership. Franklin Firearms is located in a predominantly working-class neighborhood, and its clientele, as well as its employee base, reflects the ethnic mix of white, Asian, Latino, and occasionally black shooters in the area. The range employees are mostly men, but early in my period of participant observation two young women worked there as well. Though an enthusiastic sport shooter, John gears his range and shop toward home defense; he both sells and rents handguns as well as long guns, and his range draws heavily from both the public and law enforcement communities.

In many respects, Franklin's layout is typical for a combination shop and shooting range. Visitors entering the establishment walk immediately into the gun shop. Boldly printed signs posted right up front catch the eye. These signs notify shooters that they must check in with store employees and present any guns brought onto the premises. The employee counter runs along one whole wall and the back of the store, where the indoor range is located. Standing racks fill the central body of the shop, stocking gun and shooting accoutrements. The employee counter is actually a glass case, and stored in these locked cases are dozens of handguns, both new and used. In the back area of Franklin Firearms, adjoining but closed off from the indoor range, is an area used by Manuel, an employee who runs an ammunition reloading business on the side. The walls of the store stock long guns and paper targets. Some targets are simply bull's-eyes or human silhouettes, but others are more complex, including black-and-white photographs of people (always men, both black and white) breaking into cars or buildings or even pointing guns at the camera.

The store area and the indoor range are separated by a thick cement and shatterproof glass wall, which allows the rangemaster (who works the back counter) to continually monitor all activity on the range behind him. Most ranges I visited are similarly designed: the rangemaster or another range employee checks people in and out and monitors the range itself, directly or with mirrors and/or close-circuit video cameras.

After checking themselves in with their firearms, buying or renting anything they might need, and donning their eye and ear protection, shooters walk through the small anteroom that separates the shop and the shooting range. The anteroom exists not only to allow shooters to put on eye and ear protection but also to reduce noise in the store area. Shooting is a noisy sport, and one can always spot the old-timers who've been shooting forever: they are often practically deaf.

When they first check in with store employees, shooters are assigned their own lane. Lanes are structurally similar to the lanes at a bowling alley, though shooting range lanes are separated from each other at the firing line (the marked line that shooters do not cross when firing). The top of the lane is actually a boothlike open window (usually of wooden or cement construction) with a small shelf onto which shooters rest their guns and ammunition. Shooters fire through this "open window" down the lane at their target, which is located at the end of the lane.

To affix targets downrange, shooters flip a lever on the wall of their booth that sends an automated hanger zipping toward them from the back of the shooting zone. After hanging their target, shooters flip the lever again, sending their target zipping backward into the shooting zone. Typical distances for shooting with handguns at paper targets are five to seven yards, but some ranges have distances up to twenty-five yards, depending on the size of the range itself. Shooters at indoor ranges do not cross the firing line for any reason; some are tempted because they want to pick up their "brass," the hollow casing part of their ammunition, which they can use to make "reloads," recycled ammunition. Many shooters reload their own ammunition to save money, though others use only factory ammo, as using reloads can void the warranty on some of the more expensive or finicky firearms.

Shooting by the Book

Ranges sometimes cultivate or are branded with a particular reputation and may draw a particular kind of shooter accordingly. A range may specialize in hunting, home defense, or sport shooting. According to John, Franklin's tends to specialize in home defense and therefore stocks a variety of handguns and short-range target ammunition designed for protection purposes. Likewise, the shop caters to both the general public and law enforcement communities and has hours or days oriented to the specific needs of these communities, with classes, requalifications, and intensive training sessions given by owners, employees, or independent contractors who make arrangements with the range.

Thus, Franklin, like most other ranges in Northern California, is used by a variety of people on any given day or week. In this particular regard, ranges are interesting places. They provide a space where a variety of people from different backgrounds and occupations can come together and enjoy a shared interest or hobby. Although most of the people discussed in this book would be considered middle class, shooters are a diverse group in terms of professions and lifestyles. Shooting ranges and, more specifically, shooting competitions promote socialization among diverse groups of people in ways that neighborhood parties or job-related gatherings do not. This point is particularly interesting from the perspective of civilian interaction with law enforcement: shooting ranges, gun shops, and shooting competitions provide venues where members of the public can intermingle with police officers or other law enforcement personnel. During my weekly sessions of participant observation, I regularly witnessed people at shops and ranges interacting with on- and off-duty cops, and I shot with a variety of police officers on a regular basis, sometimes chatting with them, depending on their willingness to talk with me.

John informed me at our first meeting that our introductory class would be one-on-one, and I would learn the basics of handguns from him as well as several of the other range employees, depending on their time and availability. John teaches his classes by the book, the NRA's *Introduction to Handgun Shooting*; each of the employees who taught a weekly lesson (one or two hours long) sat with the NRA manual in front of them. They used the manual to check that their answers were always technically correct and to ensure that they didn't forget to convey any information, crucial or otherwise.

The NRA's introductory course instructs new shooters on the basic aspects of guns and gun safety. Designed for absolute beginners, this course covers the different types of guns, the working mechanics of guns and ammunition, how to hold and fire a revolver and pistol safely, how to clean a gun and maintain it, and how to increase accuracy through different stances and shooting techniques. There is no real information about when guns should be used in terms of defining and advocating gun use for home defense. In this course, the NRA does not suggest appropriate and inappropriate shooting scenarios (i.e., whom to shoot at, when and why you should shoot), and the emissaries at Franklin did not take this particular opportunity to engage in more ideologically loaded discussions of gun usage.

John himself was not shy about conveying his feelings about criminals and home defense at later dates, but he did not make his feelings particularly clear when teaching me the basics of handgun safety.[1] At one point, I asked him if there was another method to learn gun safety besides basic NRA training, or if there were other organizations that taught introductory classes. He seemed somewhat puzzled by the question and said that there were other ways to learn, but "Why would you need another organization besides the NRA to learn gun safety?" I didn't really have an answer formulated at the time, and we quickly moved on to more basics. The NRA's basic safety rules and regulations as well as their training manuals and classes so dominate the world of shooting that beginners rarely look elsewhere unless they have ready access to a community of shooters already.

John and I enjoyed chatting together, and he communicated to all his employees that they should make themselves available to me for interviewing. I did manage to interview John and two other employees who self-identified as gun enthusiasts and who taught several classes within the introductory course.

John himself is an interesting man. He loves guns and learned to shoot at an early age; his father taught him about guns as a child and put him through a hunter safety course.

He is proudly politically conservative and proud of his wife, whom he identified as politically liberal and better-educated than he. He has always seen shooting as a family activity. John describes his wife as "antigun until she actually went out and shot an AR15, and she liked it." He taught her to shoot, particularly because he thought she should be able to use a gun defensively if the need should arise. Self-defensive gun training is important "because crooks have always had guns. . . . Serious drug people or whatever are gonna get the guns if they really want 'em. . . . I think our best defense against those types of things is for us to have 'em too." In keeping with this self-defense philosophy, John had me practice on the range by picking up my handgun and shooting without sighting the gun. Though these kinds of activities produced fairly inaccurate shooting on my part, John felt it was important to understand how to handle guns in emergencies. These facets of shooting practice were not part of the pleasure of shooting that he enjoyed, but he wanted his students to understand that guns are both fun and serious business.

Sierra Gun Club and Shooting Range

My second class was an all-day event at Sierra Gun Club, an outdoor range that has been in existence in the Bay Area for years. Located on a fairly sizable plot of land in a national park region of the greater Bay Area, Sierra is well-hidden within the woodsy hills and valleys. A small road sign with an arrow indicates the dirt road entrance to the range, an easy-to-miss turn off the paved county road that runs through the park region. Sierra has a small office area perched on the top of a hillside where shooters check in and buy necessary accoutrements. The ranges themselves—pistol, rifle, and long-range rifle, in particular—are spread out in a valley area that comprises the range as a whole. The club offers a yearly membership that is reasonably priced (about $85 in 1998),[2] which enables shooters to pay less each time they venture out to the range.

Sierra does not rent guns, unlike most of the indoor ranges of the area. Shooters must bring their own guns to shoot there, which means that the range is not as welcoming for beginners. Although the range shop does sell ammunition, eye and ear protection, and targets, the shop is not as extensively stocked as others in the greater Bay Area.

Shooters pull up to the range and park their vehicles, walk down a steep hill to the shooting areas (which are grouped according to target range distance: short range for handgun, medium and long range for rifles), and shoot into a large, wooded mountain of earth that slopes upward into forestland. Commands from a rangemaster are broadcast over a loudspeaker, easily audible from anywhere on the grounds. Shooters are notified of a fifteen-minute shooting period, during which time they are allowed to prep their guns and shoot. Rangemasters walk up and down the whole compound, patrolling the preparation areas where shooters are organizing their guns, loading them, and shooting at their targets. These range officers often check and assist shooters, making sure they are behaving safely and are obeying range rules.

After the fifteen-minute shooting period is over, a rangemaster announces over the loudspeaker that a break period has commenced. During breaks between shooting, shooters walk out from the sheltered preparation areas and onto the grassy grounds to their targets. They have about ten minutes to put up, check, or take down their targets. During that period, shooters are not allowed to even touch their guns, which must be visibly free of ammunition (demonstrating that the gun is safe to be left unattended). When the ten minutes is up, shooters are informed once again over the loudspeaker that the shooting period will recommence shortly. Patrolling range officers make sure that the grassy area between the firing line and the targets is clear of people before the shooting period starts again. Range officers stop to answer questions and inform shooters of the workings of the range, but Sierra has a very regimented, no-nonsense atmosphere that is intimidating to new shooters.

The introductory class at Sierra was taught by Greg, a knowledgeable and articulate Vietnam veteran in his early fifties. Greg volunteered his time as a shooting instructor and had been an influential member at the club for years. This was a group class with eight people, including a father and his teenage son. Greg is a charismatic man and an effective teacher, covering much of the same basic safety and handling instructions that I had learned at Franklin Firearms. But his overview was forcefully condensed and had an urgent, authoritarian tone, very much in keeping with the style of the range itself. The day passed quickly, culminating in a late afternoon shooting session in chilly winter rain. Greg marched behind us, shouting occasionally as we shot our handguns at paper bull's-eye targets at close range. He brusquely fixed incorrect stance or technique, quietly muttering a compliment now and then. With our brains crammed full of information about how guns work and the basics of good shooting techniques, all of the students were exhausted by the end of the day.

Teaching Shooting as Community Service

During the class, Greg emphasized the necessity of what he called "good gun etiquette," one aspect of which is never pointing a gun at another human being, regardless of whether or not it is loaded. He clearly followed this doctrine himself, and when he handled guns, he would turn them in his hands very carefully, without ever pointing the muzzle at himself or anyone around him. He reinforced the deadliness of guns, constantly reiterating the idea that although they are not "magic talismans," they do have symbolic and literal power in the hands of their users, regardless of how they are used.

In our interview, Greg spoke candidly about why he teaches gun safety and why he enjoys it. He explained that he joined the military as a young man to test both his manhood and his independence, and he credited the military with teaching him much of what he knows about firearms. His military experience aged him considerably, and his interest in guns subsided once he got out of the service. But several years later, a friend reintroduced him to shooting. Since then he's been an avid enthusiast and has dedicated several weekends a month to teaching shooting classes on a volunteer basis. He believes strongly that he is performing a community service by passing on his knowledge to his students. He talked about how people, particularly women, came to his classes both concerned about violent crime and frightened of guns. Greg feels that the media and the entertainment industry prey on people's fear of guns and crime. He believes it is important to provide knowledge and understanding of how to use guns safely and with confidence. He believes that the anxieties of living in a violent society necessitate learning to keep yourself safe, not because most people are likely to get attacked, but because the fear of being attacked can be just as paralyzing.

Greg articulated several important themes about gun enthusiasm and shooting sports for me. The most important is that some shooters are well aware that the media and popular culture can engender unreasonable or unrealistic fear about violence and crime in society. But even though that's the case, some people still choose self-defense training with guns as a means to address those anxieties. Addressing unnamed fears through preparedness is more satisfying than dismissing those fears as simply unfounded. Greg also embodies the fact that although some veterans are ambivalent or even angry about their military experience, some still find pleasure in firearms. A rejection of war or the military does not necessarily indicate a rejection of guns and shooting sports. Rather than reject guns as a symbol of killing, Greg takes pleasure in teaching others about gun safety. His attitude is that there will always be guns around, so the most responsible position a person can take is to learn good gun safety.

Hot Shots Indoor Shooting Range

I took my third set of lessons at Hot Shots, also a range and shop located in a high-rent community in the area. Hot Shots is a slightly smaller establishment than Franklin Firearms, with a smaller employee base and more circumscribed clientele. Run mostly by men, the range has a slightly macho feel that is cultivated by the owner, Jim, through his friendly but gruff style of interaction that focuses almost exclusively on the world of guns. He wasn't very interested in chatting about much else. His employees were somewhat friendly but restrained. They were willing to make chit-chat occasionally, but they were also clearly business-oriented, usually interested only in offering advice and knowledge about handling, cleaning, and shooting guns.

An indoor range with a small shop that stocks guns, ammunition, cleaning supplies, and targets for the range, Hot Shots, like Franklin Firearms, has an anteroom that separates the range from the shop. But like other ranges similarly structured, the ubiquitous sound of handgun fire resounds in the background of any conversation or transaction in the shop.

This third class at Hot Shots was taught by two female instructors, Jane and Louise, who had an arrangement with Jim to teach introductory and advanced-beginner handgun classes. Louise is a former journalist who had gone through police training, and Jane was working toward her private investigator's license at the time. This class was composed of mostly women (seven women, two men), almost all of whom were between forty and sixty-five years old. Most of these women said that they had a husband or male friend who owned and enjoyed guns. I was one of the few students who had handled guns previously and already owned a gun.

Women in the Men's Room

After the class had finished, I became friendly with Jane, and she and I shot regularly together at this range. She talked openly, as did Louise, about her feeling that the world of guns and shooting tends to be a men's club. She said that she struggled to feel comfortable and maintain her credibility at the various ranges where she shot.

Both Jane and Louise had had negative experiences at a range in the northeastern part of the area, where they felt they were patronized by male employees, even disparaged behind their backs because they are women. Both are competent shooters and instructors, and Jane in particular is an avid enthusiast and highly skilled marksperson. However, she feels her skills tend to make her the target of jealousy and even mean-spirited remarks, particularly by male shooters less competent than she. She is comfortable teaching and shooting at Hot Shots, however, because Jim treats her respectfully and she gets along well with most of the other employees at that range. Sometimes shooting ranges and gun shops live up to their negative reputation as men's clubs, and female shooters need to fight for respect in such male-dominated arenas.

This third class was an excellent conduit to a variety of other shooting experiences, not only because Jane became a friend, but also because in that class I met a woman named Thea. Thea is charming and vivacious, and after the first class, she quickly expressed interest in becoming friends and introducing me to a variety of other shooters she has known for years. An attorney, she was then dating (and eventually married) a man several years her junior, whom she identified as a "cowboy action shooter." Jonathan had become interested in cowboy action shooting after seeing some cowboy action shooters gathered at a local range one weekend. He got Thea involved, and they both introduced me to the sport, which became one of my greatest sources of information about the world of shooting sports, gun enthusiasm, and the ways that shooters express themselves through shooting. I describe the sport of cowboy action shooting in the following chapter.

Range Rules

All of the ranges I attended had in place a basic set of safety rules, or range rules, which are designed to maintain basic safety standards, as well as regulations designed for the particular specifications of the range itself. Range rules can be fairly standard rules that apply to all manner of handling guns, such as the axiom "Always keep a gun pointed in a safe direction," which is usually downrange on a range, or straight down or up if you're in a more public space. Other rules, including "Never load a gun until you're ready to shoot" and "Finger off the trigger until the gun is pointed downrange," are standard as well and are taught in introductory classes.

These rules are also often canonized on the walls of a shooting range, and they operationalize basic shooting standards that help ensure and enforce gun safety from one locale to the next. This is evidence of one way that gun owners consider themselves a community: shooters both self-regulate and regulate each other to ensure the safety of the community itself.

At Sierra, these rules are strictly enforced, and rangemasters either give warnings or throw shooters off the range for any safety violation. Critics of the gun industry are sometimes critical of shooting ranges; one critic stated grandly that "ranges are notoriously unsafe."[3] On some level, such a critique isn't so surprising: there were no formalized mechanisms at any of the ranges that I visited (when I conducted the research) that proactively measured shooters' ability with guns or their adherence to standard safety and handling rules. However, most of the ranges I visited had fairly attentive rangemasters, people whose job and own personal safety depend on their ability to keep track of shooters' behavior on the range.

Shooters offer advice or critical comments to each other while on the range or in the shop, even to outright strangers. Usually shooters appear open to such exchange of tips and information. But there is always a certain amount of inherent trust involved with shooting at a range, particularly a range that is regularly used by the general public. Shooters are often standing next to strangers, people who may or may not be competent to handle the guns they're shooting. Shooters seem to generally believe that if an individual is spending time at a shooting range, he or she can be trusted to use guns relatively safely. Several people voiced concerns during interviews, however, that shooting ranges made them uneasy: you never really know if the people standing next to you can safely handle their guns or not.

Suicides have occurred on several local ranges, and such incidents were understandably upsetting to range owners and employees. How these incidents could be prevented was puzzling for some owners. After one incident, several implemented the "shooting in pairs" rule, which means that if a shooter is unknown or new to the range and wants to rent a gun, he or she cannot shoot it alone. New shooters who rent guns must be accompanied by another shooter. The logic here is that if the shooter brings his or her own gun, then suicide is unlikely: Who would use a range when the task could be accomplished at home? But if the shooter who wants to rent is accompanied by a friend, the presumption is that a suicide is less likely to occur. One range in the area changed their policy to "no gun rentals at all" so that they would not have to worry about suicides on their premises. To my knowledge, that policy is working so far.

In general, the best that most ranges can do regarding safety is employ conscientious rangemasters who watch shooters carefully and offer to assist shooters who appear to be novices or unsafe with their guns. Some rangemasters told me that they often stepped in to assist people who were having difficulties or threw people off the range when they witnessed unsafe practices. At Franklin, range employees encouraged new shooters to purchase the "beginner's package," which included a twenty-minute lesson, handgun rental, one hundred rounds of .22 ammunition, several targets, and an hour of range time, with assistance from a range employee at any point during that time.

Manuel, who worked at Franklin, told me that the range is not legally responsible for making sure people understand how to operate their own guns properly, but range employees take it upon themselves to educate people. During our interview, he put it this way: "It's kind of scary sometimes, that somebody can somehow pass the test and get their Basic Firearms Safety Certificate and still not know how to operate a gun they just bought. So that can't be safe. There's no way that's safe." He told me he had just met two men who bought a gun from a gun show, brought it to Franklin for shooting practice, and then complained that the gun didn't work properly. "They went in there [to the range] and they come out and they say, 'It won't shoot.' They didn't know how to load it. I took it upon myself to show them, but it's not our responsibility to make sure they know how, because they've got the certificate, the person that sold them the gun [should teach them]. Any time we sell a gun out of this store we make sure they know how to use it, even if they have their BFSC [Basic Firearms Safety Certificate]."

Rangemasters said that generally most new shooters are willing to take instruction if the instructor is clearly more knowledgeable than they are. However, several also said that new male gun owners will sometimes assume a degree of knowledge and expertise that is clearly posturing, often when they're with a female companion they're (apparently) trying to impress. Every instructor I met (both male and female) said they prefer teaching women because women make better students: women are more willing to listen to their instructors, do not assume their sex automatically denotes expertise with a gun, and are not invested in proving themselves immediately capable with an unfamiliar gun. Instructors generally communicated the idea that some men seem to believe they are born knowing how to operate guns safely and properly, and as that is clearly not the case, teaching such men how to become safe gun owners is particularly challenging.

Gun Shops and Gun Dealers

Most of the ranges in Northern California have some form of attendant shop attached. A good gun shop sells a variety of targets and ammunition as well as new and used guns. The Bay Area also has several stand-alone gun shops, some of them quite extensively equipped and others somewhat smaller, crammed with more shooting accoutrements than guns.

Gun shops, like shooting ranges, develop a reputation in the area and may attract a clientele accordingly. Shooters I befriended said that they tend to visit a shop that they like in their neighborhood (or nearby), unless they have a particular issue with a shop and therefore don't want to frequent it. For example, several female shooters told me they don't like a particular shop in the eastern part of the region because the employees either ignore or patronize women. For some female shooters, this kind of behavior is unacceptable. This same shop has a reputation among several other shooters who have law enforcement ties as somewhat shady in its business practices.[4] Other shooters simply feel uneasy about this store but occasionally shop there because it is so well stocked. Obviously, there are checks and balances involved in shopping at various business establishments, and shooters make calculated choices about where they want to shop and why.

Several stores in the Bay Area actually closed down while I was doing my research, including a shop that had been in the area for decades. One, Johnson's, was located in an urban area afflicted by serious economic decline. Close to a freeway, the neighborhood is full of liquor stores, run-down sandwich shops, and always empty parking lots. Several shooters mentioned that Johnson's went under because it had been targeted by local politicians as an institution that should be shut down "for the good of the community." The shop apparently had been drowning under a barrage of paperwork, suffering from increased taxes on retailers who sell guns, bans on certain kinds of guns that sell primarily to low-income individuals, and hostility from local government.[5] My several visits to the shop before it finally closed introduced me to employees who were knowledgeable but brusque, disinterested in making conversation unrelated to immediate sales. The shop's business troubles probably explain why employees were reluctant to sink valuable time into a research project only tangentially related to their business.

Johnson's was not the only gun store in the area that had been having trouble staying solvent. Another well-known shop in the city, just as well-established but actually bigger and better-equipped, also closed down in the late 1990s. When shooters discussed these closings, there was usually a lot of head shaking, frowns, and disgusted faces. Shooters feel the local government's efforts to "eradicate the gun culture" by targeting specific gun shops is morally wrong. As far as shooters are concerned, these stores had not been engaged in wrongful business practices but rather had been selling products that some Bay Area residents find offensive. Shooters believe these issues demonstrate that local politicians simply pander to their liberal constituency and cynically target businesses that the self-appointed intelligentsia of the area designate immoral. Shooters feel that these kinds of issues illustrate that gun owners are the pariahs of the area more generally. They find the high-profile rhetoric of "making the Bay Area safer" by driving gun stores out of business to be ridiculous at best, offensive at worst.

Although the number of venues for purchasing guns has been shrinking somewhat, shooters can still purchase from stores near or just outside the main city limits, or seek out local gun dealers.[6] I met a number of freelance gun dealers (i.e., who do not operate out of a shop) during my research. Several hold dealers' licenses so that they can purchase for themselves more cheaply from manufacturers, but gun dealing is simply a side interest. Several others work in some other capacity related to the gun world and find it useful to also be licensed to sell guns. To purchase my first gun, I went back to the person who first taught me to shoot: John at Franklin Firearms.

Buying Guns

Choosing a gun for purchase can be a difficult and confusing process. First, there is an extraordinary array of guns on the market. Each gun is designed to address and reflect the personal requirements and tastes of its shooter. Dealers like John encourage new purchasers to buy guns that are manageable and enjoyable to shoot, but that can also serve for self- or home defense if the buyer wants a gun for that purpose. For my first purchase, John worked to convince me that revolvers are actually easier to manage than semiautomatics. I initially wondered if he would try to steer me in a particular direction because I am a woman (and therefore weaker and more delicate, according to my prejudicial assumptions about his prejudicial assumptions), but John basically conveyed the idea that any gun would be good for a woman if she would manage it effectively, that is, pick it up, load it, and shoot it accurately. I ended up choosing a stainless steel Smith and Wesson 687 revolver, a .357 caliber handgun that also shoots .38 caliber ammunition. This gun was my first choice because the grip fits my hand easily, its weight is substantial but manageable, it takes a standard and reasonably inexpensive caliber of ammunition, its appearance is aesthetically pleasing to me when compared to other handguns, and I can indeed shoot it fairly well.

To purchase a firearm of any kind in California, a potential gun owner must obtain a BFSC. One can either read the BFSC booklet and pass the accompanying test (usually issued by a certified gun dealer or some other legitimate party), take a BFSC course and pass the test, or take and pass the test without bothering with the preliminaries. Questions on the test revolve around correct loading, handling, and maintenance of firearms, as well as some of the more technical aspects of projectile trajectories. After passing the test, one receives the BFSC card, enabling legal gun purchase. This licensing procedure is similar to taking the written exam for a driver's license.

The more interesting part of buying a gun in California comes from the necessity of undergoing a minor investigation, or check for criminal background. A potential buyer hands over a driver's license, a passport, or a similar government-issued identification to the dealer, and his or her information gets typed into a computer by that dealer or range employee (dealers and ranges are required to have an FFL, or Federal Firearms License, which federally licenses the ability to sell firearms). Potential buyers fill out a computerized form that demands they lack three things: a felony record, a history of mental instability, and a history of criminal drug use. This form is then sent to the state capital, Sacramento, and the state of California has ten business days to determine whether the potential purchaser can legally claim the firearm. The firearm can be viewed and handled on the range premises, but the dealer is not legally permitted to officially transfer the gun to the buyer's hands until the waiting period is over. After the ten days have passed, and provided one has passed the background check and that no inconsistencies or outright untruths are discovered, the buyer is permitted to take home the firearm.[7]

Although this process is supposed to prevent felons from purchasing guns from dealers, it is not failsafe. Robby, a former army officer and part-time firearms dealer, made these issues clearer over a lengthy interview. Robby is particularly concerned that the state of California's methods for ensuring the legality of gun sales are weak at best. He said that he knows state record checkers are overworked and not always "competent," in his terms. He believes that the ten-day period is not enough time because state employees are so overworked; he estimated that only one in three background checks are actually conducted in that time period. Robby mentioned that at one point, three months after he had legally transferred a gun to a new buyer, he received a phone call from a state employee about the sale. The employee told Robby that this particular buyer had a criminal record and Robby should forbid the exchange. Utterly exasperated, Robby said the gun had long ago left his possession; because he had not heard from the state about the potential buyer after the requisite ten days had passed, he had legally transferred the gun to the buyer. The state employee's response to that information was "Get it back." Robby promptly told her that this was the state's problem, not his. His comment effectively ended the phone call.

Robby was angry that the state accepted no responsibility for its understaffing, incompetence, or oversight. On relaying this story to me, he looked me in the eye and said sardonically, "Ever try to repossess a gun?" He told me that he now refuses to sell guns to some individuals when they don't "feel right" to him. Though I tried to press him to describe who felt right and who did not, he wasn't interested in pursuing that conversational angle any further, perhaps because he thought I was trying to trap him into saying something bigoted or something he couldn't substantiate. This issue underscores one of the more interesting and troubling issues that confronts some firearms dealers. If they do not sell to potential buyers, they can find themselves in legal hot water. On what basis have they decided not to sell? Is it the race, class, or gender of the potential buyer that dissuades the dealer from continuing the transaction? But if a dealer does sell to someone who "feels wrong," he or she may find out later that the gun was sold to a felon or potential felon. This issue made several dealers with whom I spoke uncomfortable, if only because few of them had any confidence in California's apparatus for dealing with background checks.

One of the most important reasons for shooters to purchase the right guns is so that they can most easily enjoy their chosen shooting sports. Different sports demand different kinds of guns; therefore, choosing the right kind of gun for each sport is exceedingly important, particularly if a shooter wants to be competitive. For example, the first gun I purchased was completely inappropriate for the sport I ended up pursuing most frequently, cowboy action shooting. My Smith and Wesson 687 is a thoroughly modern gun, a stainless steel, double-action revolver. Its modern features make it unacceptable for a sport that demands "antique replica" guns. When I settled on cowboy action shooting, it was back to the drawing board, and the search for the "perfect" gun began again.

Shooting Sports

There are a wide variety of shooting sports available to shooters, even in an area as urban and populated as the metropolitan area of Northern California. Recreational shooting sports include highly competitive organizations like the USPSA (the United States Practical Shooting Association), IPSC (International Practical Shooting Confederation), and SASS (Single Action Shooting Society), all international organizations with local clubs that hold local competitions on a regular basis. Cowboy action shooters usually belong to SASS, which is somewhat more relaxed than the others; I discuss that sport extensively in the next chapter.

IPSC shooting is quite popular in the Bay Area. IPSC shooting matches are competitions organized around "practical" shooting scenarios, sometimes called "combat" shooting scenarios. Originally intended to replicate scenarios that police might encounter in the course of their duties, shooters compete by literally running through a course, drawing semiautomatic pistols from a holster, and aiming at human-shaped cardboard targets. The more extensive and well-financed IPSC matches sometimes have courses that imitate a would-be "home invasion" scenario.[8] Shooters negotiate their way through a stage set that resembles a middle-class American living room, replete with couches, easy chairs, and televisions. Targets pop up from behind furniture or from closets, and shooters must make quick decisions about how best to approach targets with speed and accuracy. In the Bay Area, local IPSC clubs are dominated by men, most of whom are white or

Asian, although a couple of women did compete in the several events I observed. In the shooting community, IPSC shooters have a reputation for being skilled but highly competitive, placing a premium on talent and competition as opposed to recreation and relaxation.

Several of the cowboy shooters I met who were familiar with the organization said that although IPSC shooters are certainly proficient, they "take themselves rather seriously" and are an uptight and rather joyless group. I did not find that to be true: IPSC shooters find their chosen sport as enjoyable and relaxing as other shooters found theirs, but IPSC shooters do pride themselves on being "better and faster" than other shooters. Whether or not this is empirically true is difficult to say. I didn't attempt to test it.

As to the relationship between shooting sports and an enthusiasm for violence, even shooters themselves are concerned about the question of what *really* motivates certain gun owners to take up shooting sports. These issues became more clear to me as my research progressed, and came to a head when I observed certain kinds of shooting competitions.

A Target Is a Target . . . Or Is It?

One of the most fascinating encounters I witnessed happened while I was doing participant observation at a small local IPSC match. It was late one Sunday morning, and the match was just finishing. Organizers were rushing things along because the range was going to be hosting a cowboy action shooting practice next, and the cowboy shooters were already arriving on the range, some of them watching the IPSC goings-on rather doubtfully.

The IPSC organizers were dismantling the courses and taking down cardboard-mounted paper targets, most of which had vaguely human torsos in their center. I sat chatting with an IPSC shooter, a white, slightly overweight man in his midthirties who had been competing that day. A cowboy shooter in his late fifties or early sixties, also white, with a big, bushy beard, strolled up to us in his cowboy regalia, watching the IPSC targets being disassembled. He turned to the IPSC shooter and said, "Those are your targets, huh? Looks like you're shooting at a person." The IPSC shooter looked at him rather coldly and said, "It looks like a target to me. That's all it is. A target." The cowboy snorted skeptically and ambled off, leaving the IPSC shooter to mutter somewhat defensively about snotty cowboy action shooters who thought they were better than everybody else. I nodded sympathetically, decided not to mention my participation in cowboy action shooting, and we quickly moved on to another topic.

Some shooters do feel ambivalent about how their chosen sport relates to the specter of violence and home defense. For most of the shooters with whom I spent time, shooting is a sport. A target is a piece of paper or a metal square positioned several yards away. Shooters spend their time and energy carefully and calmly aiming at these targets and pulling the trigger of their gun. Most shooting sports are exercises in skill and concentration, even when shooters are full of adrenaline, moving quickly and excitedly through a course. All this is to say, paraphrasing Freud, that sometimes a target really is just a target.

But sometimes, shooting is about preparing for the possibility of killing someone. Some shooters take classes to master self-defense techniques, learning how to conceptualize paper targets as people, focusing on "kill zones" and honing these skills to that purpose. Some shooters work to understand the process of shooting to kill and try to develop a mind-set in which they could do so. When I took my first set of lessons at Franklin, practicing with my new gun, the range employees teased me about my aim, demanding to see my targets to assess my newly acquired skills. At one point, Manuel, a Mexican American man in his late thirties who had taught one of my lessons, looked over my target and nodded his head positively, saying, "Oh yeah, he's dead, he's dead. You got him, definitely."

This comment startled me, and I realized that my own thoughts about the exercise (i.e., how difficult it was to hit the bull's-eye, how my eyes were crossing after about five minutes, how my arms were stiff) had been very different from Manuel's assessment of my activities. Manuel had grown up on the streets of the city and had quietly articulated his belief in self-defensive gun use during some of our conversations. He had apparently put me in a certain category, so to speak: a relatively young, single woman at a shooting range specializing in self- and home defense, taking up shooting for protection. He assumed that I was learning to shoot for self-defense because I felt vulnerable or was vulnerable (or both). As far as he was concerned, my efforts at learning to shoot were really efforts to learn how to better protect myself, specifically with a handgun.

In our subsequent conversations, Manuel told me that he had taught his wife and teenage children to shoot, and he believes firmly that shooting skills are important for living in a dangerous and hostile urban area. Manuel had also been in the military, and thinking about the possibility of shooting someone is not foreign to him.[9] He had experienced violence in his life and he understood its ramifications. He is not naïve about these issues. Like most of the shooters I met, he approaches this issue with gravity and spoke of this future possibility in highly abstract terms, conceptualizing it as a remote prospect that would occur only under certain conditions of extreme duress. Although shooting is an enjoyable activity for him, guns are also a tool for protecting himself, his home, and his family.

Guns in Context

Ultimately, context is the biggest determinant for how guns are thought about and used, literally and metaphorically. Kathy, a white woman in her early forties who works at a racetrack, clarified this point for me. I went shooting several times with Kathy and her boyfriend, Elliot, who had introduced Kathy to guns twelve years earlier. One of our shooting excursions took place before my beginner classes, and I had to borrow guns from them. We went to Sierra Gun Club because Kathy and Elliot both enjoy shooting in the beautiful mountain setting. After we arrived, Elliot went to register us with the rangemaster, and Kathy and I chatted as we gathered up our gear in the parking area. As we talked, I looked over at the paper targets that Kathy had with her. I noticed that on one of the targets was a vaguely human shape, a silhouette of a man from the waist up.

I was not yet familiar with the variety of targets available, or what Kathy preferred to use. I assumed that this was Kathy's usual target. I asked if she ever imagined that the target was a person so that she could start to think about the possibility of shooting someone in self-defense. She looked startled and horrified. She immediately said, "No!" rather forcefully. She shook her head and then elaborated by saying that shooting was a sport. Fantasizing about shooting people had no place on the sporting range. She was clearly uncomfortable that I had suggested such a thing and repeated several times how inappropriate the idea was.

But I was puzzled by her response because I knew that she felt strongly about keeping a gun for self-defense. She was using a target with a vaguely human shape on it. She had told me previously that she had a particular gun that she kept specifically for defensive purposes. I wondered if her denial was actually defensive embarrassment; clearly, this was an issue about which she had feelings.

Her thought process became clearer several weeks later, when I asked her what owning a gun meant to her. She said, "It's just a means to have that experience that I enjoy. . . . I mean, that's the primary reason I have guns, because I enjoy the experience of shooting them. I do have a gun that I'm not really thrilled with, one that I bought for self-defense only, and only as a carry gun. And I feel much differently about that gun than I do about the other two.... I view that [gun] as a tool, and the others as recreation. So it's very different."

Kathy understands her sporting interests to be separate and distinct from the issue of protection. Mixing the two even in fantasy is an uncomfortable idea. It was only later that I realized that the gun she uses for self-defense, which she refers to as her "icky" gun, is one she rarely (if ever) used for sport. She does conduct target practice with that gun, but she uses her sporting pistols far more frequently.

Although I didn't understand at the time, this was my first window into how gun enthusiasts place their guns into meaningful contexts. Not all shooters have a specific set of sport guns differentiated from another set of defense guns, but context determines how guns are thought about and used. This is the case even in relation to the gun-related fantasies of their owners, which is an issue that arises again and again in relation to shooting sports such as IPSC and cowboy action shooting.

Shooting sports, and the world of guns more generally, are similar to any other complex social institution in American society. The gun culture is plagued by the same kinds of (subtle and overt) sexism, racism, and classism that exists in many American social institutions. In other words, the gun culture is a part of American culture as a whole. But because gun ownership has become so stigmatized, the racism, sexism, and even violence-prone behavior of some gun owners has come to unilaterally define the public perception of gun culture itself. Members of the gun culture are now stereotyped to embody everything dark and ugly about Americans as a people. But it is naïve to pretend that only the gun culture is beset by these issues, or that guns (and gun owners) are themselves solely responsibly for the crime and violence so rife in the United States. Certainly, the world of guns has its own signs, symbols, discourses, and patterns of meaningful interaction. But in essence, the gun culture, like American culture more generally, is rife with conflict and contradiction, and is just as multilayered and faceted as the larger culture to which it belongs.

It's so real, it's like being in a movie.[1]

Cowboy Action Shooting

Throughout this book, I argue that shooters use mythic history to convey core cultural values, and guns (in symbol and in fact) are deeply embedded in both that history and those values. So what kinds of broader cultural beliefs and ideals are shooters expressing? What are shooters trying to accomplish with all their stories about the importance of guns and the social practices associated with gun enthusiasm?

Shooters are in fact attempting to demonstrate that their gun enthusiasm makes them good Americans—they value American history and they believe in the values often associated with American patriotism. Shooters in general, and cowboy action shooters in particular, are literally "performing" their status as native sons and daughters, claiming their identity as authentic American citizens.

To perform one's Americanness, to quite literally demonstrate this sense of personal and national identity, is actually a meaningful cultural practice for Americans more generally.[2] Americans frequently perform their adherence to American core values, in both public and private arenas: they say the Pledge of Allegiance at schools, they celebrate the Fourth of July with fireworks, community picnics, and patriotic songs. Children perform plays during tried-and-true American holidays like Thanksgiving and Washington's Birthday, dramatizing the myths and legends of American history that are really simply forms of "creation myths" for the nation. In these kinds of myths, the United States was founded and developed by men and women of European descent who carved out a savage land, using the values of strength, progress, and democracy, all of which was justly and fairly adjudicated by inherently moral Christian people.

In this chapter, I describe the sport of cowboy action shooting, which is the shooting sport that most explicitly dramatizes this master narrative of American Frontier history. I describe the cowboy shoots governed by the Single Action Shooting Society (SASS), the international organization for "official" cowboy shooting. In fact, dramatizing American mythic history affirms for shooters a basic tenet of pro-gun ideology—that gun owners are not just law-abiding people who happen to own guns. This is a shooting sport conducted in a venue that ostensibly gave birth to images of traditional American gender roles and forms of Frontier-oriented entertainment, literal and figurative. Cowboy action shooting presents a vision of the American Frontier in which white, middle-class good guys can create small, self-contained communities based on shared values and shared lifestyles, all of which are almost entirely self-regulated. They see themselves as true American citizens—people who deeply respect the laws, traditions, and history of the United States—modern-day good guys in every way that really counts.

Home on the Range

It's early Saturday morning at the range, and there's a definite chill in the autumn air. The trucks and SUVs are starting to fill the parking lot of the Sierra Gun Club, one of the largest outdoor ranges in the area. Wooden gun carts are unloaded from the backs of all vehicles, and shooters start to push them down the grassy knolls toward the ranges.

A sizable group of cowboy action shooters, about fifty in total, have started to gather in the rocky dirt areas near the pistol and short-range rifle ranges. Mostly men, but about ten women as well, they are laughing and chatting noisily, looking like actors off a movie set, an old-fashioned spaghetti western. The men are quite nattily dressed for the most part, some with long black frock coats over floral or suede waistcoats and shiny black dress boots over gray tweed slacks. Even those who aren't so fancy are also concerned with their appearance, fussily tucking their linen shirts into their button-down trousers and arranging their holsters to sit on their hips "just so." Most men are in their fifties and sixties, although a fair number appear to be in their forties, and several appear to be in their early and late seventies. The really old-timers have long gray beards and droopy moustaches and are slightly hunched over and squinting in the morning light.

Most of the women are dressed just like their male counterparts, in green or black button-down trousers and tailored waistcoats over white shirts, with stylish felt cowboy hats on their heads. Some women, however, are more elegant and elaborately clothed, with long silk or cotton dresses, lacy petticoats peeking out from underneath, and white lace dress gloves. Several wear notable cameos on their high-necked collars and carry dainty cloth purses on their arm. They are a bit younger than the men, most in their forties and fifties. They too wear holsters on their hips and are busy arranging all of their gear, fixing their shotgun belts so that their female anatomy won't interfere with a quick reach for a shotgun shell. Some are glancing at tiny, antique-style watches hung round their neck like necklaces. It's approaching 8:45 A.M., getting close to start time.

In the midst of all this busy preparation and shuffling of guns from carry-bag to gun cart, a lone, burly cowboy, dressed like his brethren, ambles over to the sidelines and perches himself on the grassy incline leading up to the parking lot. He clears his throat as he turns to face the crowd, smoothing down his bushy beard and moustache.

He puts his hands back up to his face and hollers for everyone to quiet down, and then waits for the crowd to settle. When all eyes are focused on him, he hollers, "Most of you know me! I'm Wild Phil Hiccup! Welcome to the fourth annual Sierra Round-Up!"

The crowd hoots their approval at this welcome, cheering and whistling, clapping and stamping their feet heartily. Clouds of dust now rise from the ground, much to everyone's further delight. Wild Phil gestures to shush them. Hands wave the dust away as the crowd settles again. Wild Phil tells us loudly that we need to pay our entrance fees, if we haven't already paid up. If we haven't paid, we're supposed to get in line to pay. He gestures toward a scraggly line that has formed haphazardly in the past few minutes in front of a card table to his right. Two harried-looking cowpokes are running their fingers down lines of papers, one checking names and making sure entrance fees are paid, the other passing out information about who belongs in which posse.

Shooters who've already been assigned to their posse move aside, discussing their placement with their buddies, and a few are surreptitiously looking around to see where the top shooters have been placed. Most are just grinning at their new (and old) compadres, shaking hands and clapping each other on the back.

Wild Phil hollers for attention again. We are informed at top volume that this is a SASS shoot and SASS rules apply. But there's more shotgun than usual, because that's what Wild Phil likes. The crowd hoots disparagingly at this, mostly just to hassle Phil, who gestures back disparagingly. But shooters are getting restless already, eager to start the competition. Phil gives us a rundown of range rules. We have to load and unload at the proper tables. Don't load the guns until you're on deck. Listen to the posse leaders because they shot the stages yesterday and they understand the procedures. After he runs down these rules, he announces that we're going to stand ready for the Pledge of Allegiance.

At that last statement, the crowd becomes remarkably quiet, and everyone turns quickly toward an American flag flying high over the range office a good four hundred yards away. Hats come off, and a number of hands cover hearts. Wild Phil loudly leads off the Pledge, and most of the shooters join in, reciting the lines without hesitation. They are focused and attentive, with little of the feet shuffling and quiet chatting that usually accompanies the Pledge at average school or sporting events.

When the recitation finishes, the crowd looks back to Phil, who shouts simply, "Have a good shoot! Eeehawww!!"

The fourth annual Sierra Round-Up has begun.[3]

The Single Action Shooting Society

No one and nothing evokes all things American quite as powerfully as the cowboy. That shooting sports should eventually meet up with a love of the Wild West should come as no great surprise. There are a variety of nationally based cowboy action shooting organizations, including the Western Action Shootists Association and the National Congress of Old West Shootists headquartered in Cedar Falls, Iowa, but the Single Action Shooting Society is the largest and best-known organization of its kind. Local, state, and regionally based cowboy action shooting clubs loosely organize themselves around the rules and regulations of SASS. Individual cowboy action shooters join SASS in the same way they would join the NRA or any interest-based association or organization dedicated to providing leadership and guidance to a constituency.

Located in southern California, SASS has approximately thirty-eight thousand members nationally, according to its Web site posting in the spring of 2002.[4] The organization provides a modicum of cohesion for as many as 166 local and regional cowboy action shooting clubs and associations (with more adding on as I write), which are located in forty-four states as well as Canada, Australia, and throughout Europe. SASS provides competition rules and regulations, general organizational blueprints, and a source for both praise and criticism for the cowboy shooters of the San Francisco Bay Area.[5] SASS was founded in the mid-1980s by Harper Creigh (who gave himself the alias "Judge Roy Bean"), along with a group of friends who wanted to share their passion for Old West paraphernalia, most particularly firearms. Their idea was to develop a shooting sport that used only "cowboy guns," was conducted in an Old West setting, and required that participants develop cowboy personae, represented by costumes, aliases, and shooting styles when competing.[6] The "super bowl" of cowboy shoots, called End of Trail, had over a thousand competitors in 1999 in southern California, as well as hundreds of vendors and approximately twenty thousand spectators.[7]

SASS is a perfect modern-day vehicle for the myths, legends, and stories of the American Frontier that are ubiquitous in American culture. These myths and legends have always articulated a wide variety of themes and do so even in contemporary society. For example, the myth that white Europeans were solely responsible for civilizing and populating a vast and desolate West has become a primary ideological construct in American society.

When modern-day cowboy shooters make their choices about the identity they present to themselves and their friends, they make good use of these exceedingly popular myths and legends of the taming of the Wild West. Cowboy shooters borrow heavily from several broad and sweeping mythic narratives that are valorized and celebrated in a variety of American cultural productions, all of which help to legitimize their modern-day interest in guns. Cowboy shooting opens a window into who these shooters choose to be on the weekends, and their choices are not accidental. They insist on identifying with "good-guy" cowboys and lawmen, metaphorically (or even literally) tipping their hats to the ladies while simultaneously keeping one hand on their holstered guns.

The earliest American archetypes, figures like the citizen soldier and the cowboy, have always owned guns, in image and reality. These are figures that have come to quintessentially define the country itself, linking the gun with the American way of life.

Local Cowboy Shoots

The Bay Area provides a good example of how the cowboy fantasy has caught on with a vengeance in the shooting community. Contemporary cowboys are not the staunch loners of yore—at least these cowboys aren't. These are the doctors, lawyers, machinists, and cops who play cowboy on the weekends and in their spare time, combining their love of guns and shooting with their love of the Wild West. These are shooters who create/recreate themselves singing cowboy tunes, dressing up like gunslingers, shooting cowboy guns by day and making quite a ruckus by night. Shooters in Northern California travel from all across the Bay Area to congregate at well-known outdoor shooting ranges on Saturdays and Sundays to participate in the increasingly popular shooting sport.

Local and regional weekend shoots in the Bay Area are designed and executed on a much smaller scale than the national shoots, drawing between twenty and fifty people for a single day's competition, and anywhere between forty and eighty shooters for weekend-long shoots. For the larger regional and even statewide shoots, whole cowboy towns spring up on local ranges (e.g., Sierra), complete with makeshift storefronts, saloons, and dance halls. Like the national organization, local SASS chapters are dedicated to the "cowboy way," which is an ethos or way of life, a fantasy world that is self-consciously designed around what middle-class Americans fantasize the Wild West was all about. Chapters name themselves after city, county, or regional vigilante groups or posses and are then responsible for organizing and financing local or regional shoots.

Shoots are often designed around a theme, a kitsch version of Tombstone or an 1800s gold-mining camp. Such themes sometimes reference generic Wild West themes and ideals, but are sometimes specific to the California context. In every case, however, these mock towns resemble not so much their actual historical counterparts as visions of how predominantly middle-class, white suburban cowboys imagine these towns and camps might have been. In other words, Hollywood representations of the Wild West loom large. Like the weekend cowboys themselves, sites for cowboy action shooting reflect an idealized version of history, constrained by the amount of time and money that local organizers can invest. But they represent what modern-day cowboys imagine the best parts of the Wild West might have been: a dance hall, a bar, and a safe and legal shootout. The words on a flyer for an upcoming shoot say it well: "Step back into the history books! At least history as we think it should have been."

Cowboy shooting, while not for the faint-hearted, is definitely a tongue-in-cheek activity; cowboys certainly *seem* to know that their emulation of western shoots and frontier towns come as much from popular cultural forms and images as they do from actual historical fact. However, few make noise about authenticating early settlers' living and traveling conditions; after all, this is weekend fun. It's hard to drive up to a shoot in a twenty-foot-long RV and make claims to roughing it in the wild.

However, cowboys do value a certain kind of authenticity: "real" cowboy clothing (jeans without zippers, leather vests with buttons instead of snaps) and "real" cowboy guns are prerequisites to competing at the shoots themselves. Cowboys don't generally bar shooters from competing when the clothing isn't "cowboy" enough, but shooters don't usually push those limits. Dressing appropriately is one of the pleasures of the activity; both men and women take great pride in their outfits.

Costume contests are held at every shoot, with categories for both men and women. Becky, one of the women most actively involved in the sport in the area, became involved soon after her husband got involved in cowboy shooting. She started the actual shooting reluctantly, not being particularly interested in guns or shooting sports. Becky had originally wanted only to compete in the costume competition, where she could make her own clothing, which she enjoyed. When she learned that only shooters could compete in the costume contest, she half-heartedly took up shooting. Becky discovered she actually had quite a talent for it, and she is now a nationally ranked competitor in the sport.

SASS also has strict rules on the kinds of guns deemed appropriate. Learning the ins and outs of period guns becomes a must; for example, the 1892 model shotgun is SASS approved because it has an exposed hammer, whereas early model semiautomatic shotguns do not and are therefore not "authentic" cowboy gear. Only cowboy guns are allowed, which means that to engage in the sport, many would-be cowboy shooters must purchase new hardware. In the words of one shooter in a conversation early in my observations, "You have to be careful to pace yourself, 'cause you don't want to end up gun poor." He referred not to a paucity of fire power but to depletion of the bank account, which does indeed suffer for the sport. A pair of six-shooters can start anywhere from $300, and many shooters spend thousands of dollars on hardware alone. The costumes and extraneous gear only increase the financial commitment to the sport.

Life on the Cowboy Range

One of the most important aspects of the cowboy action shooting is the recreation of the cultural life of the frontier, which is carefully integrated into the sport. This cultural life takes on a variety of forms. For example, cowboys indulge in that great American pastime: shopping. Shops housed in makeshift tents spring up on the range during the weekend-long shoots. Owned and managed by members of the cowboy action community, these shops sell a variety of items that are necessary for the maintenance of one's cowboy persona: cowboy clothing, some antiques, replicas of frontier-style dress for men and women, boots, hats, curios (watches, billfolds, belts, spurs, etc.), and of course, antique and antique-replica firearms. Some of the merchants make a living traveling from shoot to shoot almost every weekend, and their faces and wares became familiar after about three or four shoots.

A variety of peripheral industries are also attached to this commerce: I met a metalworker who carved elaborate and quite beautiful designs onto firearms, a gunsmith who did on-the-spot repairs, even a hatmaker who custom-made "authentic" and substantial felt cowboy hats while you waited. There is also a very talented dressmaker who sells her own and other designs; her business is booming, so orders take about four to six months to fill.

Another important aspect of the cowboy way comes in the form of the evening entertainment, which follows on the Friday and Saturday nights of weekend-long shoots. Saturday evening is usually the most elaborate night for entertainment, which can include the reciting of cowboy poetry (written by a local cowboy or a published poet), the telling of frontier stories and legends by another, dancing to a live country-western/pop band (dressed to the hilt), an intense game of poker in a makeshift saloon or casino, and always, without question, copious amounts of alcohol. These evenings are usually raucous occasions and the drink flows heavily. The festivities begin long after the guns have been put away, a rule that is strictly applied. I heard quietly murmured stories and gossip about how a couple of cowboys from shoots past had mixed their drinking and their shooting, or were witnessed drinking and handling or displaying their guns. They were supposedly promptly kicked out of the competition, in effect run off the range.

This kind of self-policing carries more weight when handled by law enforcement, and in fact a sizable number of cowboy shooters (at least in the greater urban area) are members of local police and sheriff's departments. So on some level, police regulation is built into the activity itself. That cowboy shooting is enjoyed by so many people in law enforcement seems somehow appropriate; these are folks who are used to thinking of themselves as "the good guys," defending themselves and their community from "the bad guys." At the end of the day, projecting themselves into a Wild West fantasy (the sheriff of Tombstone, perhaps?) doesn't really seem like much of a stretch.

John Wayne Meets Buckaroo Bonzai

Cowboys use aliases, which are officially registered with national SASS Headquarters (along with joining and membership fees), and SASS sends back an official badge (which looks like an old-fashioned sheriff's badge) and a membership number. Cowboy aliases are the source of great amusement for shooters and are often film characters from favorite westerns, plays on words, or a really bad pun. Shooters can live up to their aliases: "Jackie Slow Draw," "Major Disaster," and "Frank Lee Terrible" convey a sure sense of those to avoid, if only jokingly. I was nicknamed "Abby Oakley" by some cowboy friends and the alias stuck, although I never officially registered it with SASS.[8] Aliases are treated with varying degrees of lightness and seriousness, meaning that at times they indicate an actual persona and sometimes they don't. Some cowboy shooters seem to choose their aliases based solely on the humor value.

However, some aliases are serious business. Although some cowboy shooters have been involved with the sport for over a decade, they often know each other only by their cowboy name, despite the fact that some have national reputations. Some of the most talented shooters in the country actually live in the Bay Area. I was taught how to hold and shoot a shotgun for the first time by Becky, who regularly outscores almost everyone at the shoots she attends. She, like many others, is known mostly by her cowboy alias and is referred to in SASS newsletters and gun magazines by her alias (though at times her real name is mentioned).

Aliases are chosen to represent one aspect of an identity that the shooter is interested in projecting and so can provide clues as to how a shooter envisions himself or herself. For example, one shooter chose a short, masculine, frontier name for himself and cultivates a corresponding persona, that of a solitary, hardened, gentleman rancher. Several friends and I were surprised to learn later from other shooters that he is married, the father of three daughters, and working a white-collar job in a blue-collar industry. For reasons known only to him (and perhaps his closest friends), he had carefully crafted an alternative identity for himself and is patently disinterested in sharing his real life with his cowboy compatriots. The cowboy shooting community apparently provides some form of escapist pleasure for him, and he works hard to keep his two worlds separate. As another shooter said to me during an IPSC match (which functionally produces the same kinds of relationships), "These gatherings are odd because you can know someone for years, have hundreds of conversations about guns and shooting, and not really know anything about them. It produces a strange kind of skewed intimacy." This intimacy is precisely the kind that some people want: it is clearly on their own terms, which makes it so inherently appealing.

The Shoots

A weekend shoot usually starts on the Friday before, and some of the shoot organizers take the day off work to help set up the shoot. Setup entails creating different stages for the competition. A stage is a self-contained course that the shooter must complete as quickly as possible using four different guns (two revolvers, one rifle, and one shotgun) to shoot at several different kinds of targets. The shotgun targets are stationed closest to the shooter, usually about seven to ten yards away, followed by pistol targets (ten to fifteen yards) and then rifle (thirty to fifty yards). Targets are usually metal plates shaped in squares, circles, and rectangles, all of which clang when struck by the shot from a shotgun or the regulation all-lead bullets. If the posse who organized the particular shoot is well-financed, the targets can be more elaborate, shaped like a cartoon-inspired buffalo or the SASS symbol, a kitsch cowboy who looks remarkably like Yosemite Sam, complete with bowed legs, a huge Stetson, and a droopy mustache. One shooter who is only occasionally involved in the cowboy shoots told me that years ago, the cowboys shot at metal Indians. But this shooter took it upon himself to point out to organizers that some people might find such targets offensive. Slowly, the Indian targets were weeded out and replaced by the geometric metal targets. The shooter who shared this story is a master at tall tales (hence my skepticism about his role in this changeover), but in any case, Indian targets are no longer in evidence.

Each stage is arranged differently so that the order in which a cowboy shoots at targets changes with every stage. Some of the stages at the larger and longer shoots are quite elaborate, a veritable shooter's obstacle course. At one of the countywide weekend shoots I attended, the organizers had created a small, dark barn complete with stacked hay bales and an open window in the back. Shooters had to load quickly in the dark and shoot out of the window in the back of the barn. The barn would fill with smoke from the gunpowder and shooters would fling the barn door open after they had completed the stage, coughing and waving their arms to clear the smoke from their face.

Another stage at a different shoot involved a small iron pony that rocked back and forth on its stand, similar to ones found in front of supermarkets in the 1970s for children to ride. Shooters had to mount the pony, draw and shoot their pistols and rifle, and then load and shoot their shotgun, all the while rocking back and forth. There were a number of bruised shoulders and grumbling cowboys after that particular stage. I was so bruised that I wanted to quit for the day, but another female shooter convinced me to keep going. She took me aside and told me to put a feminine napkin in the hollow of my shoulder to support the butt of the shotgun, which was not very cowboy but certainly more comfortable.

Toughness, the necessity of being "hard," is part of the sport. Shooters enjoy pushing themselves to the limit. Sadie, a petite and vivacious, nationally ranked competitor, described one particular shoot in great detail, emphasizing the need for physical strength and competency. Though this particular shoot was not typical because of the hardship involved, it provides insight into the ways shoots are conceptualized and the pleasure shooters take in pushing themselves to physical limits. Cowboys may be a largely professional group, but they pride themselves on knowing how to work and work hard.

> There were three stages, and fifteen people finished, and Becky and I were the only women. . . . one of the stages started by doing six shotgun, you know the deal, picking up a box that supposedly was filled with gold, which was fifty-five pounds, they weighed it later. You had to run down the fifty-yard berm,[9] diving through three different holes, and pushing the fifty-five- [pound] thing through, picking it back up as you get back—picking it back up, diving through another one, diving through another one. . . . you get down to the end of the berm and you have to shoot your ten pistol and then reload for ten more and then you have to pick the box back up and put it on top—'cause it was a bail of hay, structured three of 'em or four, whatever it was, so that you had to go under a bail of hay. On the way back you had to put the fifty-five-pound thing on top, dive under, you know, it was. . . . And then another stage, which was our last stage, which Rusty Waters, whose legs just wouldn't move anymore. Oh yeah. This was—two people bowed out. . . . And there was another stage that was eighteen shotgun—I mean, this was crazy, in the third stage we had eighteen shotgun and you had to carry a saddle with a shotgun on it, blah blah blah. Anyway, they're making up T-shirts, "I survived the Toughest Muchacho." I didn't know if we were gonna make it to Shasta the day after we get back from the Caribbean. I don't know, but if the T-shirts are there, I'm drivin' up. 'Cause we earned those T-shirts.

Each match usually has between five and ten stages, and shooters divide into smaller groups called posses. Each posse has a leader, a de facto rangemaster who has usually shot the whole course already (on the day before the official start, if the shoot is a longer one). These posses are created for organization's sake; each shooter competes as an individual, but the posses provide structure and allow groups of people to be introduced to each stage in smaller, more tightly knit groups. Posse leaders clarify the order of the stage, the order of the shooters, and generally serve as small-group facilitators or leaders.

Each posse has a timer who starts the clock on the posse leader's say and stops it after the last shot has been fired. Cowboys shoot each stage one after the other, and guns are not loaded until you are on deck, two positions away from shooting the stage. When a posse arrives at a stage, the leader describes how cowboys are to shoot it: what order to shoot and what kinds of additional actions must be taken. For example, on one stage a shooter might need to start by picking up a hand of playing cards, glance at them, shout "You no-good cheatin' varmint!!!" and then draw his revolvers and shoot at the metal targets in a particular order. Shooters get points deducted for such things as missing a target, mixing up the correct order of targets, or messing up their lines.

These rules never seem to be hard or fast at the local or even regional matches. Some shooters are older and less mobile, and dashing from here to there with cups of hot coffee, for example, means various mixups, spills, or goofs. Sometimes posse leaders and timers have difficulty assessing how many hits and misses there are: if a shooter is quick, it is difficult to register the succession of hits on the target. Usually posse members who are watching are enlisted to count misses, but because everyone is required to wear eye and ear protection at all times, keeping track is tricky. Counters listen for a plink against the metal target, which signifies a hit. Misses are an absence of plink or a bullet that sends up a puff of dirt beyond or near a target.

Each stage is timed down to a tenth of a second. For some, the competition is fierce. There are categories for judging the match, such as traditional (guns are pre-1899, with fixed sights and standard gunpowder loads for ammunition), modern (guns are pre-1899 but have adjustable sites), black powder (cap and ball or traditional cartridges, all with black powder), women, juniors (shooters age twelve to seventeen), seniors (age fifty-eight to sixty-eight), and grand master (age sixty-nine and older). At some of the more tongue-in-cheek matches, the categories include "real men" and "real he-men," in which shooters have to begin and end each stage smoking a lit cigar that remains lit through the entire stage. Points are indeed lost if the cigar goes out halfway through the stage. These kinds of rules and regulations demonstrate that shooters don't take themselves too seriously, nudging and winking at the ludicrousness of the kind of hypermasculinity that Hollywood (and pop culture more generally) has lionized.

Shooters break for lunch, which is usually meat and potatoes fare or occasionally a barbecue. This meal, as is at least one of the dinners (usually Saturday night's), is catered, and cowboys usually prepay for their meals. The afternoon is devoted to completing the stages, and the shoot itself usually finishes around 3 or 4 P.M. The rest of the afternoon is for shopping, relaxing with beer, and general socializing. Dinner is served around 6 or 7, and the hard drinking and partying begins around 9. If a band has been hired, people dance and continue to socialize until midnight or later. At the end of the evening, folks head off to their trailers or campgrounds and don't rouse until 9 or 10 the next morning.

Team Shoots and Award Ceremonies

On the second day of the shoot, cowboys gather midmorning after the yawning and bleary-eyed greetings have finished, and a team shoot is held. Die-hards are eager to get back to the serious business of shooting. Team shoots involve all shooters, men and women, organized into six or seven teams of eight to twelve, depending on how many shooters sign up to begin with and how many show up after the previous night's partying. Several stages are set up as they had been the day before, but these stages are now designed to be shot by a large group. There may be several shotgun targets set up at varying distances as well as ten to twenty pistol targets and several rifle targets set up in the distance. Team members line up side-by-side on the firing line and, at the signal, blast away at the targets until all have been knocked down. On another stage, a huge wooden log may be hung from a wire strung between two poles, and time is called after shooters have shot the log in half, which can take anywhere from fifteen seconds to several minutes, depending on the accuracy of the shooters and the size of the log. Sometimes certain shooters are designated by their teammates to aim at certain targets or take up certain positions, if such shooters have demonstrated skills in these areas. At one countywide shoot, a skeet shoot was incorporated into one of the stages, and one team member was usually chosen to handle this more difficult aspect of the stage. These team shoots take between two and three hours, depending on the size and number of shooters involved.

The last activity that is conducted during a shoot (which are most elaborate on weekend or four-day shoots) is the awards ceremony. Shooting awards are based on the best scores for each category of shooter, and because there are several exceptionally talented people who participate regularly in the area, these shooters tend to consistently win awards. Prizes, which are often donated to the shoot, consist of a variety of items that are necessary for shooting in general or cowboy shooting in particular: ammunition, gift certificates to the traveling stores that pop up on the range during shoots, books on cowboy life and Americana, and other shooting paraphernalia.

Occasionally, at some of the more well-financed or regional shoots, shooters are awarded guns. Sometimes guns are raffled off.[10] Plaques are also awarded; some shooters showed me a wall of plaques they had collected over the years. Other prize categories, including best costume and the "good sportsman" award, are designed not only to award shooters for participating, but also to share the prizes and accolades more widely through the usual group. Because some shooters do well so consistently, other regular attendants get left out fairly regularly. More general prize categories reinforce a sense that everybody has something to contribute, though how effectively is a matter of opinion.

The awards ceremony also provides an avenue for observers to catch a glimpse of who constitutes the movers and shakers in the community. These are shooters who have had a long history not only with the sport generally, but also within the cowboy action shooting community in the metropolitan area in particular. The cowboy shooting community in which I participated has an "in" crowd, named for a fictitious Bay Area vigilante group. This in crowd consists of a number of popular and (for the most part) friendly shooters, most of whom had been tapped by one of the first cowboy shooters in the area, Harold. They paid their entrance fee to Harold, who governs the club, and in return they get a gold-plated sheriff's badge (that resembled the SASS badge) with their club number and the name of the vigilante group.

I had some difficulty discerning exactly what merited inclusion into this group. Some shooters grumbled privately that you have to have money or standing in both the cowboy community and beyond to be included. These status markers probably are important, as is a willingness to demonstrate group loyalty through consistent showings at shoots. Those tapped also had to be generally well-liked and respected by the cowboy shooters on the whole. Though shooters generally consider inclusion in this particular subclub to be positive, some shooters who hadn't been invited to join said quietly that the whole business denoted an unnecessary cliquishness. Several seemed hurt by their exclusion. Other "outsiders" are unfazed and just park their trailers on the outside of the circle created by "insider" trailers and get on with the business of shooting. But this cliquishness eventually garnered enough resentment that several sets of people created splinter groups, still under SASS regulation but under the auspices of being more open and community-minded (i.e., ostensibly less concerned with status and standing).

Cowboy shooting is quickly becoming one of the most popular and recognized shooting sports in the United States. If shooters are asked why they enjoy the activities, the answers are not surprising. Shooters speak of the pleasures of spending time with like-minded folks, average cowpokes who enjoy getting sweaty and dusty on the cowboy trail. They are tried-and-true gun enthusiasts, loving the flash and the bang and, in some cases, the intricacies of expensive but temperamental firearms that need a delicate touch. Cowboy shooting is an elaborate costume ball almost every weekend in which men indulge their closeted desire for sartorial splendor and women can be tough and feminine simultaneously, with no one batting an eyelash. This is "Halloween for adults," in the words of one shooter, where shooters can be Wyatt Earp or John Wayne, and the only limitations are budget and imagination.

The Wild West in the Suburbs

Cowboy shooters are using their sport and their love of guns to keep the West alive in a wide variety of ways. By ritually reenacting "how the West was won" on a local community level, cowboy shooters are using the Frontier as the idiom to express their pride in their American heritage. This is what cowboy action shooting is about: predominantly white, middle-class Americans claim a national identity, or even a white middle-class identity, using the "authentic" Wild West of the cowboy range as their venue. This is one of the primary ways that shooters use mythic history to contextualize their love of guns. Guns are so thoroughly intertwined with mythic history that shooters cannot think about guns without referring to images of citizen soldiers defending the republic or hardened cowboys riding across lonely western plains, carving out civilized spaces in the hostile American wilderness. American mythic history conveys the sense that the earliest American heroes and patriots wielded their guns almost naturally, so naturally that it's almost impossible to imagine them without their guns. This is the principal reason that mythic history links guns so powerfully and persuasively to broader American core values for shooters.

Performing mythic history during cowboy action shoots thus serves several purposes for these suburban cowboys. These shooters are ostensibly performing culturally meaningful rituals. They are working on a "cultural problem (or several at once), stated or unstated, and then work various operations upon it, arriving at 'solutions'—reorganizations and reinterpretations of the elements that produce a newly meaningful whole."[11] In the context of cowboy action shooting, shooters focus on the most important symbol, the one that holds these rituals together: the gun. The cultural problem they're addressing is the stigma attached both to guns and the people who own them. By analyzing a "ritual symbol" like the gun, we can thus attempt to understand the questions "of structural conflict, contradiction, and stress in the wider social and cultural world."[12] In other words, analyzing what guns mean to shooters, we can understand why guns are important cultural symbols more generally. We can then more easily understand the kinds of cultural stresses and frustrations that shooters face in their lives more generally, which will provide a window into stresses and frustrations that all Americans face, whether they choose to own guns or not.

PART TWO

The Meanings of Guns

The possession of arms is the distinction between a freeman and a slave. . . . He, who thinks he is his own master, and has what he can call his own, ought to have arms to defend himself, and what he possesses; else he lives precariously, and at discretion.[1]

Citizen Soldiers

Colonial America and Early Republicanism

In the 2000 movie *The Patriot*, South Carolina farmer/landowner Benjamin Martin (played by Mel Gibson) reluctantly rejoins the colonial militia to take on the British during the Revolutionary War. With his wily bravery and unorthodox battle strategies, Martin embodies the ideal citizen soldier, displaying the kind of courage and principle that Americans have always imagined marked the early militiamen. *The Patriot* assures viewers that abstract political principles can have significant personal impact, and that in American mythic history, wars and violent conflicts forge timeless links between manhood, citizenship, and patriotism. Such mythic (re)tellings continue to resonate with how Americans process their own history, as the success of such movies demonstrate at the box office.[2]

There are a number of philosophical strains that contributed to how colonial Americans understood citizen gun ownership. These philosophies were carried over with early colonists from seventeenth-century Britain but were reshaped and reformulated relatively quickly in the early American experience, eventually providing the ideological foundations of the American Revolutionary War. Eminent historians have pointed out that one of the most important of these philosophical paradigms was republicanism, also called civic humanism.[3] This paradigm was so ingrained in the rhetoric of late colonial theorists and activists that it would be impossible to ignore as an important component of the configuration of early American principles and values.[4]

Republicanism at its most basic is an ideological system that was used to both support and critique the British monarchal system of government. A republic is a state governed by and for "the people," those citizens who literally and figuratively compose the state. The political ideology of republicanism had its roots in classical antiquity: the Greek and Roman philosophers who wrote of patriotism and a love of virtue and liberty were the earliest republicans. American colonists contrasted their idealized vision of a classic republic with their own time and their political struggles with the British system. They perceived the British monarchy as a corrupt power that challenged their own "provincial" but heartfelt values of freedom, liberty, and rustic purity.[5]

Colonial governments required citizens to arm themselves and form citizen militias. Because the government recognized that armed citizens were needed in specific areas for the protection and maintenance of the local economy, the government called for volunteers or drafted quotas from various companies. In the years before the Revolution, officers complained about poor training (e.g., their men wouldn't march or obey orders, displayed poor soldiering skills) and poor attendance. Yet colonial Americans recognized the notion of militia as inherently valuable, in part because it represented a departure from the notion of a standing army, but also because its conceptual vagueness meant it remained in the colonial mind as synonymous with the idea of defense itself: against general emergencies, Indian attacks, or foreign aggression.[6] Early European colonizers realized quickly enough that they were ill-prepared for such a harsh wilderness. Thus, the militia was more a *concept* of defense, practiced very differently than its organization on paper would suggest.[7]

The mythology of the American citizen soldier rested in large part on his skill with a rifle. Despite the fact that seventeenth- and eighteenth-century firearms were inaccurate and cumbersome, these guns were indispensable for settlers in terms of hunting game, protecting land from predators, and confronting or defending against hostile Indian forces.[8] American colonists brought with them some decidedly English attitudes toward arming themselves, not simply for militia purposes but also for self-defense. However, the ways these customs were modified in the new American colonies differentiated them from their practice in England.[9] The need for firearms in all areas of life was so great that early colonial governments encouraged the notion of an armed citizenry, which in turn gave birth to a new and strongly held vision of civic responsibility.

State governments recognized, however, that guns in the "wrong hands" could present dangers to the larger imperialist project. Colonial governments thus saw fit to regulate existing gun ownership and use.[10] For example, state governments regulated firearm use to avoid confusion and dangerous kinds of misuse. Because muskets were fired to sound an alarm and signal an emergency, the Massachusetts government prohibited nonemergency firing of a firearm at night to avoid panic. A Virginia law of 1637 encouraged citizens to hone their shooting skills, not only to ensure the procurement of wild game and protection against Indian invasion, but also so that colonists developed firearms skills at private expense.[11] Standing armies were expensive, and the colonists brought with them from England a deep-seated distrust of the concept of a standing army; such an army was considered the "universal tool of despotism," easily capable of strong-arming the very people it was supposed to protect.[12] Thus, gun control, as well as gun ownership, was a part of the colonial experience, even when those gun controls were designed to arm as much as disarm the population as a whole.

Colonial governments used laws about guns to help structure and maintain this patriarchal social structure,[13] while republican theory fueled the political rhetoric that legitimized armament for white propertied men. There were governmental restrictions on gun ownership for certain members of colonial society, notably women, Indians, black servants and slaves, and non-property-owning white men.[14] In the seventeenth century, selling or trading guns with Indians, a practice that occurred occasionally, was strongly prohibited and could even incur the death penalty.[15] Even poor whites were restricted in their access to arms. For example, when a white servant ended his indentured servitude, he received what was called his "freedom dues." The colony of Virginia "included a musket in the list of freedom dues, which usually contained clothes, land, corn, money, and tools. A freeman was to be an armed citizen who owned his own gun."[16] Laws such as these reflected the desire to maintain white control and supremacy over all others in colonial society.[17]

Gun control is thus not a twentieth-century invention. An armed white populace during the colonial era was desirable at the time not only because it served a particular political purpose, but also because it helped maintain certain social needs and institutions. In that vein, the regulation of firearms and restrictions on guns to blacks, both free and enslaved, strongly characterized the southern states during the nineteenth century. These gun regulations were designed specifically to disarm free black men who were not under the control of a vigilant slave master. Guns in white hands but not black ones meant that whites could more easily maintain control over the black population.[18]

While different statutes and laws reflected different state and local concerns, one regulatory constant was that these statutes and laws were intended to facilitate race control for the white power structure. In other words, both gun ownership *and* gun control worked synergistically to systematically and structurally disadvantage particular members of colonial society. On a more symbolic level, the fact that guns were restricted or prohibited to classes like Indians and blacks simply confirmed their status as outsiders, inferiors, noncitizens.[19]

Thus, the American government has been regulating and controlling gun ownership and use from the earliest incarnation of the republic. The point of both gun ownership and gun control laws was to keep in step with the political, social, and economic dictates of the era. Both the social practice of owning guns and the body of law that governed this practice reflected the social and political realities of the colonial era. What this era of American history makes patently clear is that gun ownership and its control have always been complex and contentious issues, particularly in relation to race, power, status, and social control.

Myths Are Born

A particular portrait of the citizen soldier emerges from the translation of history to mythology, born out of the colonial experience in seventeenth- and eighteenth-century America and celebrated in mythic imagery. In republican theory, a citizen of the republic was implicitly gendered as male, was of European descent (i.e., was white), owned property, and was devoted to the collective security of the republic's virtue and stability. All of these qualities were theorized as literally and figuratively embodied in the individual citizen. One of the most important facets of classic republicanism is the idea that citizenship and civic virtue are deeply moral qualities, and those that espoused that particular vision of citizenship were demonstrating their "inherent" moral qualities as members of a new social and political order.[20] Citizenship and virtue were demonstrated through one's participation in the public sphere—in other words, the political arena. The public sphere before all else, to be defended through the citizen's willingness to put the needs of the polity before his own.[21]

Thus, the early American citizen soldier was his own man, white and propertied, willing to serve the new republic. He was ready to defend his rights and his freedom with his firearm skills and able to respond to the demands of a new concept of civic responsibility, befitting him both as an individual and a citizen of the nation. He recognized the moral force inherent in his rebellion against tyrannical authority, and he responded with a violence that was justified by the ideals of liberty, freedom, and progress.

The more subtle aspects of the citizen soldier have fallen by the wayside as the history of this figure has transformed into mythology. This mythologized and romanticized vision of the freeman fighting for independence developed shortly after the Revolution, and it fed the already developing sense of national identity even for colonial Americans in the eighteenth century. The archetypal citizen soldier was embodied in the mythic qualities of such patriots as George Washington, a man who, despite a lack of aristocratic birth, demonstrated leadership skills and succeeded through perseverance, integrity, and, indeed, and willingness toward violent action. These kinds of mythic figures served to justify and legitimize early Americans' imperial conquest as inherently righteous in its moral purpose and essential for the birth of a new nation. These figures also provide, along with myths about American history more generally, the context that shooters use to understand and make meaningful guns in their lives now.

Contemporary Citizen Soldiers

When I interviewed shooters about their gun enthusiasm, several key questions elicited answers that frequently involved early American notions of republican service and ideology.[22] Several shooters raised the example of the American Revolutionary War as an important aspect of what guns mean for Americans, not only because it was the birth of the nation, but also because it occurred during a period of history when Americans collectively recognized the need for an armed populace. When I asked shooters "What does owning a gun mean to you?" and "What does the gun symbolize for you?" these were the questions that often generated such responses as "Independence" and "Freedom." Shooters talked about how these are the core values that are symbolized by guns, and owning guns means attending to these core values in their lives. Several shooters asserted that their gun enthusiasm represents a form of civic responsibility, actualized in a variety of behaviors that may seem contrary to the notion of a modern "civilized" society. They were not talking about swearing allegiance to any formalized militia system. Rather, civic duty and citizenship are deeply intertwined with the concept of keeping and bearing arms. In these ways, shooters are both implicitly and explicitly modeling their beliefs and behavior on notions of the citizen soldier ideal.[23]

Of the values and ideals that shooters frequently discussed, freedom was the most often mentioned and the most strongly felt. On a broader social level, social scientists have documented how fiercely and tenaciously Americans believe in a notion of freedom: it is "perhaps the most resonant, deeply held American value" and is complexly interwoven with individualism and self-reliance.[24] Freedom and individualism are part of the American Creed, which includes liberty, egalitarianism, individualism, and laissez-faire capitalism. The American Creed is one of the nation's most sweeping ideologies, and subscribing to it is often what many think of as "Americanism."[25] Freedom, both political and social, is generally thought of as freedom from the demands of others and the ability to be and act in any way one chooses, which is why American ideas of freedom have always existed in tension with the creation and maintenance of community. But freedom as an ideal has "historically given Americans a respect for individuals; it has, no doubt, stimulated their initiative and creativity; it has sometimes even made them tolerant of differences in a diverse society and resistant to overt forms of political oppression."[26]

Shooters in the study stated frequently that freedom is one of the most important core values or symbols that they identify with gun ownership. They talked about the relationship of gun ownership to freedom in a variety of ways, most of which demonstrate just how inextricably linked freedom and gun ownership are to them. This relationship was discussed primarily in terms of its historical significance, both its literal impact on historical events and the more metaphoric connotations of freedom in terms of personal expression.

Historical events loomed large when shooters discussed the relationship between guns and freedom. Being able to own guns at all is seen by many gun enthusiasts as a basic freedom that Americans can enjoy; shooters understood gun ownership to be a key aspect of citizenship under a democratic government. Some shooters suggested that this is one of the freedoms that was fought for during the American Revolutionary War; when they make overt historical references to firearms, guns are understood to symbolize freedom. Firearms guarantee freedom in the most literal sense: they were used by citizens to fight and win the War of Independence and thus "made" Americans free. Freedom is also metaphoric: colonial Americans were fighting for the freedom to govern and protect themselves, and as such, they were fighting for abstract freedoms, like the right to own whatever thing they wanted, even a gun.

Most shooters are very aware that many socialist and fascist governments do not permit firearms to be owned by the general populace, and some theorize that this kind of gun control exists because gun ownership can potentially threaten the foundations of government through a citizens' revolt. These shooters therefore see gun ownership as a hallmark of living in a country that is indeed governed by its citizens. Paula referred to historical events to illustrate this point: "Why did Independence Day come about? What caused the Independence Day? I think it may have had something to do with guns. I just go back to—that's what made America. America stands for one thing, it's supposed to be freedom, but that's falling apart because people aren't going back into history and they're just being blinded. They figure, 'Well, that's old stuff.' It carries on all through, and they're not doing that." Paula suggested that one reason people are opposed to firearms ownership in modern times is because they are either unaware of the historical foundations of gun ownership in the United States, or they assume that this historical relationship is irrelevant in current times. Shooters sometimes alluded to the idea that they are indeed carrying on an honorable tradition in American history by honing their marksmanship and enjoying the practice of shooting in general. Because they view guns as an integral part of securing a political and moral victory over political oppression historically, continuing this practice today is a constant reminder of how early Americans were willing to defend themselves and their country.

Some shooters asserted that the antigun stance is part of an unwillingness to serve one's country, or, on a larger scale, a lack of respect for the United States as a nation. Harold touched on this point when he discussed his willingness to serve in the military: "But it is, generation after generation we lose more and more freedoms. And nobody today knows what America means. I mean, I'd go to war again today as old as I am if they asked me. For the country. I'd do it in a heartbeat. I'll bet you could take ten people out there and you'd only find maybe two or three that would be willing to go. And this is what's hurting the country."

Harold also feels a strong sense of outrage against what he perceives as the deterioration of his "gun rights" when he thinks of his current gun enthusiasm in relation to his past military service. He feels that the political and social opposition to gun ownership is hypocritical: when he was in the military, his interest in guns was understood, even lauded, as patriotic and civic-minded. At that time, Harold believes, social and political forces deemed him a "responsible" party because he was a young soldier in the Marine Corps. His interest in guns was therefore legitimized: he was serving the interests of the American government. Those days are long over, however, and he believes that his status as a gun owner is now in question. I asked Harold what guns mean to him: "Yeah, it's freedom. That's what I fought for when I joined the Marine Corps. It's my right, my choice as a citizen, as long as I don't infringe somebody else's right with it I should be allowed to own a nuclear device if I want. That's my personal opinion. And that's what it really represents, I think, is freedom. If they want to take that away, f——— this country. It's freedom of choice. Either you want . . . [a gun] or you don't want one, it's your choice."[27]

The idea that his interest in guns should need to be legitimized through the authority of the state (when in his mind he was fighting for the freedom to own guns) is frustrating for Harold. He thinks of gun restriction as a governmental abuse of power. Harold also believes strongly that his gun ownership has not literally hurt anyone, and as long he does not infringe on the rights of others, he should be able to continue with his interest in guns. Some shooters feel that the very ability to own guns is in serious jeopardy when some politicians express a desire to ban all or certain kinds of guns.

Part of what is voiced in Harold's anger is a sense that his right to own guns is inherent in being a responsible adult. The suggestion that he should be prohibited from having guns attacks his sense of status. He feels demoralized and offended by the notion that he should be viewed, in his mind, as a ward of the state, reliant on state agents (i.e., the police) for his own protection.

At the root of this issue for Harold is what he sees as hypocrisy perpetuated by the state when it continues to pass more gun controls. The government requests or even demands that citizens give their lives for their country in the form of military service. And yet gun control presumes that these same citizens actually *lack* the status to decide how and when they should be able to defend themselves, ironically using the same tools the government deems appropriate for national defense. Harold sees no distinction between himself in the past, a soldier, and now, a civilian. That the government should make these distinctions, potentially undermining his ability to defend himself, frustrates Harold enormously.

Harold also locates the shifts in political and social acceptance of guns in what he understands as profound changes in American society. He perceives not only a shift toward more lenient parenting attitudes, but also that certain kinds of demographic changes have changed political attitudes in the

United States. He spoke in frustrated tones about how he believes that the freedoms, rights, and value systems of gun owners are disparaged and ignored in public/political arenas because politicians respond to "special interest groups" that are hostile to guns and gun owners. Though several other shooters voiced frustration with politics and their lack of political representation on the state level, Harold's discussion was especially aggrieved, suggesting anger over not only his loss of status as a gun owner but also his loss of status as a white male in particular.

Harold identifies as unfair or corrupt the contemporary disparagement of gun ownership in public culture. He fondly associates a past America with an unquestioning acceptance of gun ownership. He mentioned his own boyhood adventures with guns often; those were times when no one ever questioned his pleasure in shooting and guns. He believes, perhaps not surprisingly, that this past America viewed gun ownership as positive, moral, obviously much less contentious than it is viewed today. Today's America does not understand gun ownership and gun owners the way it did during Harold's childhood. He told me the following narrative:

When they first passed the first assault rifle bill, I went up to Sacramento, I closed the store down, took a bunch of friends, we all went up there, went to a big rally, went inside and lobbied all the people not to vote for it, and I was never so upset and disgusted with our governmental system. It would just make you want to vomit. Everything was all prearranged, they didn't listen to anybody, they could care less. We went all the way upstairs. I don't know if you've ever been to the State Capitol, but there's like a peanut gallery where you get to watch what they do. And it's like first come, first serve, as far as getting admission to the peanut gallery. So there's all of us gun people there, and we were in line . . . and we were waiting for them to open the peanut gallery, so we could sit there when they go through the legislative process. . . .

So we're all standing there waiting. Pretty soon, all these Hispanic women come up with these signs, "No on Assault Rifles." And they couldn't speak English for the most part. And they take 'em past us and they seat 'em inside, and we're saying, "Hey, wait a minute, this is first come, first serve. What's this? What kind of crap is this?" "Oh, these are all guests of Senator Roberti." He was the guy getting the bill passed to ban the assault rifles. So not one pro-gun person was allowed to sit in the peanut gallery. So all of these people up there with their placards, "No on Assault Rifles," made the news media. When the news media takes a picture up there it makes it look like everybody's against it.

Then they took all of us downstairs and put us in this room, where we could watch it on TV and listen to it. And then they come in and turn the TVs off and would only allow us to listen to it. And I was just so fed up. I mean, I realized then that they could care less about us. They don't listen to us, they don't give a crap about what it is, whatever they want, you're gonna get it. Because when it came time for the vote, finally, they started the vote and they realized they didn't have enough votes to pass it, so Willy Brown stopped the voting. He didn't allow it to be—like they took a pre-vote. There weren't enough people. So he said "Okay, we're gonna redo the vote tonight at eight o'clock." He sent an airplane down to San Diego to pick up two more assemblymen who weren't there to vote. Flew them up, and then they voted at eight o'clock at night and they passed the bill. And this is the way our politics—now, if Willy Brown didn't want the bill, he would have accepted the vote.[28]

The shift to a more multivocal and, in this example, multicultural discussion about the legitimacy of guns in American society has led Harold to several rather bitter conclusions about the political process and his own place in it. For Harold, the gun debate is really about the loss of status of gun owners in American society. His narrative exemplifies the complexity of the issue in relation to power and politics. Harold is not simply remembering a mythic, past America that had more respect for gun owners. Acknowledged or not, he is also recalling an America that unilaterally privileged white male voices in the political arena. The America Harold remembers as sympathetic to gun owners was also an America before the eras of feminism and civil rights, and certainly before the Clinton administration's courting of women's and minorities' political interests. His disgust at the political participation of Hispanic women who "couldn't speak English" conflated with his frustration as a gun owner. Harold seems relatively unaware of how, in the not-too-distant past, he was able to exercise a certain amount of political clout not because he is a gun owner (and America respected guns back then) but because he is a white, middle-class male. His status translated into social and political power, and it was that status (more than his interest in guns) that was uncontested. The ease with which he could advance most of his social and political interests undoubtedly helped protect his gun rights, whether he recognizes this social fact or not.

Harold now perceives himself to be in a minority position, and it is an unfamiliar and uncomfortable place. He perceives himself embodying certain "intrinsic" social attributes that denote authentic American identity (i.e., he is white, male, middle class, a small business owner, a conservative, and a gun owner). He thus ostensibly perceives himself to be articulating the voice of the *real* America. Because guns have come to symbolize for Harold every-thing that he believes the real America stands for (i.e., freedom, individual-ism, and equality), those who are antigun are not real Americans. These gun control advocates also have several other attributes Harold identifies as "less" or even "un-American" (i.e., they are nonwhite, non-English-speaking, fe-male, and antigun), all of which makes the situation that much more outra-geous and intolerable for him.

The final indignity for Harold is that the antigun position was being heard and accepted by powerful politicians, but his pro-gun position was not. All this has led Harold to conclude that America's contemporary social and moral order is collapsing, and rapidly. For Harold, gun control signifies all of these things, and its continued status as a cause célèbre is strong evidence that the United States is no longer being run by true Americans. Harold's beliefs are not necessarily shared by all (or even most) of the shooters I met, but his articulation of these issues provides insight into why some gun enthusiasts sound so bitter and jingoistic when discussing the politics of gun control.

The stance against perceived political oppression takes on powerful sym-bolic meaning for other shooters as well. For John, the ability to freely own guns is a kind of individual freedom that expresses his individual choices and behaviors. Living in a free country means being able to practice a certain free-dom of individual expression, including the ability to express oneself through gun ownership. Both John and Peter, an Asian American graduate student in his twenties, presented this view, each by alluding to different circum-stances. John believes that living in the United States means the state should respect citizens' choices, particularly with regard to physical rights. The state operates for the people, not the other way around. The government should take a "hands off" approach to regulating behavior. John explained:

> But it's the freedom thing, I think. The issue is freedom, and Americans, they love that, and they don't like it when you try to take away their freedoms. You see how it goes, you know, they get huge rallies going and stuff like that. Like the abortion issue, look at that. Which I'm pro—I think a woman's right, that's her freedom, that's freedom to me . . . [the] government has no idea, got no idea, but they have no right to tell a woman what to do with her body. I think that's totally wrong and I don't side with the Republicans on that at all. That's the same freedom as I want with my guns. And that's all I'm saying: Leave me alone.

Gun ownership to John is a basic right with which the government should not interfere, and therefore gun ownership defines his notion of freedom itself. Despite his self-professed political conservatism, which he identified several times through the course of our discussion, he bucks his chosen political affiliation on the issue of abortion. He made this offering in an almost quid pro quo fashion to illustrate the strength of his conviction on the gun rights issue. Peter voiced a similar position: "[Gun ownership means] the freedom to indulge yourself in whatever interests you, as long as you don't step on the rights of the next person. That's a big part of it. Kind of a libertarian slant. I don't believe inanimate objects should be outlawed for a person's own good. It should be up to you. If you do something wrong with it, then you pay the price. It's about freedom, I guess."

Peter voiced a sentiment that is shared by many shooters with whom I spoke. Gun ownership is a freedom to be revoked only after it has been abused. Shooters perceive the limitation of gun ownership by the government as an attempt to control the fully legal choices and behaviors of individuals, men and women who are supposed to have guaranteed rights on this issue.

In this vein, gun control is understood as a misguided attempt to constrain the behavior of the few by controlling the behavior of all. Shooters perceive this logic as inherently indefensible. As far as shooters are concerned, guns can be used for a variety of purposes, both positive and negative. Governmental restrictions on gun ownership are viewed as an attempt to regulate a tool, a machine that is used in conjunction with action, be it toward positive or negative ends. Because shooters understand themselves to be engaged in a variety of positive actions and behaviors with guns, they are angered and offended by the notion that their positive individual actions should be restricted by the negative (i.e., dangerous) individual actions of others. By regulating or banning the gun itself, the government is only serving to restrict the tools by which action is accomplished. In other words, neither gun crime nor its root causes is addressed by these kinds of controls on gun ownership.

For shooters, the guns themselves are not the crux of the issue, as Peter pointed out. Shooters' perspective on this issue is their own take on the paradigm of individualism that runs through so much of American discourse and thus for shooters is at the heart of the discourse on guns. Individualism means controlling your own actions, not having your actions controlled by others, be it the state or antigun activists. Louise and Jane, the two women who work as shooting instructors, gave this answer when I asked them what guns symbolize:

Jane: The first word that came into my head was freedom.

Louise: Yeah, I thought of that too, power and freedom. To me those are kind of synonymous words. . . .

AK: Because of the freedom that the gun—the freedom to own one or the freedom that—well, how so? . . .

Louise: It's probably tied in with . . . something. I don't know what it is. I can't pinpoint it. I get frightened when I shoot my gun. It's just this feeling. . . .

Jane: I mean, there's not a lot of things I get really pumped up about, and shooting is one.[29]

The American core values of individualism and independence, freedom, and rights and responsibility are clearly intertwined. So while concerns about freedom and the ability to enjoy certain freedoms are understood to be guaranteed in the conception of citizenship for shooters, so too are the concepts of individualism and independence.

Individualism and Independence

As I mentioned earlier, one of the most important American core values is individualism. Because of the vastness of description and definition, I use a very broad notion of individualism as a touchstone. Individualism can be "broadly conceived as the view that the individual human subject is a maker of the world we inhabit . . . [and] whose experiences and history, whose will and values, whose expressions and preferences are essential constituents of reality."[30] Because the primacy, as well as the agency, of the individual is so reified in American culture (in the very laws and institutions of society itself), it is not surprising that the notion of individualism would appear in various forms and guises in discussions of gun enthusiasm. However, one of the most interesting facets about modern incarnations of individualism is its close conceptual relationship to independence, which is illustrated in the thoughts of some shooters.

Though some gun enthusiasts did address the notion of how gun ownership related directly to their notion of individualism, the definitions and characterizations of this relationship emerge more subtly and indirectly. For example, some shooters do not want to be lumped into any kind of category with other gun enthusiasts despite the fact that they might share common ideas or beliefs about gun use. They implied that their ideas could or should not represent others' ideas, nor should I assume that they could do so. These shooters are uncomfortable with the idea that their words or ideas could represent anyone but themselves. Some shooters even resist the idea that my analysis of their gun ownership could tell me anything of value about them, in the sense that it would raise false assumptions or stereotypes about their character. There may indeed be some validity to that idea, but safe to say here that they see their gun enthusiasm as part of a theme of individuality, which is central to their sense of self-identity. Elliot illustrated this point concisely: "[People assume] . . . that I was part of kind of a macho gun culture, that [my gun ownership] . . . defined who I was, and I kind of resist any kind of real definition. I don't like to be pigeonholed. I don't like to be pigeonholed as a gun owner, I don't like to be pigeonholed as a . . . [commercial artist], I don't like to be pigeonholed as anything really. I like to define who I am myself. Generally my definitions are just too complex to have a label like that."

On a related note, many shooters have negative or even hostile reactions to the idea that there exists a "gun culture" in the United States. To these shooters, the idea that they would be associated with other individuals who are not serious about shooting as a sport or vocation, or who are sloppy or irresponsible about guns in general, is offensive. Other shooters simply feel that the reasons and justifications for an interest in guns are too diverse and complex to be summarized in the concept of a gun culture. Shooters come from such a variety of class and ethnic backgrounds, many shooters felt, and to classify them as a culture is misleading.[31] In John's words: "I don't see it. . . . I don't think there's like a culture. I mean, I don't subscribe to any particular culture. I'm an NRA member, but I think that's just a whole bunch of people I just told you about, blue collar, white collar, whatever. There's such a wide range of Americans [involved with guns], including black Americans, Asian Americans, Mexican Americans, and so on."

This belief in the inherent diversity of gun enthusiasm as it's practiced is interesting for several reasons. Chiefly, John is harking to the basic idea that a shooter is the archetypal everyman, a person not necessarily distinguished by class or ethnic heritage. This idea has resonance with a basic ideology of American identity, invoked in a variety of situations and contexts: the United States is not a stratified society but one without socioeconomic class and class prejudice. We are all Americans under the skin, after all. In fact, shooters see themselves drawn together not by their exterior characteristics or their background but by their interest in guns. The end result is that shooters dislike being represented as anything but a collection of individuals who are different in many respects but drawn together by their respect for guns and what guns mean.

More specifically, shooters see gun ownership as relating to individualism in two primary ways. First and foremost, guns serve as a way of symbolically stating the primacy of the individual and his or her ability to be independent. A gun-owning person does not have to depend on any other person, institution, or community, by definition. A gun owner is not hostile to community per se. But guns can define an individualistic life, which is therefore an independent one. Greg's discussion of why gun ownership and use is important to him sheds light on this idea:

> I became interested in handguns because they're weapons of our culture. If it was a thousand years ago I'd be interested in swords and bows and fighting axes . . . I would be interested in man's ability to take care of himself. I'd be interested in my ability to be independent. This has a lot to do with my family, too, that I would want to be my own person. And one way that you can be your own person is—this is puerilely self-apparent, but is to not be dependent on other individuals. Well, what is it that you need to live your life? What does a person need to live their life? Well, food, shelter, and clothing. . . . You need safety. You need to feel that you can exist in the world, that you're not prey. That you're your own person, that you're not dependent on Daddy taking care of you, if you will, whether Daddy is the state . . . whether Daddy's your literal daddy, whether Daddy is Bobo in the cell that you're forced to share because you broke some law. . . . As far as symbolism goes, it is symbolic of your ability to take care of yourself. . . . It's the ability for you to address the deepest archetypical fears that everyone has, the things that go bump in the night. . . . So guns give you a base. They give you the ability to move on and live the rest of your life. . . . When it comes down to you and some guy looking at you with evil intent, you're on your own.

The first idea that Greg expressed is that being an independent person who does not rely on others in any way is very important to him. The ways that people can be dependent—by relying on the state for protection, relying on other individuals for literal or even symbolic protection—are unacceptable. Greg gives voice to a tenet that many shooters share, and that is a basic understanding that independence is a necessity in a complex society that presents a variety of threats to both public and individual safety. In Greg's view, threats to the individual are omnipresent in society and have been for centuries. The individual's experience of these threats is felt as a generalized sense of anxiety or fear, not related to specific people or events, but what could be thought of as "free-floating anxiety."[32] Or this fear can be embodied in the form of criminals or human "predators," known abusers or dangerous strangers, people who harm and attack everyone else. Such predators do physical harm but also psychological damage, specifically by compromising the peace of mind of individuals who feel vulnerable. Greg believes that people are always vulnerable to a certain degree unless they take steps to ensure that they can take care of themselves. For Greg, the solution to this dilemma is fairly basic. Gun ownership and use provide the means by which the individual can survive on his own.

Greg expanded on the kinds of literal threats that people face in their daily lives, and he also talked about how fear or anxiety over these threats could affect people's lives:

> [The idea] . . . is that you can live your life, you can be whatever you want to be, absolutely anything. You can be an artist, a poet. You can be a construction worker. You can be a neurosurgeon. But when it comes down to it, when an emergency occurs, none of those things make any difference. When you're faced with the abyss, all of that, whatever it was that you've done, all your training, it may increase your self-confidence, maybe you have a lot of self-confidence, so you'll stand and face your fate with your chin held high. That's great. If you have the tools, though, to be able to say, "I have the right to exist, I have the right not to be prey, I have the right to be my own person, whether I'm a laborer, a drug dealer, or a neurosurgeon, I have the right to exist, to be my own thing." And so this handgun gives anyone in any profession, in any capability, at any age, at any sex, any race, any religion, any sexual preference, at any anything, the ability to be themselves, to not be victims, to not be prey. . . . But to me it's something that's very important.

Greg feels strongly that it is not only the literal threats that people experience in their daily lives that hinder their ability to do what they want and be who they want. These fears prohibit people from achieving self-actualization. Threats are internalized and become symbolic obstacles, equally threatening though not as concrete. The antidote to both these concrete and more ambiguous fears is to become trained in self-defense. In fact, becoming competent with guns (as a means toward independence) is in some ways a practical imperative, insofar as the institutions on which many people rely to provide basic safety and protection (the police or the military) do not reliably ensure personal safety. Greg's point is that should the need arise, he and his students will be capable of responding to that threat with force. In Greg's view, you cannot be who you want to be if you're afraid. A gun can ensure your personal sense of safety. By literally protecting the body, the individual can literally and metaphorically actualize the self.

As I mentioned in Chapter 2, Greg perceives certain aspects of his gun enthusiasm as civic duty. For example, he works as a shooting instructor on a volunteer basis. He views this service as a way to educate individuals about how to use firearms safely, and he feels strongly that his instruction is instrumental in helping people overcome their fears about being a victim of crime. He understands that the chances that most middle-class individuals will experience a home invasion by a criminal is statistically slim. However, Greg argues that it is the *fear* of victimization that is so limiting. He feels that he is doing a service to his community by educating people on how to own and use firearms safety. He stated:

> I feel—it's very gratifying for me. When I can help somebody realize their own self-ness, their own value, and give them the means with which they can defend that. It's a very powerful thing for me. The person who sits at home, afraid, there's things going on in the hallway outside, and they sit there, and they buy extra locks for the door, and they cringe every time there's a loud noise, and they can't live their life because they feel like prey. If I can instruct them to where they can start thinking, and override that fear and anxiety, then they have the tools with which to ultimately, because as I say in the class, the chances of your ever having to shoot anyone are really small. It's not gonna happen. It's very likely not gonna happen. But the thousand and one times in your whole life, from the time you're old enough to own a handgun at twenty-one to the time you die of old age at eighty-five, during that whole time, when you're sitting at home, and the handgun's in the home, and you know that you know how to use it, and you know that you can defend yourself, your home is your castle, that home is your redoubt, that home is your place of rest and respite from the horrors and the tribulations and pettiness of the world, and you can make it so. It can't be wrested from you. You have the ultimate argument for someone who is going to try and take your life, your peace, your home, away from you, by violence, you can answer that.

Greg also demonstrated his sense of civic duty in the most obvious way: he served in the military. He is honest about how he saw military service not simply as a way to express loyalty to his country, but also as a rite of passage, a means by which to achieve adult status in society. For Greg, and even for shooters more generally, being a shooter means being willing to commit to acts of violence in a variety of contexts: to protect yourself, your family, your community, or your nation. Owning a gun and being willing to use it indicate for shooters a willingness to take up arms toward these ends, at a moment's notice. This willingness recalls the well-regulated militia in its historic sense: citizens being ready to defend against a variety of threats, local and national. Greg's willingness to serve is interesting because it served as a mediating point between the belief in an independent existence and the importance of serving the state as a politically active citizen. This willingness to serve becomes a kind of bridge between maintaining the theoretical concept of living an independent life (serving as such guaranteed this independence) and providing a service toward a stronger nation-state.

Rights

There is a vast amount of historical and legal scholarship discussing the American concept of constitutional rights, and in the past several decades, much of it has been dedicated to the Second Amendment.[33] A good deal of this scholarship has revolved around the exact meaning of the Second Amendment. Legal scholars and historians are questioning whether or not the language the Framers used does indeed guarantee an individual right to gun ownership, or rather, affirms the right of citizens to own guns if they serve in a militia capacity. Because there is so much contention with regard to the meaning of the Second Amendment, I've restricted myself to discussing how the Amendment is understood by shooters and how they feel it has had an impact on their own lives.

The concept of having rights in a governed society is intertwined with the concept of having status, and therefore certain kinds of rights are designated by status.[34] For example, civil rights are those possessed by virtue of being a citizen, human rights are possessed by virtue of being human, and so on. When shooters talked about their right to own guns, they often invoked a variety of institutions or concepts that will be familiar to Americans, shooters and nonshooters alike. When shooters stated that they are exercising their constitutional right to own guns, they were obviously invoking the Second Amendment. But they were also invoking a particular set of historical circumstances that led to the formation of the Constitution, as well as the amendments to that Constitution. Just as some shooters referenced Independence Day and the winning of the Revolutionary War to invoke a notion of freedom, others invoked the Second Amendment and the Constitution to convey a sense of the rights inherent in being an American citizen. They view their right to own guns as a unique political right guaranteed by the Second Amendment and affirmed by the participation of citizen soldiers in events like the Revolutionary War.

For shooters, the Second Amendment is a living doctrine that illustrates in strongly worded terms their political rights as American citizens. These rights do not simply ensure that the government remains within the control of the American people, but also ensures that average Americans can maintain a strong defensive position against anyone (i.e., another citizen) who is dangerous or threatening. The Second Amendment confers on American citizens the right to use deadly force to protect themselves not only against tyrannical government, but against other individuals who threaten them or their family with bodily harm. Shooters asserted that this social and political "fact" is unique in the American historical and modern register. Manuel explained:

It means—I was gonna say that it means I'm exercising my right to own a gun, but I'm not really—I'm not gonna say [anything] political . . . like that, where people are not so much yelling about their gun rights being taken away or whatnot . . . because I can [have a gun], because I live here in America, and we can, where some places they can't have guns. So I guess I am exercising my right to have guns. And I guess it's important to me that I do have that freedom, where other people don't. It means that if I had to I could defend myself with it, and do it safely. I know how to use it. I've been in the military and I've been here [working at the shooting range] a couple years. So I feel qualified. If I had to, I could.

Other shooters demonstrated that this right is meaningful by sharing stories of times and places where gun rights were revoked or nonexistent for all or certain kinds of citizens. Such narratives often invoked circumstances illustrating the opposite of the political rights and freedoms that shooters believe Americans enjoy. Shooters used stories about a lack of gun rights as moral lessons that illustrate the abuses of power that can occur when citizens cannot own guns. By pointing to times when guns were taken away, shooters are attempting to throw their own rights into sharp relief. Implicit in these kinds of narratives is the understanding that a citizen who is stripped of his gun rights is a citizen with less status in the eyes of the state. Elliot explained:

But it was really hard for me to justify demand for gun ownership simply because I wanted a [gun] collection. Or I wanted to shoot at tin cans on weekends. I felt that the most important thing politically was, I think people have the right, guaranteed by the Constitution, but they need the right to protect themselves if they need to, just like they need the right to have abortions if they want. That was politically as far as I was willing to go. . . . The fact [is] that people live by the fact that they want the right to own guns, and that [right] . . . also

allows people access to Uzis and the ability to shoot up crowds. . . . And this is
the kind of carnage that is part of the by-product of demanding that guns be
legal. That's one end of it. And the other end is being—is giving up everything,
is giving up the right to defend yourself. . . . If in fact we were ever attacked,
hiding behind a telephone pole with your gun, irrespective of what it is, against
an invading army, is a little ridiculous. On the other hand, if an invading army
did something similar to what the Nazis did [i.e., prohibiting firearms ownership by Jews], if every Jew had a gun, and if every Jew killed the first Nazi that
came to the door that was gonna take him to the concentration camp—I had
family that was extinguished at Buchenwald. If every one of them had taken
out the first Nazi that was coming through the door, just the first one, there
were nine million people extinguished there. So each one killed one German
soldier. That means nine million German soldiers were not at Hitler's command, and I think that that might have changed things. I like to think that
won't happen again, but I don't know.[35]

Elliot's narrative is powerful for him because it re-envisions a past that he
finds personally troubling and very painful. His story also demonstrates the
ways that narratives can blur the boundaries between historical circum-
stance and interpretive experience; therein lies his story's power and moral
authority. By pointing to a historical moment in which select individuals
were stripped of their rights (i.e., the Jews under the Third Reich in Germany), Elliot bolsters his argument that the deterioration of gun rights can
have deadly consequences for disenfranchised citizens.

Such "if this, then that" narratives have enormous emotional power, derived in large part from their moral undertones. Few would question the bla-
tantly immoral actions taken by Hitler and the Third Reich, who perpetrated
some of the greatest crimes against humanity that history has ever witnessed. To suggest that the Jews might have at least struggled or put up a good
fight had their guns not been confiscated earlier is an appealing (if ques-
tionable) argument.[36] By using the example of a victimized group, Elliot
used the moral authority of their victimized status to argue for a possible
history in which they might have been able to save themselves, however fu-
tile that struggle might have eventually been.

Over the years, Americans have used their discussion of rights to articulate their vision of citizenship—of what being an American actually means
in terms of legal rights and political status. But the question of the right of
individuals to own guns is particularly contentious. Critics of the concept

of gun rights have often asserted that such a concept illustrates the ultimate in selfishness: the triumph of the individual gun owner's desire for guns over basic community safety and security.[37] And in fact, many shooters do see their guns rights as a basic right conferred on them as American citizens. Some even believe such gun rights may add to problems of public safety.

But most shooters see gun rights as a means to confer safety to individuals *and* social groups; gun rights enable individuals to protect themselves and their family, their community, and even their nation. The issue is not so much that gun control supporters believe in public safety and shooters do not. The difference is in how public safety should be achieved. Shooters believe gun rights allow them to promote collective as well as individual safety. In their minds, a lack of individual gun rights means that only government agents and criminals would remain armed, and citizens would be vulnerable to both.

Responsibility

Shooters also talk concretely about how gun ownership is not simply a right but a responsibility. The interweaving of rights and responsibilities is yet another way that shooters hark to notions of the earliest citizen soldiers, who recognized that rights did not come for free. Contemporary shooters use the term to denote several things: owning guns responsibly means being safe in your usage and storage, and recognizing that you have a powerful tool at your disposal. Most say they take the responsibility of safety very seriously. Jeremy, a former police officer in his late twenties, made this point when I asked him what gun ownership means to him: "Responsibility. Period. You can have fun responsibly, but it's a core value to owning a handgun. Especially—and I guess this falls into the whole education and enthusiast category, I enjoy some of the benefits of owning handguns, recreationally, work-related, personally in terms of personal safety. But they all carry responsibility. I have a lot of fun. But it's still responsible. I can't get away from that." Most of the shooters with whom I spoke attempt to differentiate themselves from those they consider "amateurs," people who do not take gun ownership and handling seriously, or who do not recognize the literal as well as symbolic power inherent in a gun. Tobias, a man in his late twenties who worked in the computer industry, links the notion of gun ownership with learning how to be a responsible person, which he had to prove to his parents through taking a course on gun safety as a child:

It's a responsibility. That's something that I learned from Peter Parker, the Amazing Spider Man, back when I was eight years old. With great power comes great responsibility. And as I said, guns are a tool of power. They're a hammer of might, and with that comes responsibility. That's why I wasn't allowed [to do anything], other than to touch the gun when I first got it, it went back in the case away until I completed the courses and proven to my parents and [had] gotten that little piece of paper that said, I've taken a gun safety course. It's a responsibility of knowing how to maintain, respect, and use the power that's invested in that piece of metal. Or plastic these days. So that's what it means.

The issue of responsibility is, of course, one the most contentious issues with regard to guns. Critics of gun ownership repeatedly point out that there are few mechanisms in place to ensure that people do use their guns responsibly, such as following safety rules and storing guns in locked safes so that children or housebreakers cannot get access. A number of shooters argued that one of the primary reasons safety is a problem is that people assume that gun handling is simple and straightforward, but at the time this research was conducted (in California), shooters were not legally required to take classes or pass stringent tests of knowledge. The Basic Firearms Safety Certificate exam is at best akin to the written part of a driver's test, and does not demand that shooters physically demonstrate that they can handle and shoot their firearms safely.

But rigorous certification and education requires an institutional structure for conveying knowledge. Many organizations and social groups are opposed to gun education, particularly for children, on the presumption that any gun education conveys the notion that gun ownership and the gun culture are somehow socially and culturally acceptable.[38] Thus, federally legislating that gun owners or anyone who may be exposed to guns must take mandatory classes to learn gun safety is unlikely to occur. Certain states might also see federal efforts to mandate safety and education as an infringement on state gun law and therefore hotly protest.

But there are any number of sources in American society that "educate" people about guns. For many gun users who are beginners, media images drive appropriate gun behavior. In my security guard training class, I watched several of the men joke and play with their unloaded pistols, pointing them straight in front of them (but not at each other) with mock-threatening body gestures. They flipped their pistols sideways and gestured with them, posturing to signify the kind of urban toughness so popular in television shows and movies. When the instructor noticed, he pointed out with polite annoyance that this posturing was not only dangerous but also technically incorrect, as it would be impossible to hit a target without looking down the front sights of the gun. Shooting a gun held sideways would produce wildly inaccurate shooting; movie and television messages to the contrary are simply wrong.

These shooters were not raw novices, and they immediately recognized that the instructor was right. They even acknowledged his point. However, I watched them continue to play in the same vein when the instructor was otherwise occupied. Apparently, television and movie images of what constitutes hip and cool with guns had more weight than the instructor's chastisements.

I later discussed the issue of enforcing safe and responsible behavior with Jane, a friend and shooting instructor. Her response was somewhat frustrated and typical of shooters on that issue: "Jesus Christ, Abby . . . what are we going to do? Put chips in people's heads?" Her point was that it is exceedingly difficult to *force* people to be responsible, even if there were some basic consensus on what is meant by responsible behavior with guns.

These are difficult issues both to address and to resolve, and they lack easy solutions. One of the inherent difficulties with gun laws differing from state to state, even county to county within a state, is that safety (in the broadest sense) is not standardized, and individuals are held accountable only to themselves, their family, or their locally regulated community and state. Being safe with guns in one state may mean keeping them unlocked and fully loaded because the perceived danger lies in criminal attack, not in the guns themselves. In another state or city, simply having a gun in the home is construed as the greatest danger and is thus illegal. Thus, shooters themselves think about safety in their own home as an issue of individual choice and custom, maintained by local dictates and local legislation. Although many shooters may be comfortable with this state of affairs, they assert that they take safety and responsibility issues very seriously. But most of the shooters with whom I spoke also talked of times when they themselves were appalled by the behavior of some gun owners.

Guns and Personhood

One of the reasons that some shooters are so opposed to allowing more stringent government regulation of gun ownership is that they believe that being able to own guns is synonymous with being recognized as a full-status person in the eyes of the state. In fact, historians have long recognized that the vast majority of individuals living in colonial America did not have legal sanction to own guns: the ability to "keep and bear arms" was a right afforded only to white, propertied, adult men. By implication, then, those who were prevented from owning and using guns did not have equal status. Slaves, indigenous peoples, women, children—all of these people were afforded fewer rights than white, propertied, adult men.[39] In relation to the broader question of what constitutes a good arbiter of personhood and political status in any given society (historically and contemporarily), shooters argue that legal access to guns is a particularly powerful statement of how the state recognizes the power and status of the individual. By extension, access to guns can become an arbiter of status among groups of citizens, particular citizens who clash with each other over a wider variety of rights, privileges, and powers.

These symbolic associations resonate even today. Shooters implicitly believe that the symbolic associations between guns and personhood so deeply entrenched in the American cultural and political cosmology are still meaningful and important. In the following fieldnote, I documented a discussion that took place at an IPSC shoot, in which shooters were chatting about some fairly sensitive topics:

> We all waited as the timer and the referee got set up on this particular stage, and as we waited, the men chatted and told jokes. They arrived on the topic of different kinds of sporting events, and someone mentioned the "politically incorrect" sport of "midget tossing." There were some head shakes and general expressions of disbelief at the outrageousness of such an activity, but the guy who mentioned it stated vehemently that he had heard this activity was considered a pub sport in England.
>
> This prompted another shooter, my contact Robby, to mention that he had a good friend, another shooter in the group, who was Italian, and apparently "Italians think that seeing a midget, or touching one on the head, is good luck." He went on to say that at one point, he and his friend had had a couple drinks one night before a shoot, and his friend wanted to drive around town and find a midget for good luck, and even pat the midget on the head. There was a round of slightly disbelieving but amused laughter at this, and Robby insisted that it was true. His friend thought that touching a midget on the head was good luck.
>
> Then another shooter, a heavyset man in his late fifties who had been one of

the leading forces in the conversation up to that point but had remained skeptical about the midget tossing, crossed his arms, shook his head, and stated definitively, "Well, if he's packing, you'd better ask his permission first." There was a murmur of agreement, and the conversation moved on from there. (fieldnotes, 17 October 1998, IPSC match)

To "pack" a gun, or wear it on your person, is to determine your own fate, ensuring not only your own safety but also personal respect. Carrying a firearm enforces personal boundaries and ensures being treated with dignity. These shooters were using packing status as a shorthand way to illustrate these connections. These shooters knew that what they were describing is offensive even though they also found it funny.[40] The shooter who had the last word (by reminding everyone that "even a midget" could be packing) subtly reminded the crowd not only that everyone should be treated with respect and dignity, but that even those who don't look it can potentially enforce that respect should the need arise. No matter what his size or stature, a person who's packing is in a position to dictate for himself how he wants to be treated. Shooters believe guns ensure a balance of power interpersonally, which is important because people will take advantage of each other if they think they can.

As I discussed, the United States is a nation founded first and foremost on the political philosophy of republicanism. As such, the earliest Americans believed in the concept of the citizen soldier: responsible, adult citizens who had a right and an obligation to arm themselves to protect their nation. In early colonial republican ideology, such citizen soldiers were considered the civic ideal. They were responsible for community defense and formed the backbone of America itself, willing to be armed and proud to defend their colony against threats both internal and external. More contemporarily, American mythic history encourages the belief that the concept of the citizen soldier is synonymous with both freedom and independence. Shooters subscribe strongly to these mythic connections and ascribe to the citizen soldier very modern notions of being a responsible, full-status adult in American society.

However, they are also aware of the extent to which concepts like responsibility are exercised differently by different people, and the reality is that in modern-day American society, there are no agreed-upon definitions of how to be responsible with guns, even if Americans do have a right to own them. But because this latter point is not one on which shooters believe there is a consensus view, they are often willing to agree that the freedom to own a gun and exercise one's gun rights should always trump the government's ability to control who has access to firearms. To relinquish this basic American right would spell disaster for shooters because, as some shooters mentioned, it is the Second Amendment that guarantees the ability of Americans to enjoy their other constitutional rights. The citizen soldier lives on in theory if not in actuality.

Cowboy Lawmen

Americans have long romanticized the American West and the frontier as places that forged some of the most legendary heroes of American history, people who came to embody the country itself: strong, proud, independent, and free. Guns were woven into the social fabric of that era as well, and the myths and fables that grew out of the period reflected the complexity of guns and their uses.

The relationship of western frontiersmen in the mid–nineteenth century to American Indians also has bearing on understanding the complexity of the historic frontier. Frontier rhetoric of constant vigilance against fearless and savage Indians made the need for armament seem crucial. Even when pioneers did *not* encounter hostile Indian forces on their travels west, settlers tended to "reimagine" such Indians when reflecting back on their travels in memoirs and stories about westward expansion. In other words, "Indians played a crucial symbolic role in giving this 'pioneer' past meaning."[1] "Remembering" the conquest of a land populated by bloodthirsty Indians affirmed for pioneering Americans that a certain kind of courage and toughness was inherent in the experience of westward expansion.

The revision of the not-too-distant past, even during the late nineteenth century itself, was a process fueled by the scientific rhetoric of the day: evolutionism. Evolutionism was a popular paradigm even before Darwin published the *Origin of the Species* in 1859. When evolutionism combined with the religious fervor of middle-class Americans, the annihilation of the American Indians seemed a moral imperative. In this vein, Indians were conceptualized as the savage and barbaric holdovers of a country that *needed* to be conquered by good government, commercial expansion, and Christianity.[2] By the mid–nineteenth century, the image of Indians in the public imagination was so dehumanized and barbaric that "the destructive march of progress could not only proceed but also claim a moral victory over the forces of barbarism and evil."[3]

The social role of guns in this time period also got a major boost by one of the most important entrepreneurs of nineteenth-century America, Samuel Colt. "Colonel" Colt was one of the first arms manufacturers and dealers, a brilliant businessman and the quintessential American mythmaker.[4] Colt introduced his particular kind of firearm, which in effect revolutionized gun violence through the action of "repeating" gunfire at a time in American history that was ripe for his product. A master of self-marketing and publicity, Colt soon made the image of his guns synonymous with the most celebrated aspects of western frontier life: tough, reliable, and straight shooting (literally and figuratively), an image that suited the tone of the times. Colt was enormously helpful in drawing conceptual links between guns as a symbol of power, status, and masculinity.

As the frontier diminished as an actual proportion of the United States land mass in the late nineteenth century, it grew in symbolic significance as an embodied, nostalgic concept onto which Easterners projected images of frontiersmen and cowboys as superior individuals.[5] The frontier became the Frontier, a mythic space and ideological construct. This mythic Frontier is what looms large in so many contemporary imaginations, predominantly because it is not bound by the facts and reality of actual American history. Thus, it has served as an ideological repository for Americans past and present, a legendary place where men could best test their strength and courage, and where the ideals of freedom, liberty, and equality were played out in their most primitive (and therefore most pure) forms. Guns were an essential part of those Frontier myths and images, so ubiquitous and common that it is almost impossible to imagine the scout or western cowboy without his trusty firearm.

Real versus Mythic Cowboys

In both myth and fact, cowboys have always been gun-toting.[6] In the nineteenth century, cowboys were apparently the most heavily armed civilians outside of professional hunters, carrying large-caliber revolvers and repeating rifles. Cowboy mortality rates were high not simply due to intentional homicide but also from accidental shootings and general firearms accidents (guns falling out of pockets or tipping over and discharging, etc.). One of the most frequent kinds of provocation for cowboy violence was the notion of *nemo me impugnit*, "No one impugns me." This variation on the theme of violent action to redress personal insult resulted in relatively frequent unpremeditated homicides, especially when combined with group situations involving alcohol. Interestingly, these kinds of scenarios were infrequent on the trails, and focused mainly on cattle town sprees, when hard-working men took breaks from trail work to spruce themselves up and spend their money on fancy food, drink, gambling, and prostitutes. Thus, cattle towns boomed during the cattle drive season, when various townsfolk put up with cowboy rambunctiousness to cash in on cowboy spending sprees.[7]

Despite their image as the strong and upright heroes of the frontier, cowboys were considerably less romantic and moral than legend would have it. In fact, although cowboys were usually dependable and hard-working when sober, they were notoriously mean and unpredictable when drunk. The origins of the cowboy myth emerges from history with some difficulty, but actual cowboys did exist nonetheless. In fact, "cowboys, in short, were lower-class bachelor laborers in a risky and unhealthful line of work. They were members of a disreputable and violent subculture with its own rules for appropriate behavior." For the cowboy to become and remain such a treasured cultural icon demanded a bit of moral surgery, transforming the belligerent drunk sleeping off a night of gambling and whoring into a crusty mounted protector with a heart of gold.[8]

The men responsible for maintaining law and order on the western frontier in the mid–nineteenth century fed these myths and images of using controlled violence to contain chaotic violence. This job fell to men who became legendary in the annals of western frontier history: Wild Bill Hickok, Wyatt Earp, and William Barclay "Bat" Masterson, all examples of men who would stand up to dangerously reckless cowboys and fight firepower with firepower.[9] For the more hardened criminals, the cattle rustlers and highwaymen, local law enforcement gave way to local vigilante groups, which dealt with more serious crimes by hanging or simply shooting outlaws in their jail cells. In some respects, vigilantism ironically provided community cohesion, as it entailed community members becoming organized enough to take punitive measures against outlaws or criminals without resorting to the formalized legal system.[10]

Separating the cowboy as a historical figure from the colorful and mythic narratives that he inhabits is difficult at best. The scope and power of Wild West narratives are perhaps most identifiable in their modern incarnations:

movies and television programs. Such classic films as *High Noon*, *The Shootist*, and *Stagecoach*, more modern films like *Tombstone* and *Wyatt Earp*, and even television programs like *Bonanza* and *Lonesome Dove*, are not all simply westerns. These iconic productions were/are American myths and values writ large.[11] The heroes of these films and TV shows embody familiar and idealized qualities that have resonated in American culture for decades, particularly for the white middle class.

As the movie industry prospered and moved beyond the silent pictures, the western as a genre, with its formulaic plots and straightforward moral lessons, grew immensely in popularity. A historic epic emerged, one that celebrated the conquering of the West as a triumph of civilization over savagery, of whites over Indians, and of civilization over nature.[12] The cowboy was the perfect hero for this particular vision, as his image was tightly linked with moral courage and lonely individualism, a hero who was destined to repeatedly save a society to which he would never quite belong. Although the mythic stories embodied in movie westerns don't enjoy the tremendous popularity that they did in the 1950s and 1960s, the cowboy himself remains a powerful icon in American popular culture.

One primary reason for the continued fascination with the mythic cowboy is that he never fully integrated himself with society, despite the inherently social tendency to serve that society and work with his peers. The cowboy thus embodied an interesting ability to mediate the tension between stark individualism and adherence to community, both in spirit and in actuality.[13] The cowboy's six-shooter came to embody his individualistic brand of justice, enabling him to shoot straighter and faster than others, encouraging the sense that even when he took the law into his own hands, he did so with an unerring sense of virtue and righteousness. These values ostensibly justified his vigilante actions.[14] Classic movie westerns reiterated this lesson at every turn: when the hero of *High Noon*, Sheriff Will Kane, returns to town to face his enemies, he does so not because his community asks him to but because his pride and sense of duty demand it.[15] Everybody knows that a bloody showdown between good and evil is the only ending to the story when the bad men come to town.

Western Myths and Myths of the West

Cowboys on the mythic Frontier, which was both a geographic place and an ideological construct, have had tremendous impact on the development of the American national character and the imaginations and identities of the citizenry. Two of the most famous contributors to both the Frontier and to cowboys (in myth and image) in the past two centuries were Frederick Jackson Turner, a historian and professor, and William "Buffalo Bill" Cody, a premiere entertainer of the Wild West.[16] This unlikely duo presented two very different images of the American Frontier during the late nineteenth century. Turner's image of the Frontier, which has been referred to as his "Frontier thesis," presented a rather bucolic image of the "taming" of the American Frontier. His heroes were farmers, always gendered as male, forging their way through the American wilderness, which took on a decidedly Eden-like cast, while American Indians watched quietly from the sidelines. Turner's argument helped foster the idea that a man was not born American. Rather, he became American through his action and his vigor, which proclaimed his new identity more loudly than any document or speech could possibly do. Europeans could become American by performing their Americanness, by this active and transformative process.[17]

William "Buffalo Bill" Cody also recognized the importance of action and performance as "authentically" American, action and performance in all their uses and meanings. Frontier history, as presented in Buffalo Bill Cody's Wild West and Congress of Rough Riders, a historical reenactment and rodeo show featuring "authentic" sharpshooters and cowboys, was about combating wild animals and savage, menacing Indians.[18] Buffalo Bill's West teemed with people and ferocious wildlife, and his Frontier heroes were the hunters and cowboys, frontiersmen and scouts who combated their "natural" enemies and defeated them in literal and moral victories. The show turned the westering movement into a morality play: white frontiersmen represented the forces of "good and civilization and Indians and a few errant White road agents symbolized evil and barbarism."[19] Once Cody's show had run its course, it was quickly replaced by the traveling rodeo, an equally dazzling opportunity for Americans to see "examples of modern men who reflected western toughness, raw courage, and natural strength, living proof that the pioneer spirit of the West remained intact."[20]

These two different images of the American Frontier in the nineteenth century, Turner's Frontier thesis and Cody's Wild West show, had wide appeal for Americans. Both explained the forging of an American identity in ways that Americans understood and were already romanticizing. It was an identity created out of the conquering of the American Frontier. This was the time when particular constructions of masculinity, including physical strength, a willingness to confront and commit violence, and a stoic resolve to "push through" and "civilize" the world, were highly valued commodities.

While these characteristics were certainly employed in the service of the literal conquest and settlement of the West, they took on their own mythic qualities as they were employed to convey the magnitude of the accomplishment of claiming the West. This was a West that demanded the "authentic masculinity" that middle-class Americans treasured, a far cry from an increasingly urban and industrialized East. This "authentic masculinity" found a distinctive home in the mythic West and came to signify an authentic American character in significant ways. In the early twentieth century, the West was understood as the great repository for the individualism and freedom already woven into the American ethos. Journalists and other cultural producers learned quickly that myths sold more easily than reality because myths informed Americans how to *be* Americans with far more flair and color than any other kind of narratives possibly could.[21] These mythic visions of the West also came during a time when Americans were concerned that the "real" West was closing, that the boundaries were now visible on what was first conceptualized as a boundless economic and phenomenological opportunity for growth and progress. How could progress, literal and metaphoric, be demonstrated with the "closing" of the Frontier?

The answer is that Americans create new frontiers, in a variety of different ways. The Frontier, in myth and image, continues to serve as a powerful metaphor for American progress and entrepreneurial spirit, and as a symbol in the service of American industry and business.[22] In the early and mid-1990s, the nascent information technology industry referred to itself and was referred to as the "next American Frontier." The Frontier is also kept alive through television and film; the American West still looms large in popular culture as the landscape for epic American drama. And finally, Americans ritually reenact "how the West was won" on a local and community level, creating Frontiers for play and self-expression, using the Frontier as the idiom to express their own pride in their heritage.[23]

Modern-Day Cowboy Lawmen

Shooters harked constantly to images and ideals that are now linked inexorably to American's western past. For the men and women who love the sport of cowboy action shooting in particular, guns are emblematic of a host of principles and values that speak largely to the American Creed.

Self-Reliance

Cowboy shooters, like modern-day citizen soldiers, talk about how guns provide a means by which they can become more self-reliant. This self-reliance is intimately connected with their notion of being more individualistic. A shooter is capable of relying on himself, being his own person. Jonathan, a white administrator who worked at a large university, explained:

> Why do I like guns? To me it's just like—because I can shoot really well with them, I just have this affinity for them. I love to read about them. I like the history that goes with guns . . . when I go out and shoot it relaxes me, very meditative and such. Owning a gun, it kind of means that you are determining your own fate. . . . I don't call 911. It really is true. You aren't dialing 911 [when you have a gun], you handle it yourself. And besides, if you're gonna wait for those police to show up, they never show up in time anyway. So it's like, you don't have to rely on the police, you know what I mean? You have to know when to use them and what you're gonna use them for and such, and since so many people out there have [guns] already, you kind of feel like, like when I do security work and stuff, it's like I feel better having one.

In this sentiment, Jonathan is similar to Greg, who also expresses a desire to be able to determine his own fate, primarily because of his willingness and ability to own and use guns. Jonathan also expresses a desire to not rely on the police for protection, and in this way he is very similar to most of the shooters I befriended. Many of the shooters I interviewed spoke of how they do not want to have to rely on the police, or any peacekeeping officers, to feel and actually *be* protected in their home or community. Rarely are these shooters actively distrustful of the police, nor do they exhibit a lack of respect for police (in fact, far from it).[24] They generally feel, however, that the police are rarely able to react and arrive in time to save someone from harm, an example being if an intruder is breaking into the shooter's home or attacking him or her on the street.

Some shooters found this to be true from their own experience. Jennifer, a white attorney in her early fifties, provided good examples. She often served as a divorce attorney for women who had been battered by their former husbands or partners. She shared several narratives about times when she felt her life had been threatened during the course of her work. In one instance, she was taking a deposition in her home office. The man she was deposing became enraged during their exchange and started toward Jennifer, yelling that he would kill her. She reached into her office drawer, drew out a handgun, and pointed it at her would-be attacker. He stopped short. She ordered him out of her office, and he quickly left the premises. She also described how a client's husband had threatened her verbally and did in fact try to break down her office door on one occasion, presumably to attack her as he was screaming that he would. She called the police while he was trying to get in and then also called her boyfriend (now husband). Her boyfriend arrived within five minutes with several of his friends in tow, and these men managed to frighten the would-be attacker off the property. The police arrived some fifteen minutes after them. Jennifer capped off these narratives by stating that a number of lawyers in her acquaintance feel the need to be armed in their daily lives.

Shooters in general reflect a good deal of knowledge about the degree to which the police are legally required (or are not, as the case may be) to assist someone at home against an attacker or intruder, and the amount of response time that calling the police for assistance usually entails. In fact, the police are not legally required to arrive in time to save lives or actively prevent incidents from occurring.[25] Shooters offered this information to illustrate the necessity of being able to protect oneself from an intruder in the home, because the police are neither capable of nor liable for doing so.

Most shooters noted, however, that actual home invasions are rare. But the rarity of the incidents does not necessarily affect the desire for guns for self- and home defense. Should the need for protection arise, one should be vigilant and prepared; to rely on institutions like the police or similar protectors is the height of folly.

Equality

The principle of equality in the United States is closely intertwined with the idea of a lack of class distinction. Many Americans conceptualize the United States as a strictly democratic and classless society. Therefore, all individuals, regardless of age, race, gender, and socioeconomic level, are in principle equal, certainly in terms of equality of opportunity. However, social critics and scholars have long held that Americans are not all equal. The complexity of social factors and their impact on social structures and institutions makes the notion of equality dubious, particularly in terms of access to social services and benefits. Yet Americans cling to the ideal of equality, holding onto this ideal as a foundational principle that should be practiced in all areas of legal, social, and political life.

Shooters' notion of equality is a complex one and can be linked directly to notions of equality that stem from the mythology of the Frontier and all its ideological associations. Shooters are principally interested in two related issues: social equality, the idea that all individuals should have equal access to societal benefits, and political equality, the idea that all individuals should have equal access to political power (broadly understood as political rights and guarantees). Shooters employ the basic assumption that Americans are supposed to enjoy these kinds of equality, which should be woven into the fabric of society. However, what emerges from their discussions of these issues is that they do not feel that the principle of equality is currently being applied to people who own guns. Several of the shooters who spoke most eloquently on this topic related their notion of equality to class. They argued that gun ownership as it relates to class is deeply problematic. For example, Lewis, a white craftsman in his late thirties with some Native American heritage self-identifies as working class. He believes that the poor and disadvantaged have a greater need for guns for protection. But the poor feel the brunt of strict gun controls more frequently than the middle or upper classes. He explained: "Oh yeah. [In this township], you know, the same week that they passed the welfare reform law, they passed the Saturday Night Special 'law,' to keep poor people from being able to own guns. So what is that saying about what the government's trying to do? You know, Clinton tried to keep people in subsidized housing from having guns. You know, it's like, 'Well, we can't trust people'."

Lewis first refers to a measure in California in the early 1990s in which state legislators banned the so-called Saturday Night Specials, small, cheap handguns that are supposedly used so frequently to commit gun crimes but are believed by some to be useless for self-defense. Although there is criminological evidence that refutes both notions, state and local legislation that restricts the purchase of Saturday Night Specials continues to crop up as a means of combating gun crime.[26] Lewis objects to this kind of legislation on the grounds that are frequently used to oppose it, which is that restricting the sales of certain kinds of guns (particularly cheaper ones) ostensibly means that certain populations are being pointedly denied access to guns simply because they cannot afford the more expensive (and therefore legal) varieties.[27] Lewis lumps this kind of legislation in with similar reforms that penalize Americans who are poor (i.e., certain kinds of welfare reform). He argues that this phenomenon derives from the politicians' stereotypes of the poor, one example being the bigoted assumption that links being poor to being inherently criminal.[28] He continued:

I come from a very poor family, and when they start passing laws like gun taxes and making it where poor people can't afford to protect themselves, and they're the ones that need to protect themselves, you know, they act like everybody in the ghetto is a criminal. Well, 99 percent of the people in the ghetto are fine people. . . . [They are] more likely to be victims and have less to lose, but that little means more to them. So if they pass laws or taxes or federal taxes or tax on ammunition, and make it to where only the elite can afford to [own guns], it goes back to what happened in Europe, where the rich were able to hunt, to own guns, but the poor were put to death if they hunted on land. So this country's about equality. Money's not supposed to not give you more rights.

Political Equality

Other shooters have similarly vehement arguments centering around the idea that prohibitions on gun ownership are class- or even race-based. Shooters broadly understand attempts to restrict gun ownership from certain segments of the population (as in the case of the banning of Saturday Night Specials) as representative of class struggles in American society in which the poverty-stricken are made more vulnerable by the elite, who are capable of controlling the forces of law and order through political influence. Jonathan, who emigrated to the United States as a child, also believes strongly that banning guns is a way to penalize the poor, in effect denying them a right to self-defense. He stated:

What does owning a gun mean to [me]? Autonomy, self-determination. . . . It always worries me when the elitist power structure, all the rich people, don't like you to have guns, because they want their military to have them, and they want their police to have them. The people that buy and own the police, like in . . . [wealthy neighborhoods], [rich people] want those guys to have [guns] because they own those people, and those people will do what they tell them, but they don't like other people having them. . . . I've seen what it's like to be on the side that doesn't have the guns, and what [the elite] can get away with. They can keep you poor and on the dole and uneducated, no right to vote. . . . No. I think anyone . . . [should be able to own guns], no matter if they're liberals or conservatives.

What is fascinating about the lessons of American history for some shooters is that they do not relate to the notion of whites settling the land or making the wilderness "safe" for other Europeans. Some shooters feel more kinship with the indigenous populations of the Americas who lost their land to whites in protracted and violent conflicts. The idea of a gun as an equalizer has power and resonance precisely because some shooters identify their ethnic heritage as American Indian. If their ancestors had had firepower, they argue, then the settling of the American Frontier would have played out very differently. Lewis proudly lays claim to both a "cowboy and Indian" heritage, and has numerous family stories about both sides of his family on the actual frontier of the nineteenth century. Having already learned about his ethnic heritage, I asked him to discuss this heritage in relation to how whites and Indians interacted:

AK: Now, it's interesting . . . with regard to the cowboy shooting, because you have the family heritage of both cowboys and Indians, as it were. Does that ever create any kind of tension in your mind about allegiances or . . . I mean, I know part of the same frontier history. But does the Indian part of you ever have some resentment about the way Indians were treated. . . ?

Lewis: Oh absolutely. Sure. I wish they would have had guns earlier. Instead of having the Pilgrims *over* for dinner, they would have had the Pilgrims *for* dinner [emphasis added]. They could have been a lot different if they'd been armed earlier. . . . It's like—I think of the Jews in Europe. Their guns were confiscated, and once your guns are confiscated, you're subjugated to whatever the power is. Once you disarm a population, they're helpless. You do what you're told or you're killed. At least you can stand up and fight if you have the means. And that's why they [the Framers] were so adamant about the Second Amendment. The Second Amendment protects all the other freedoms we have. . . . Without it, you don't have any chance.

Mythic history is a powerful tool not simply because it reimagines historical events to make a more timely argument, but because this mythic history can be shaped and molded to meet the psychic needs of its creators and audience.[29] Because such rearranged events did not occur exactly as told, there is no way to know how they might have affected history. But these myths have power and resonance precisely because of their imaginative quality, which makes them meaningful and timeless. Revisionist history is powerful and satisfying because it can right moral wrongs, even if only on the level of the personal or collective imagination. Lewis's statement in particular illustrates the flexibility of pro-gun ideology in its ability to articulate not only cultural concerns about equality and rights, but also more personal concerns about how families and different social groups stood in relation to the early American state. Lewis essentially argues that if history had been different, if the

Indians had owned more guns, then European settlers would not have defeated them so easily. Pro-gun ideology speaks directly to the issue of how certain populations have experienced aggression by the state, or aggression from those claiming the authority of state power within the framework of imperialist conquest. But guns on both sides would have truly equalized the fight.

There are a number of historical factors that make this argument refutable (e.g., the sheer numbers of whites colonizing the North American continent, the disease and starvation that decimated Indian tribes, to name but a few factors), but Lewis finds meaning in the "what might have been," had his ancestors been equipped with guns. He makes the same argument about Indians that Elliot makes about Jews and the Third Reich: an armed population is an empowered population; a disarmed population is at the mercy of its enemies. These are the kinds of arguments that redress old psychic wounds and fire a sense of righteous anger over the "social injustice" of gun control. Shooters see modern-day gun control efforts as contextualized by historical events that illustrate the untrustworthiness of government, American as well as European.

The examples Lewis and Jonathan used also illustrate their notions of class struggle and class vulnerability. Referring back to the Frontier saying "God made men; Colonel Colt made them equal" makes this point more clear. Shooters understand guns as symbolic as well as literal equalizers. In this context, when guns are denied to vulnerable populations but accessible to aggressors, guns then come to symbolize status and personhood. Lewis recalls the Jews and their disarmament. Jonathan recalls a childhood in which he felt vulnerable to police and the militarized state, which he believes is controlled by society's elite. Lewis and Jonathan are equating a lack of societal status with tight restrictions on gun ownership, and they firmly believe that these restrictions are aimed at the poor and working class, people who are less powerful than elites, who are able to exempt themselves from these same restrictions.

Some shooters suggested to me that repeated calls to reject guns in favor of "alternative" defensive methods (e.g., calling the police) reveals an elitism that underscores what shooters consider the hypocrisy of a white, middle-class critique of gun ownership. Writing in response to what he considers this hypocrisy, attorney Jeffrey Snyder argues that there is something deeply disturbing about expecting police officers (who are often working or lower-middle class themselves) to put themselves in dangerous situations for people who are apparently unwilling to defend themselves. He puts it this way:

Is your life worth protecting? Is so, whose responsibility is it to protect it? If you believe that it is the police's, not only are you wrong—since the courts universally rule that they have no legal obligation to do so—but you face some difficult moral quandaries. How can you rightfully ask another human being to risk his life to protect yours, when you will assume no responsibility yourself? Because that is his job and we pay him to do it? Because your life is of incalculable value, but his is only worth the $30,000 salary we pay him? If you believe it reprehensible to possess the means and will to use lethal force to repel a criminal assault, how can you call upon another to do it for you?

Snyder is launching a critique against what he sees as the elitist belief that only the backward and uncivilized want guns. He argues that this elitist mentality is directed toward the project of "civilizing" the masses, those misguided Americans who need to be weaned off their foolish need for self-defense. Stating that the battle against gun control is waged by the "common man," Snyder attacks both liberals and conservatives by arguing that elitist liberals take a "moral high ground" vis-à-vis gun ownership, and elitist conservatives simply concede to this liberal framework because it's easy to do so. Snyder suggests that often politicians have "taken upon themselves the terrible burden" of civilizing the masses, but these politicians' lives illustrate that they believe "laws are for other people," not themselves.[30] Snyder demonstrates that the issue of gun ownership for self-defense is a way for shooters to understand and articulate class tensions and frustrations while packaging them in an ideological stance that manifestly celebrates American ideals of autonomy and equality.[31]

For shooters, when a specific group is purposely disarmed for "the social good" but other members of that same population are not, the symbolic statement is clear: the disarmed group is not equal in the eyes of the state. The state cannot trust this group to own or use guns because this group is perceived as a danger to themselves or others. Disarmament is symbolically infantalizing: disarmed populations become wards of the state, with no ability or means to protect themselves from criminal aggressors, or even the aggressive state itself. Additionally, the lack of status inherent in selective disarmament suggests that there are no legal, social, or political means of retaliation for disempowered groups. This mode of understanding gun control has led some social critics and commentators to argue that even in the United States, issues of nativism, racism, and gun control are intimately intertwined in complex ways.[32] Different social groups have "different experiences with organized violence, and differences in victims' ability to rely on government for protection, explain attitudes toward private armies and collective self-defense."[33]

The point is that both historically and contemporarily, both gun ownership and gun control have facilitated the elite white power structure's control over American society.[34] How individuals and social groups locate themselves on the spectrum of gun rights versus gun control is influenced not just by their reading of the present but also by their reading of the past, particularly in relation to their perception of the relationship between gun control and social control. This is one of the reasons that both gun ownership and gun control continue to be contested issues, and race, class, and gender do matter in these debates. Both gun ownership and gun control have been used throughout American history to advantage some and disadvantage others. Such laws, and the social practices that are structured by them, eventually influence how symbolically significant objects like guns are perceived by their owners and by groups prohibited from owning them.

Thus, it is not only personal experience that determines an individual's attitudes toward self-defense. Familial experience and knowledge of one's ethnic heritage has bearing on the issue as well. Beliefs, individual experiences, and family memories fuse with cultural values and ideals to produce a complex understanding of how individuals and ethnic groups stand in relation to the state, specifically in terms of either protection by or vulnerability to both the state and criminal aggression. Those who feel strongly that their own ethnic or racial group has suffered a long history of victimization may also feel a sense of vulnerability in relation to the state, as well as a reluctance from the state to offer protective services. For these reasons, some communities are distrustful when informed that their access to guns is to be restricted for their own good. When the state restricts access to guns for protection but refuses to offer other concrete guarantees of safety, some gun owners become that much more suspicious of the state. On both literal and symbolic levels, such actions are viewed as incompetent at best and downright sinister at worst.

Individuals and social collectives note how other groups are treated by the state as well, and these observations make a difference to understandings of these issues. Although the predominantly white, middle-class shooters discussed here do not necessarily perceive that their own ethnic groups have received abusive treatment from the state historically, they believe that gun control is one of the primary ways the state can abuse its power. When any social collective (regardless of ethnicity or class) is denied access to guns by the state, that group is made more vulnerable. The experiences of African Americans throughout American history and the Jews prior to and during the rise of the Third Reich in Germany provide cautionary tales to any group of concerned gun enthusiasts, regardless of ethnicity or social class. Public narratives about the experiences of politically subordinated groups vis-à-vis access to guns can have broader impact on the ways contemporary gun enthusiasts understand what it means to be subordinated, even while they understand the experiences of their own ethnic groups to have been relatively privileged. These examples illustrate the extent to which guns and gun control have come to articulate a certain understanding of how much political and social power the individual and his or her ethnic group maintain in relation to a (potentially abusive) state.

Clear Moral Codes

One of the most frequent and powerful sentiments expressed by shooters, cowboy shooters in particular, is a longing for what they imagine was a simpler kind of life in the Old West. For such shooters, cowboy action shooting is a way to reminisce about what is romanticized as a less complex moral arena: there was good and there was bad, everybody knew which was which, and everybody could make straightforward choices about which side they wanted to take. This reductive vision of moral order, simplistic though it may be, is also a neat and totalizing (i.e., mythic) way to explain the status quo of how we "won the West." In this context, guns provide a way to reenact a simpler time when moral codes were black and white, very straightforward, and the good guys always defeated the bad. Mick, a real estate assessor in his early fifties who is a naturalized American citizen, explained:

> What's right, what's wrong. And to this day, when we go out to the range and we all get dressed up like cowboys, it's (a) absolute escapism, (b) it's very safe and comfortable because when I grew up, there was right and there was wrong. There was no variation. And if you were right, you were one of the good guys. And if you were bad, evil befell you. So it's very simplistic, it's very comforting to, on Sunday mornings, get up and get dressed up like a cowboy and get a latte and . . . then sashay ourselves out to the range. And have everything black and white, right or wrong. It's escapism. . . . And everybody is in synch with the fantasy. . . . Yeah. If you give your word, you say you will do something, you do it. You can walk away from a range with a $5,000 rifle and say to the guy, I'll give you the money next week, and he says, That's fine. Whereas, in your business, you wouldn't extend $5,000 credit to somebody you just— whose name you don't even know.

The appeal of cowboy shooting is strong for several reasons. As I mentioned in the first chapter on cowboy shooting, this is a highly enjoyable activity. It is, in Mick's words, absolute escapism. But the escapism isn't simply about escaping from the stress of a demanding job or a hectic city life, or a yearning for open Frontier spaces. Mick yearns for a time when it was easy to identify right and wrong; back then, these concepts were firm and reified, as simple to understand and identify as white hats and white horses. These simple indicators for right and wrong have been drilled into middle-class Americans at an early age through dime store novels, 1950s television shows, and, most important, movie westerns. Cowboy shooters are united in their love of a romanticized vision of a Wild West past, where everybody knew where everybody else stood. The bad guy got what was coming to him, and the good guy rode off into the sunset, secure in the knowledge that his actions were justified by the legitimacy and consistency of his moral code. Mick explained:

> So guns were a way of dealing justice. It was the difference between right and wrong, along with white hats and white horses. White cowboy shirts. So it was very simple, it was all black and white. The movies were black and white, the lessons were black and white, good versus evil, good wins. Cowboys carried really cute . . . guns. . . . [I used to think to myself that] one day I'm going to go to America and be a cowboy. And so that is my interest in guns. My interest in guns is old guns, is only cowboy guns, because it's absolute escapism. And it goes back to my childhood. One time I had an AR15, but that was not a fun gun because that was the gun that was used in Vietnam and that wasn't a shining example of what a gun does. That's the other side, that's the down side of the gun, so I don't like those guns. I like the cowboy guns.

Mick differentiates between the kinds of moral values that he associates with different kinds of guns. Modern automatic rifles offer him no escapist pleasure because he associates them with moral ambiguity, if not outright immoral behavior, as with the Vietnam War. But his association with cowboy guns is far more pure and pleasurable: these guns provide an avenue to a fantasy of the Wild West, a time that middle-class Americans continue to mythologize as the best of American progressivism, moral purpose, and the romantic dream of founding a new and ideal nation. Cowboy shooters revel in what they've made for themselves with symbols of "true" Americana that are borrowed from a time imagined as less morally ambiguous, even though conquest and imperialism was the norm. Through cowboy shooting, mostly middle-class Americans can assure themselves that they have not lost the strength of character that "won the West." Baby boomers can reengage through ritual what they feel is lost through the over-civilizing processes of obtaining white-collar jobs, Winnebagos, and houses in wealthy neighborhoods. Guns are an integral part of this ritual because guns are the quintessential symbol of "regeneration through violence"—the means to tame the wilderness and ensure a moral victory over decadence and over-civilization.[35]

Romancing the Frontier

Cowboy shooting thus celebrates a very particular reading of the American Frontier experience: cowboy shooters are a relatively homogeneous group of people, collectively selecting elements of Frontier life for emulation. There is very little ethnic diversity in the cowboy shooters of the Bay Area, despite their occasionally defensive insistence to the contrary. In some ways, this is not surprising: the vision of the Frontier as "good guys and bad guys," in Mick's words, is a relatively privileged experience of "how the West was won." It is not incidental that local and regional shooting clubs name themselves after vigilante groups that actually existed, or use local place-names to create modern-day vigilante groups for the purposes of cowboy competitions (e.g., the San Jose Regulators). Nor is it surprising that shooters are organized into posses for shooting competitions. These kinds of devices hark to the notion that this is a sport for the "good guys" and quietly reinforces the sense of celebrating a moral victory over forces of ambiguity inherent in postmodern times. Cowboy shooters are embracing a vision of the Wild West that made America what it is today, where it's a darn good thing to be a cowboy action shooter. Cowboy shooters know they're living the good life, the best that American society has to offer, and as far as they're concerned, they've earned it.

The idea that people are able to make self-conscious choices about the life they lead and the identity they choose to project to their social peers is a quintessentially American cultural value. The ideology of choice in relation to identity, in being whoever you want to be, is a powerful part of the American Dream. Within this ideology, individuals are not supposed to be judged on who they are (their intrinsic qualities, such as ethnicity or sex), but rather on the lifestyle choices they make and on the personal qualities they've chosen to develop in themselves. These are the choices that involve what is sometimes called "character," which (supposedly) stems from moral choices and free will. In other words, Americans are made, not born. More than that—Americans make themselves.

This way of thinking about identity and choice is also fundamentally middle class: within this framework, identity is entirely about choice, and is not (or should not) be constrained by money, status, power, or historical forces beyond one's control. And perhaps it takes having money and being middle class to pretend these factors don't matter. Refusing to recognize that the playing field is not actually level and that some Americans find their choices fairly limited is one of the ways that the American Creed masks profound prejudices and inequalities that hinder some Americans while promoting the advancement of others.

However, abundant opportunities for choice come with a potent set of anxieties as well. To be middle class in the United States can cast doubt on one's ability to be free and independent, to attend to other aspects of the American Creed. Certainly, these anxieties are not as painful as living without material resources or being unable to maintain a degree of economic solvency. But living the American Dream can be stressful: to be middle class in American society is to be tied to a job, a family, and a dense web of responsibilities that may constrain one's ability to be free in those romantic ways of the Old West cowboys. Few cowboy shooters would argue that they are disadvantaged by their assets or their access to social and economic resources, yet they are far from free and unencumbered by responsibility. Their real lives reflect the "unromantic" realities of debt and taxes, mortgage and car payments, the complexities of modern marriage and raising children in the crowded, expensive San Francisco Bay Area. Nowadays, with these stresses and the alienation that comes from the commodification of so much of one's lifestyle, yearning for an idealized Frontier of self-reliance and simple living is not so difficult to understand, even if the actualities of that Frontier were far less appealing than they seem now.

This focus on middle-class values and interests serves to provide a sense of solidarity and unification while simultaneously deflecting away from the issue of race and ethnicity, which could be potential sources of conflict if addressed more critically and self-consciously. Some shooters were somewhat ambivalent about this issue, insisting to me that cowboy shooting was a friendly sport that welcomed shooters of all backgrounds and ethnicities. And indeed, cowboy shooting is not necessarily hostile to people of color. Rather, it is a space in which whiteness is the norm, unquestioned and uncriticized, literally there in its presence and figuratively there in its values and reference to mythic rather than actual history. As in Turner's Frontier thesis, nonwhites are moved aside, more unnoted or simply absent than actively shunned. This is partly because cowboy shooting's vision of the American

West is so heavily reliant on Hollywood movies and westerns, where people of color were absent or painfully stereotyped until the 1990s, and even then, still without accurately measuring the dynamic participation of blacks, Latinos, and Asians on the historic frontier. Like the popular and even some academic histories of the region, the histories and visions of people of color are simply ignored, reduced to the margins of the cow towns and the shoots themselves.

The soft lighting of mythic and idealized history thus blurs the edges of a less appealing history, the history of brutal and far-reaching imperialist conquest, the conquering of an entire continent of land and people. Cowboy shooters acknowledge that the slow and almost complete annihilation of whole groups of indigenous peoples was certainly not a positive accomplishment; a number of cowboy shooters discussed how sympathetic they were to the plight of the American Indians, for example, nations of people who were sometimes described as fallen heroes who certainly didn't deserve the horror that befell them. But the romanticized past of the American cowboy is somehow more powerfully appealing in part because the cowboys "won." After all (as everybody knows), the cowboys were the ones with the guns. The outcome of that particular battle was decided from the start.

But the sport of cowboy action shooting helps highlight the good times and sweep away those difficult and ambiguous issues. Cowboy shooting offers a metaphoric space in which shooters can celebrate the fact that they have succeeded socially and economically, and are able to relish the privileges and pleasures that only a relatively comfortable socioeconomic status can provide. Indeed, at first blush, cowboy shooting seems like a celebration of distinctly European (i.e., white) status and privilege, and there is considerable power in this observation. Cowboy shooting celebrates a time in American history when whites were consistently mythologized as the good guys, the heroes who hailed a new era of progress and democracy. And in a modern era of multiculturalism, in which sorting through the competing social, political, and ethnic interests has distinctly moral ramifications, cowboy shooting provides a welcome break. Nobody on the cowboy range has to think reflexively about being white.

Some shooters are in fact acutely aware of these issues. Marcus, one of the few men of color who participated in the local cowboy shoots, put it this way: "I think a lot of times—until just recently, maybe in the early '60's, when you used to see western movies, you didn't see black faces. But I knew ever since I was a kid that there were [black cowboys], because we had pictures of guys, like around 1901. . . . They don't make many western movies

American River College Library

now. But at least you see [blacks] now. And before the '60's you really didn't see it. . . . I think that was Hollywood making what people wanted to see at the time." It is with this knowledge, that there were indeed black cowboys, that Marcus can comfortably legitimate his participation in the construction of the master narrative embedded in cowboy shooting. His recognition of his familial and ethnic contribution to the historical frontier adds to his pleasure and enthusiasm for (re)creating a mythic one. And interestingly, save for the color of his skin, Marcus is very much like most of the other shooters on the cowboy range: he is a well-educated, middle-class professional with a home and family, has a profound love of the historic and mythic Frontier, and is a firm supporter of pro-gun ideology. Even his cowboy alias lends itself to the dominant narrative, harking to the famous Buffalo Soldiers, the African American cavalrymen (and former Union soldiers) who patrolled the actual frontier alongside their white compatriots, fighting Indians and Mexicans, carving out their own space on the mythic Frontier.

Ironically, in helping to correct for a forgotten real history (i.e., that there were, in fact, black cowboys), Marcus is reinforcing dominant mythic images of settling the American Frontier.[36] Cowboy action shooting provides him with a legitimate venue to be included, to contribute to the ritual reenactment of this legendary time in American history. Ironically, people of color colonized the frontier as well, and their participation in this process (whether given freely or coerced) can now be viewed as just as patriotic as it is for their white compatriots.[37]

Ultimately, cowboy action shooting dramatizes a central theme of American mythic history: that American identity itself is reborn, remade, through violent conflict.[38] This is a profoundly important aspect of pro-gun ideology, and lies at the heart of what guns symbolize to gun enthusiasts, cowboy shooters in particular. Shooters ritually reenact this mythic theme not only through their cowboy shooting (and also with shooting competitions like IPSC, complete with images of self-defense and the ubiquitous home invasion scenarios). Shooting sports like cowboy action shooting demonstrate the power and pleasure in employing controlled violence toward moral ends; ritually reenacting this basic theme is the underlying subtext of the cowboy lifestyle. In this vein, guns are righteous tools to be used for righteous ends, and shooting sports provide a venue to make this ideology into meaningful social practice, every single weekend of the year.

Tough Americans

Americans have long prided themselves on their toughness. Americans make tough business deals, athletes play a tough game, and consumers buy products like tough trucks and tough tools. Tough men of history—Generals Sherman and Patton, activists like Malcolm X, and greatly mythologized characters of fiction and film like Captain Ahab and Dirty Harry—all invoke images of an American character that included strength, determination, bravery, and moral fiber, definitive (if idealized) characteristics of American masculinity that can be summarized in one simple word: tough.[1]

Historically, toughness was celebrated and mythologized during America's Revolutionary and Frontier periods. During those eras in particular, toughness was wedded to masculinity, as well as to republican and revolutionary ideologies. The American Revolution stressed a model of manhood that demanded autonomy and independence, qualities that were embodied in the idealized persona of the citizen soldier.[2] Early American republican ideology explicitly intertwined manliness with strength and virtue, civic involvement, and a willingness to fight and die for the protection of the new republic. One of the first successful American comedies, written by Royall Tyler in 1787, entitled *The Contrast*, centered around the eponymous "Colonel Manly," who embodied those qualities so important to revolutionary America: "The Colonel was brave, frank, independent in thought and feeling, and free from submission and luxury."[3] These manly virtues celebrated the republican spirit of the era and were explicitly juxtaposed against the supposed feminine qualities of submissiveness and weakness.

During the Frontier era, the harshness of frontier scouting and pioneering reshaped notions of masculinity, which was immediately celebrated and romanticized by nineteenth-century Americans, eastern and western alike. General George Custer wrote of Wild Bill Hickok, the scout who eventually became the notorious lawman, "Of his courage there could be no question; it had been brought to the test on too many occasions to admit a doubt. His skill in the use of the rifle and pistol was unerring; while his deportment was exactly opposite of what might be expected from a man of his surroundings. It was entirely free from all bluster or bravado."[4] These kinds of portraits, which explicitly linked masculinity with courage, virtue, and toughness, embraced the notion of a personal moral code as firmly as they did any notion of respect for law and order. Throughout American history, manhood and toughness encompassed not only physical strength but also moral character, all of which crystallized in a celebration of the core values that are present in American society even today. Although its manifestations are heavily influenced by such factors as gender, class, religion, and ethnicity, toughness is recognized and lauded by American men as a quintessential mark of their Americanness.

Tough Men

The constellation of values and behaviors best described as "American tough" have their most colorful and exaggerated manifestations in modern-day popular culture. Toughness embraces a variety of characteristics, including self-reliance, mental and physical strength, and readiness to take action, all of which are apparent in a variety of American cultural and social formulations. The tough guy is ubiquitously characterized as masterful—brilliantly capable of self-control and control over his environment. He is competent and capable of manipulating social, political, and economic situations with equal ease. He is without social class, though he can embody the physical strength associated with the working class; the manner, speech, and morals of the middle class; and the confidence, power, and mastery associated with the upper class. The tough guy is the everyman, but he still manages to be a hero, a celebration of all the core values that are demonstrated in his every word, thought, and deed.[5]

That guns should figure into this vision of masculinity and thus American toughness shouldn't be too surprising; guns have long been associated with literal and symbolic power, control, and dangerousness. Thus, guns fit almost "naturally" with toughness in both the historical and contemporary American imagination. Toughness is now an ideology that connects gun ownership to wider cultural expectations about appropriate forms of masculinity and femininity in contemporary society.

Manhood and Family Responsibility

One of the themes that arose over and over again with male shooters was their association between guns and pleasurable memories of growing up—learning about shooting from older male relatives, and learning about becoming a responsible man through safe gun usage. Male shooters clearly linked guns to becoming a man; shooting was a family tradition, something they learned from a father or another male family member. These shooters talked about how they take pleasure in the guns that have been handed down through generations in their families, making them meaningful for that reason in particular. Bob explained: "I have a gun that I owned as a child when I was nine years old. I have the same gun. It's been in my family all that long. I have a shotgun that belonged to my father and his father before him. These are in our family and have been there and will be there. They'll go to my sons."

Other male shooters fondly recalled times that a male family member taught them how to shoot, which they saw as a rite of passage to manhood. Those were times not only when they did something pleasurable and exciting with a family member, usually male, but also a time when they were learning to become a man. Andrew explained:

> The first person who taught me how to shoot was my uncle in Las Vegas when I was about six or seven years old. He used to have a farm out there. . . . And he taught us how to shoot. 'Cause he wanted us to know how to shoot and he thought it would be—and he said, 'It's a right we Americans have and you should know how to use one.' Instead of, you know, picking [one] up . . . not knowing how to use it and killing yourself. So after that—after shooting a gun as a kid, I think it felt neat, it felt good, how much power was in a gun. . . . Oh god, the thing kicked me and threw me back on my ass or something. . . . I was bruised, you know, it's like the manly thing, I don't know.

For shooters like Bob and Andrew, learning about guns as children was an important part of growing up, of becoming an adult male. However, teaching children about gun handling is obviously a contentious issue, particularly for those who feel that children of any age have no business near guns. Critics have long taken issue with the idea that any child can learn about guns safely; guns are obviously tempting to children, who presumably cannot begin to comprehend the inherent danger of handling them. Why would any responsible parent want to introduce his or her child to a gun?[6]

It's important to remember that shooters do not make the same symbolic associations with guns and violence that critics of gun ownership make. For shooters, to teach children about guns is to teach them about being responsible and knowledgeable about something recognized as dangerous. On the most obvious level, as Andrew points out, there are a lot of guns around, and better to know how to deal with a gun than reach for one in ignorance. Thus, Andrew recalls his outings with his uncle as rites of passage that not only taught him about respecting something powerful and dangerous, but also becoming familiar with an item his uncle thought Andrew might encounter later in his life.

Some Traditions Die Hard

Male shooters link their belief in protecting themselves and their family with the basic notion of being a responsible man. But some shooters conceptualize the issue of responsibility differently, or suggest a kind of responsibility that connotes a different set of duties and obligations than simply being safe or recognizing the power of guns. Although most male shooters did not state directly that defending their family was an explicit responsibility, the question of defending the family clearly weighed on many minds.

The issue of being a good protector emerged when I asked shooters if they keep a gun for home defense. All but two of the thirty-seven shooters (both male and female) said that they did, and many stated that defense of family is important to them. This phenomenon may also be a long-standing echo of the early American tradition of coverture, in which a head of household had a duty and responsibility to maintain the physical safety of those dependents under his roof. For shooters, keeping a gun is simply understood as the easiest way to protect the family. When I asked him if he keeps a gun in his home for defense, and if he would use it as such, John stated, "I do. . . . I would, if someone came in my house, yeah, I would use a gun. Only because if they come in my house and they know I'm there and they know my family's there, they're not there to do me any good, and I think that they could probably hurt one of my family members. I have this strong love for my family, and I would never jeopardize that, and I'll use whatever tool I have."

Bob stated that defense of self and family is one of the only reasons he would take another's life, which he insisted he took very seriously. I asked him to describe the circumstances in which he would use a gun defensively. He stated, "Only in the defense of my life or the life of another. What I have in my home, no matter what it is, is not worth taking human life over. If they want to come into my home and take my property, so be it. . . . But the only time my gun comes into play is in the defense of my life or the life of another. Because I'm not gonna let some scumbag put me under the dirt till I'm ready to go. And if it means defending myself with the use of a gun I will do so, or defending my family."

For some male shooters, there is an implicit assumption that gun owner-ship demonstrates one's responsibility to family. Here, then, is how this vision of American masculinity is performance-based: being a good man (and father) means being a good protector, taking steps to ensure the safety of the family. One shooter, a single man in his midforties I knew quite well, remarked that if he needed to, he would absolutely use his gun to protect himself. He added that if he saw that I was in danger as well, he would not hesitate to protect me, too.

There is perhaps an inherent sexism in the idea that men should ideally protect women (even from themselves) because women are supposedly weaker than men, or lack the ability or nerve to take responsibility for protecting themselves. However, the politics of gender in relation to self- and home defense are complicated. The sense of responsibility that some male shooters feel and demonstrate does not necessarily indicate a belief that women inherently lack the capability to protect or defend themselves. The shooter who offered to protect me was ostensibly doing so under the auspices of a gendered form of responsibility and obligation to community (as well as personal) safety. Many of the male shooters interviewed did articulate a concern with protecting their wives and children, but several said explicitly that women (and in some cases, older children) should try and protect themselves. For example, Bob's wife, Paula, is a former police officer, eminently capable of protecting herself: she had been a good cop and had voiced her personal ethos of toughness to me several times. John offered another example: he taught his wife to shoot despite her initial disinterest in guns. He believes that if his wife should ever find herself in a situation where her life is in danger, she should be capable of protecting herself.

Ironically, some men who have heard the messages that the women's movement has been communicating for decades may feel they are in a double bind. Even while they may be embodying certain patriarchal prerogatives by taking it upon themselves to try to protect the women they know, if they pretend that these women don't face real dangers (dangers that demand some form of proactive response), they in effect dismiss or minimize the ways that (largely) male violence continues to endanger women. If a man sincerely believes that guns provide an effective means of self-defense, and he recognizes that the women around him are occasionally vulnerable, how would he be *more* responsible if he advocates that women should stay away from guns?

For the female shooters who commented on men and guns, being a shooter is something to be lauded in male partners. Several women were comfortable with the idea of protective male force. Thea explained: "I think of men who have guns as somebody who would be more likely to be able to protect me than somebody who didn't. I know that with respect to my daughters, that as I'm talking this through, and I've never thought about any of this stuff before, that having somebody who will protect them is very important to me. . . . I know this last boyfriend that Ellen had, Edward, was such a wuss. I mean, a really nice guy, and talked literature and books and movies and fit right in and he was just a nice guy, but I never had the sense that she was protected." Thea herself certainly ascribes to a vision of toughness and does not find her own ability to be tough incompatible with a potential partner's desire to protect her. She explicitly harked back to a certain conception of masculinity that centers on a willingness or a potential to do violence. While she couches this violence as defensive, and thus ostensibly morally legitimate, her comments raise several important issues that have been highlighted by the critique of defensive gun ownership/enthusiasm[7] offered by antigun critics of the gun culture, particularly gender theorists and academicians interested in the gun debate. I discuss this issue later in the chapter.

It's All-American: "Plain Man Patriotism"

One of the ways that toughness is expressed by male shooters is in their description of gun ownership as simply a convention of American masculinity: they see familiarity with guns as the status quo for American manhood. However, for some shooters this assertion has a distinctly patriotic undertone. The toughness exemplified by owning guns was woven into shooters' narratives, particularly ones that touched on American history and tradition, incorporating the colonial and Frontier ideologies to give their rhetoric a firmly "all-American" flavor. These narratives provide a window into what Rupert Wilkinson calls "plain man patriotism," which encompasses strength (both physical and of personality), attention to history, civic virtue, and love of country, all of which come together to form the foundation of a modern-day heroic everyman.[8] One of the most powerful ways that some shooters understand their gun ownership is to equate it with simple Americanism.

The shooters interviewed here are not literally "plain men"; for the most part, these shooters embody a middle-class professionalism and worldview that differentiate them from the early American republican portrait of a true patriot. However, early American patriotism as a standard and an ideal echoed through many shooters' pro-gun ideology, demonstrating the extent to which guns symbolize a vision of citizenship and morality. It is in "plain man patriotism" that shooters demonstrated their most populist tenets, as gun enthusiasm expresses patriotic sentiment through a celebration of and attention to local, anti-elitist concerns. The sentiment reflected in this conceptual paradigm also recalled the nineteenth-century middle-class easterners' romanticization of the western frontiersman, who by that time were already mythologizing themselves.

Bob, a white cowboy shooter in his late forties who worked as a range manager and gun dealer, illustrates the plain man sentiment effectively. Inherent in Bob's notion of being a shooter is the assumption that owning guns does not necessarily indicate straightforward aggression. Rather, it signifies a willingness to stand up to those who would hurt or abuse others. Guns maintain a balance between aggression and defensiveness. This balance would not exist if guns remained the sole property of either the state or violent criminals. For Bob, gun ownership indicates the potential for different social collectives to balance each others' aggressive and violent tendencies. He stated:

> We want to live in a safe culture. We want to live in an environment where we can come and go as we please and not have to worry about the bad guys. That's an ideal culture. Well, the gun helps us to keep that ideal, to keep things balanced a little bit. If the bad guys knew that none of us were allowed to carry guns and none of us did, then we would be at their mercy. We would be prey for the bad guys. I would be beat up. You would be raped, or your kin, murder[ed], whatever, at their whim. The ideal is that we need a balance in our culture. We need a balance that says, maybe I got something that'll keep you from doing this to me. And there's only one way you're gonna find out. Maybe you should just kind of back off. Maybe it's our attitude, maybe the way we speak, the way we walk. Maybe it's the persona we present, when we're out there alone. Maybe it's that intensity in the way we ward off somebody. Maybe we just give them thought for a minute. . . . Maybe she's not as fragile as maybe we think she is. Maybe we should go around and go the other way. Maybe we should find another prey who is weaker. Symbolism? I don't know. An ideal? I think so.

The sentiment expressed here quite effectively reflects the attitudes of most shooters with regard to crime and society, and their relationship to both. If strong gun controls are passed, then the law-abiding will be inherently disadvantaged. They will be at the mercy of criminals. By the same token, shooters simply do not believe that gun restrictions or prohibitions will disarm the population most capable of violence. Such a situation would seriously threaten or even destroy the integrity of the social body and the body politic. In short, gun control signifies a breakdown of the social and moral order—the very fabric of society itself. On the other hand, gun ownership denotes defending the social and moral order; in short, being tough. Tough individuals create tough communities, which in turn create a tougher nation.

The Tough Bind

Shooters understand gun ownership as part and parcel of a willingness to stand and defend yourself and your moral values. But being tough is not simply a matter of a willingness to act; it is also a constant vigilance centered on the possibility of being vulnerable. This was as true for male shooters as for female shooters, though for men it is articulated in more abstract terminology. Both men and women pointed to specific incidents in which they had felt or had been threatened, and both men and women generally advocated a vigilance that is as important metaphorically as it is physically. A lack of vigilance can have serious ramifications. One shooter who was not formally interviewed said to me during an academic meeting, "It's almost worse knowing that you could have acted, but somehow you were prevented from doing so." He continued to explain that he is uncomfortable with the idea that in some future emergency, he might be able to do something, but for some reason won't be prepared at that moment or will be actively prevented from doing anything. To this shooter, such a scenario is worse than believing he never could have acted in the first place. Manuel said that this idea haunts him as well, to the point that vigilance has become an integral part of his life: "I've had dreams of people coming in my windows at night, weird dreams. And it's weird, because every dream that I had like that, I'd have a gun but have the wrong ammo. And I don't know why. And I couldn't find the ammo to save my ass. But it always worked out somehow. I've had, like, four or five dreams like that in the last three years, where I had the gun but no ammo for it. So I don't know if that's why I make sure I've got plenty of guns and plenty of ammo. So I'll figure out which one goes in where before anything happens."

Manuel's narrative also exemplifies shooters' belief that competence, as well as vigilance, is necessary to living safely in a violent society. Accepting responsibility for their own safety and that of their family demands that they are always ready for an impending attack, and although having guns does not guarantee that safety, guns go a long way toward ensuring it (as well as peace of mind). This sentiment may also reflect a concern with moral impotence that is articulated in more concrete, physical concerns: How can you do the right thing when you are actively prevented from doing so? Similar beliefs are echoed in Greg's previous discussion of the necessity for preparation and defensiveness, for honing skills with the tool that provides the best symbolic (and in this case, literal) equalizer.

The American focus on vigilance and defensive preparedness is long-standing. Historians have pointed out that for nineteenth-century middle-class Americans, the institutions so strongly associated with society itself, business and industrial society, were thought to breed softness and laziness. An overt reliance on the workings of society was believed to be making Americans morally impotent.[9] Thus, nineteenth-century Americans romanticized that mythological Frontier value: self-reliance. Add to this a willingness to train for defense, and being a shooter in modern-day America becomes one means of soothing ever-present anxieties that are voiced as an issue of personal safety. Greg stated:

> What do guns symbolize for [me]? Can we get the American anthem in the background? . . . The fact that guns are a tool that enables one to be self-sufficient, that enables one to feel that one is not a victim and not afraid. . . . Because, man, there's nothing scarier than the abyss. So if we can leave the abyss out there as an archetypical fear, then we can just deal with . . . [the] predator trying to hurt me. I will prevent that from happening, that's easy to work with. The things that go bump in the night and the horrors of history and humanity, and serial killers and all this stuff I'm currently studying, all of those horrors are always going to be there. [If] you can take care of your own little bailiwick, you can take care of yourself.

One of the ways that shooters cope with the instability and anxiety of contemporary society is to grasp onto objects of safety, control, and profound symbolic meaning: guns. The value of guns lies in their historic and contemporary sociocultural meaning as much as their solid, crime-fighting allure. In the powerful mythology of colonial and Frontier America, guns make heroes. And they continue to do so even if those heroes are the stuff of imagination more than reality.

The anxiety and distress that some shooters feel is not only centered on abstract concerns; it is also indicative of local issues. Shooters recognize that violent crime has real consequences, and the urban parts of the San Francisco Bay Area have their fair share of violent crime. Shooters consistently complained that part of the problem of crime today is that violent criminals harm and kill innocent people but then refuse to take responsibility for their actions; they blame their upbringing, the people around them, or even society itself for their criminality. Because shooters understand themselves to be deeply invested in society and the maintenance of law and order, such a lack of personal responsibility is absolutely enraging, particularly to those shooters who have been directly or indirectly victimized by crime.

Tough Women

American women can be just as tough as men; former First Lady Rosalyn Carter, former Attorney General Janet Reno, and American film icons from Bette Davis to Sigorney Weaver have all demonstrated their own brands of female toughness. Toughness crosses gender boundaries just as it does ethnic boundaries, and is celebrated by a wide variety of "true-blue" Americans.[10]

American women have learned to combine toughness with femininity in a way that makes their toughness seem as natural as their "inherent" ladylike manner. Examples from American history illustrate this point: in the fall of 1776, amid crushing American defeats by the British, Abigail Adams wrote to her husband, "We are no ways dispirited here, we possess a Spirit that will not be conquered. If our men are drawn off and we should be attacked, you would find a Race of Amazons in America."[11] A century later, Annie Oakley, the celebrated frontier performer in Buffalo Bill Cody's Wild West show, negotiated that fine line of gender-appropriate behavior exceedingly well, demonstrating a distinctly "manly" marksmanship ability, all the while embodying the essence of Victorian womanhood in her "modest, quiet, ladylike appearance."[12] Her performances, undoubtedly that much more ladylike because of her engagement with such masculine sport, exemplified the ways women can embody, challenge, and reject qualities that have been considered the sole prerogative of their male counterparts.

Whether or not women were characterized as tough, either by their contemporaries or the historians who later documented their lives (or didn't, as some feminist historians have pointed out),[13] American women have alternately been lauded and demeaned for demonstrating the kind of toughness designated as peculiarly American. The fact that toughness has been and continues to be considered a feature of masculinity more than femininity has meant that if and when women demonstrate their own tough tendencies, the result can be an ambivalence that finds expression both within themselves and in wider social arenas examining their behavior. Although toughness was a respected if not necessary quality for American women historically, its expression has always been shaped and molded, attentive to the demands of the gender-appropriate behavior of the day.

Perhaps not surprisingly, what are considered acceptable expressions of toughness have been configured differently for men and women, both historically and currently. Men and women also *experience* what it means to be tough differently. The same could be said for any behavior, but toughness in female gun enthusiasts in particular demands a discussion of several politicized issues. Foremost among them is the issue of how women who use violence to repel attackers are thought about and discussed by feminists and other social critics. Women who actively carry guns, particularly for self-defense, tend to run afoul of those who argue that gun ownership for women is not an "appropriate" way to resist attack. However, female shooters believe that defensive gun use is not only legitimate but morally acceptable, particularly because guns are an exemplary way to challenge the broadly construed system of patriarchy.[14]

Some women frame their toughness as convention, but point out that it is implicitly gendered as male despite its seemingly neutral and gender-free connotation. Such tough-minded women suggest there is a double standard for physical power operating here. If the toughness that men take for granted is overtly advocated for women, it is criticized as traitorous to the feminine ideal. D. A. Clarke puts it this way:

> We do respect people who "know their limits," who cannot be pushed past a certain point—just as we mistrust and disrespect those who have no give in them at all and overreact violently to every little frustration. We respect people who can take care of themselves, who inform us of their limits clearly and look prepared to enforce them. Women are traditionally denied these qualities— the "no means yes" of male mythology—*and one reason for this is that we are denied the use of force.* To put it very simply, little boys who get pushed around on the playground are usually told to "stand up to him, don't let him get away with it," whereas little girls are more usually advised to run to Teacher.[15]

Toughness, which Clarke describes as the ability to stand up for oneself and use force to impose physical boundaries, is not advocated for girls or women despite the lip service paid to "respecting limits." Clarke points out that women have always been criticized and penalized for behavior that enforces their physical boundaries: they are denounced as acting out, being aggressive, or being "ball-busters." Women who enforce their own physical boundaries are sometimes even accused of encouraging violent reactions in men: bad things happen to women who are "asking for it."

As several feminist firearms researchers have pointed out, this kind of backlash comes from both conservative and liberal quarters.[16] While conservatives deem the use of force as betraying femininity, liberals frame the use of force as betraying feminism. In fact, liberals have argued that women who use force, particularly the "excessive" force embodied in gun ownership, are betraying a feminist ideal, which is that women must end patriarchy (thereby achieving true equality) through nonviolent means. If they use violence to counter violence, they model no new paradigm for a more peaceable society; they are only perpetuating patriarchal paradigms. The poet Audre Lorde is often invoked to make this point: "the master's tools will never dismantle the master's house."[17]

Thus, women who are willing to employ force by taking up guns in a variety of contexts (e.g., in the military, the police, or on their own behalf) are viewed in anthropological terms as "liminal": they are "betwixt and between," not one thing or the other. Liminal figures are viewed as a source of ambivalence and discomfort even by themselves. One of the ways that women work to resist and challenge these discomforting categorizations is to find broader cultural paradigms and values that normalize not only their life situations but their responses to those situations. Being tough is a culturally appropriate and meaningful way to do this because toughness situates female behavior in a historical context of frontierism, pioneerism, and certain expressions of womanhood throughout American history. Being considered tough can legitimize a woman's independence, strong-mindedness and strength of will, vigilance, and willingness to stand up to bullies. Standing up to bullies, fighting fire with fire, so to speak, is the quintessential mark of being a female shooter; it is what makes a woman tough. It can even make her a "good woman."

Tough Women with Guns

How many American women own guns? Although the popular media in the late 1980s and early 1990s played up the idea that women were increasingly becoming armed, social scientists remained more skeptical.[18] A study by gun manufacturer Smith and Wesson purported to find that between 1983 and

1986, gun ownership by women went up by 53 percent. However, some social scientists argue that contrary to the media and firearms industry, the best available data suggest that of the entire population of American women, between 11 and 12 percent own a gun and between 4.5 and 8 percent own a handgun, figures that have remained constant for decades.[19] Stange and Oyster argue that the number of women armed with guns is between 11 and 17 million, which ostensibly covers all of these figures by providing a fairly broad range.[20]

Regardless of exact numbers, the fact remains that there are American women who own guns, and some of them consider themselves gun enthusiasts. Several feminist researchers have argued relatively straightforwardly that many American women find guns empowering because guns are tools of power, literally and figuratively.[21] My own discussions with female gun enthusiasts supports that argument, though I argue that pro-gun ideology is empowering because it links gun ownership to a variety of cultural themes and values that affirms these women as independent, capable, strong-willed, and responsible. In short, tough.

Toughness for Neutralizing Aggression

Many female shooters illustrate not simply how and why guns are meaningful to them, but how gun use is a vital part of behavior that went beyond the question of gun enthusiasm per se. Several of the eleven female shooters interviewed talked about gun ownership as a part of a larger paradigm of being resolute, arguing that being protective of themselves and their family was a way of life for them. They embraced the belief that they were obligated to protect themselves and their family; this was part of being a responsible person as well as a responsible woman. They were ostensibly arguing that their toughness, particularly their gun ownership, is a formidable way to challenge chauvinistic male behavior.

The irony of their argument lies in the fact that critics of gun ownership have often argued that gun ownership in and of itself actually signifies "traditional hegemonic masculinity," a set of masculine behaviors that includes being controlling, being violent, and using violent force to maintain social and political norms. Because critics of guns see gun ownership as inherently violent, owning a gun means being a part of "the problem," not a part of the solution. However, female shooters don't understand their own gun ownership in these terms. They tend to view themselves as challenging patriarchal order and norms in a wide variety of ways. They very explicitly assert that they perceive those abusive and dangerous aspects of the patriarchy to be the reason they own guns. Because gun ownership helps make shooters tough, and tough women defy the patriarchal belief that women are weak and subservient, female shooters argue that being tough by owning guns is exactly what challenges the patriarchal tendencies of violent men. Basically, female shooters see their gun ownership as a way to communicate to the people around them that violence is *not* acceptable, and the only way that women are going to stop abusive men is by literally stopping them.

All that said, toughness is not simply an obvious and literal manifestation of traditionally masculine (and presumably aggressive) behaviors and characteristics. Toughness can also be understood as an attempt to balance or neutralize aggression. Being tough can mean simply standing one's ground and refusing to be either passive or aggressive. While the threat of violence may underscore this posture, its manifestation is a "brick wall," designed to challenge the "traditional masculine imperative" of perpetuating violence against those who are weaker and more vulnerable. Female shooters see themselves as eminently capable of being tough in this fashion; in short, they like to stand up to bullies. Female toughness can be a means of empowerment through which traditional frameworks themselves can be dismantled.

A defensive stance does not necessarily hinge on gun ownership for some shooters, though it may be the most literal and obvious form of expressing defensive attitudes. Paula, a former police officer, is trained in martial arts. She believes that training enables her to stand her ground in dangerous situations. She knows that men who intend to hurt or victimize women often expect to be able to do so quickly and easily. A diminutive woman, Paula believes that her stature and her sex mislead others into thinking she will be easy to manipulate or intimidate, and she takes a grim pleasure in contradicting them, if only by her unwillingness to show fear to would-be aggressors. She told the following narrative about a time when she worked for an eye wear company:

> I had another [situation]—you talk about beating up women. I had a lady come in to pick up her glasses. . . . I said, "Okay, I'll get them, have a seat." In storms either the boyfriend or the husband, whoever he is, in his late twenties. . . . And they were—she was quietly arguing with him because he had come in and he was kind of loud. And I'm watching the whole thing, and he hauls off and he slaps her. Whack. I mean, just hauled off and smacked her good. She immediately sat down in the chair and just sat there. And I'm like, "Uh uh [shakes her head], this is not gonna happen." He pissed me off. So I walked out there, and I told him to leave. And now it's like, "Yeah, who are you?" He

turned on me. We had a [store] counter between us. But I told him to leave. And he basically said I can't tell him what to do. And I informed him that, yes I could, and it's really funny, when you're trained, you position yourself in a certain position, when you're doing it, and your brain's clicking, if he comes over the counter I can do this, if he comes around here I can do that, and all you're doing is looking at target zones. And I'm standing there, and he said, "Why don't you call security?" I said, "I don't need security." I said, "You got a choice. Either leave on your own or I will make you leave, one of the two. You can make it easy or hard." And you could see he just wanted a piece of me, so bad. Just so bad, and I just stood there. I was hoping he would come over at me, hoping, 'cause he'd made me mad. Just like, "Go ahead, please."

[He] turned around and walked out. . . . Just turned around and walked out. Didn't bother him hitting a woman at all. Didn't bother him in the least. . . . But I didn't just sit down. I stood up to him, and he knew something wasn't right. And most of them, they're used to—they're bullies, they're used to getting what they want by fear and force, but it's almost rare they ever get stood up to.

Paula's narrative also underscores a point that is sometimes difficult to remember amid the constant rhetoric of armed defense. For most shooters, the defensive posture does not necessitate killing. It is coy to suggest that using guns for self-defense does not sometimes come down to shooting someone, yet adopting a defensive posture may be the only necessary action required. For Paula, bullies get what they want because they expect people to react with fear and passivity. When someone stands up to them, bullies often back down. If a person stands her ground, that potential victim is insisting upon respect. In the mind of shooters, that person earns respect, even if it is not immediately forthcoming. The underlying point is that it is strength of will and personality that command respect, not just physical prowess. Paula takes pride in the fact that she did not need to hurt her would-be aggressor in order to demonstrate that she wouldn't back down, or that his violence against others was unacceptable.

Paula also places a premium on her own self-control. She could have hurt the aggressor—she even felt a desire to do just that. But she believed that any more action on her part was unwarranted, and thus her defensive posture served its purpose. These kinds of narratives also exemplify shooters' belief that their defensive and tough posture is a necessity because, in Paula's words, "there's always somebody out there that can get you." Shooters must always be ready to take action and be ready for anything. For several, particularly some of the female shooters for whom toughness is a way of life, the idea of vigilance has been borne out in their personal and professional experiences, particularly after being on the receiving end of either aggression or a potentially violent attack.

Stick to Your Guns

Toughness is not simply about demonstrating physical strength or assuming a defensive posture. Toughness is also about strength of will and an ability to stand up to threats and bullying. Gun ownership for some female shooters also indicates that they are not afraid to "buck the system" or work for their own sense of righteousness, even if doing so incurs the wrath of others. The idea of strength in the face of opposition crystallizes in the defensive stance, which appears repeatedly to literally and metaphorically signify core aspects of values that illustrate American national character. Thea stated that she understands gun ownership to be synonymous with forging one's own destiny and taking an active stance against bullying and violence:

> I never think of people who own guns as pussies. I think of them being kind of in charge of their destinies and kind of, not gonna take a whole lot of shit from people and being willing to stand up for themselves. And I think maybe that's another reason why this is something that's good for me now, is that I am traditionally not a person—I'm a person who loves to stand up to bullies. I mean, that's kind of my nature. Because of my old man, he was such a bully. But not ever ever ever standing up for myself, and so this is a very new skill that I'm learning to cultivate. It's very hard for me. And this makes me feel strong. . . . I don't think gun owners by and large are passive people, and that's what I mean by pussies, obviously. I think they're more active. . . . I think maybe—I don't think they live—I don't think gun owners by and large live in their heads. I think they live more in a physical reality.

Interestingly, Thea juxtaposed toughness with being a "pussy," derogatory slang denoting weak and cowardly femininity. She implied that being feminine can signify weakness or subservience. Thea symbolically associated gun ownership and shooting, on the other hand, with standing up for herself, something she perceives as a struggle for her. She spoke at length about how important it was to her that her partner, Jonathan, who introduced her to guns, be capable of protecting and defending her because she feels that she cannot always rely on herself. Thea also mentioned being violently victimized as a child by a colleague of her father, and this victimization further accentuates her desire for protection here and now:

I mean, like my friend Rex, former OPD cop and my chief investigator at the bar, called me Crusader Rabbit, that's kind of who I am. I made a career, personally and professionally, of empowering people. . . . But as good as I've always been about standing up for other people, and I said this earlier . . . I'm not the least bit good about standing up for myself. And so it's very important to me to have somebody—I mean, I didn't have a clue how important that was until I was with Jonathan, to have a man protect me. And I feel like he is completely protective of me.

This willingness to "do the right thing" and take an active stance against opposition is interesting in light of debates about the legitimacy of gun ownership. The kind of protectiveness that Thea described not only helps to highlight the conceptual differences between antigun and pro-gun advocates, but also underscores a basic theoretical similarity between these two camps, so virulently opposed to each other. As I discussed in earlier chapters, antigun rhetoric often emphasizes a need for individual, community, and societal safety. Antigun advocates understand guns as threats to safety regardless of how they are used. But one area in which antigun advocates are usually silent, except in terms of advocating what *not* to do, is the question of how potential victims should deal with violent conflict, or how they should actively make their immediate world safer.

Some antigun advocates suggest that would-be victims should simply run away from their attackers.[22] Others, particularly from the religious community, advocate that victims simply yield to attackers, even in the case of rape, to avoid responding with violence themselves.[23] More recent incarnations of the gun control movement don't address the issue directly at all.[24] The tactic in most current gun control rhetoric is to treat the issue as largely theoretical, which allows for endorsing collective political action as the most appropriate way to deal with the issue of confronting violent behavior. Taking guns off the streets through gun control would presumably make the issue of how to respond when an attacker is armed largely irrelevant; in the future, attackers presumably will not be armed at all.

By side-stepping the issue of the most "appropriate" response to being attacked, gun control advocates can therefore stick to the bottom line: responsible citizens shun guns. Eventually, these macrolevel policies will also be reflected on the micro level, and everyone's physical environment will be that much safer. However, most shooters simply don't buy this argument. Their distrust for this position (which they consider naïve at best, dangerously foolhardy at worst) is reflected in ubiquitous pro-gun bumper stickers and slogans like "If guns are outlawed, only outlaws will have them." Female shooters take the broader view that guns are one aspect of being vigilant and constantly defensive. They argue that women cannot afford to take an abstract, theoretical approach to the question of what to do when someone attacks; attacks can happen at any time, anywhere. Their argument is echoed by the few feminist firearms researchers who have considered the issue: better to recognize that the dangers to women are real and that owning a gun can be an effective tool in preventing someone from trying to harm you.[25] Feminist firearms researchers have put the issues into more political terms: advocating a politically active but interpersonally passive stance is fairly precarious when you're worried about your physical safety on a day-to-day basis.[26]

Women's Self-Defense

The issue of women losing their fear after learning self-defense is echoed in the thoughts of some shooting instructors I met, both male and female. Greg in particular felt good about teaching women to shoot, as he explicitly acknowledged that women often articulate a fear of being victimized to him but come away from his classes feeling tougher. He stated:

> I have taught so many women who were so afraid before, and who see me at the range and they come up and they go—and this makes me feel so good, they come up and they say, "You know something? I don't have to take any shit from anybody who wants to hurt me. I used to sit at home scared, and I'm not scared anymore. I live my life. I go out and I do things. . . . I go home, I feel comfortable, I have a good lock on the door. If somebody tries to hurt me, man, I've got my firearm, I know what to do, I'll call the cops, took a class, know exactly what's going on, I feel so much better because all of it was this vague fear."

Critics of women's gun use often argue that when women take up guns, they add to the carnage or endanger themselves through this inherently dangerous and untrustworthy device.[27] Ironically, such critics unwittingly invoke the exact stereotypes that feminist pro-gun arguments are designed to dismantle: that women are helpless and incompetent in the face of violent, "masculine" tools. Martha McCaughey argues that fear and concern about violence have been incorporated into women's experience of their own bodies (as weak and helpless), which can explain in part some women's unwillingness to act forcefully or violently, even when doing so would save their own lives. She argues that women have been taught to fear not only male violence but their own capacity for violence, which is one of the reasons that some feminists are so concerned with women turning to guns for self-protection. This hesitancy is a by-product of a patriarchal system that is invested in women's submission and fear of self-empowerment. She argues that "women are afraid to fight for the same reasons they are afraid of guns—in either case, women's size or strength is far less relevant than the social investment in a female body that does not exert coercive force."[28] When women learn self-defense, they often change their notions of their own body, as well as their sense of the appropriateness of fighting back against an attack.

Several overt critics of gun ownership for women have argued that armed women will only drive up the homicide rate.[29] Such critics are in effect reiterating unfounded assumptions that do not address any research on female gun ownership. Or they rely on the public health literature on guns, which has been rigorously critiqued by criminologists for employing flawed methodologies and ignoring the complexities of the context in which gun crime occurs. Feminist scholars who support women's defensive gun use assert that critics of women's gun use have glossed over data and analysis on women and homicide. Public health researchers in particular have ignored the fact that female gun owners do not contribute substantially to high homicide rates in the United States, and that when women have used guns to kill, it is usually in the context of self-defense.[30]

In considering female gun ownership, it is tempting to argue that women like Thea exemplify a form of "false consciousness," unable or unwilling to understand how their position on gun ownership and protection locks them into a cycle of domination and submission at the hands of men, if only at the hands of men who say they offer protection. Such women are supposedly therefore complicit in the patriarchal system that either protects or dominates them. This argument raises the question of how women's self-defense should be considered, in both the personal and the political realms.

In fact, critics of gun ownership have underestimated the ways in which the proposed solutions to ending gun violence also contain hidden class and political interests. Gun control doesn't spell any kind of reduction of patriarchy either, as an increasing number of vocal pro-gun blacks, feminists, and gays are now pointing out. Groups like the Pink Pistols (a pro-gun gay group), the Second Amendment Sisters (a pro-gun women's organization), and the Tenth Cavalry (a pro-gun group formed by and for blacks) demonstrate that pro-gun ideology is not embraced only by white middle-class men and that gun ownership is adopted by a broader spectrum of Americans than antigun social critics would like to believe.[31] These disputes also illustrate one of the central flaws in liberal support for gun control as a main method for reducing violent crime. Gun control presumes a "trickle down" theory to violence reduction: gun control laws are passed, the laws slowly work to get the guns off the street, eventually fewer people have access to guns. In the long run, violence is reduced.

But what pro-gun gay advocates assert, along with pro-gun feminists, is that gun control leaves them vulnerable *now*. Because stringent gun control hinders law-abiding citizens from getting access to guns when they need them, liberal theories of gun control ostensibly suggest that certain individuals might have to be killed on the way to making communities safer. Pro-gun groups argue that even if one concedes that gun control will eventually protect vulnerable groups like blacks and gays from gun violence, gun control will take time before it is effective, and because of that, more people who could have protected themselves will have to die. For the Pink Pistols, the bottom line is that they'd rather take their chances getting tough and becoming armed than wait for the rest of society to put into practice the liberal paradigm that a safe society is a disarmed society. This is the central premise of most forms of gun control. Janis Cortese, a pro-gun lesbian and third-wave feminist activist, puts it this way:

> So I want to change society. I want to help somehow. I want to support shelters that will allow women to get out of abusive situations, rape counseling centers that will help us recover from sexual assault. I want to see schools improve so that kids in disadvantaged areas can look forward to more in life than an early death while seeing their friends die around them. And if I'm killed in the meantime, I can't do that, can I? I want all of that, but I also want to stay alive. I want the twenty-year solution of improving the world. But I need the twelve-second solution that will keep me around to do it should I wake up one early morning at 2 AM and see someone crawling in through my bedroom window.[32]

The fact that pro-gun ideology can effectively combine a liberal understanding of contemporary society with a belief in armed self-defense demonstrates that it is broader and more flexible than critics who equate it with patriarchy have recognized or conceded. For pro-gun advocates, the very ubiquity of American violence, which both liberals and pro-gun advocates agree is intolerable, has become the very thing that most clearly justifies and legitimates the case for widespread citizen armament.

McCaughey suggests that certain kinds of behaviors are always discussed and framed in relation to traditional forms of masculinity, regardless of whether both sexes partake in those behaviors. Her point is echoed in the narratives of several female shooters who talked about why they enjoy using guns. For example, Louise, a shooting instructor, described why shooting is an enjoyable activity:

> Yeah. I just—I like being able to do something that most people can't do. And I like—I have to—I don't know why, but I do like the kind of feminine aspect, that it puts you, it's something that traditionally is a male thing, and that males seem to have a certain domination in that field, and it's considered a masculine, fearless sort of a sport. Not a wimpy [one] . . . So I like being able to be a female that can do that. Without becoming like a total macho human being, sort of. . . . Yeah, it's a dual existence. It's sort of, "I can do this . . . I can do this kind of thing." I don't know. I think it probably ties into something really deep . . . some Jungian thing, like some survival instinct that's very in there for all of us. All those mysteries I don't know about. I think some of that's in there somewhere.

It is precisely this sense of transgression, of being a woman doing a "masculine" thing, that several female shooters found so pleasurable. One of the most important elements in this symbolic cosmology is power, and the way shooting engages directly with power. Both guns and masculinity are associated with power, and being a woman who is competent with a man's tool can find shooting to be thrilling, empowering, and inherently satisfying.

It is important to recall, too, that while guns can be a symbol of masculine aggression for some, and have indeed historically bolstered and maintained the traditional patriarchal framework of domination and submission in the American context, within this same framework, gun ownership has also historically signified personhood and status in American society (one of the reasons that guns owners have traditionally been white and male). As I pointed out earlier, in seventeenth-, eighteenth-, and nineteenth-century America, women and people of color were for the most part not considered full citizens, and as such were usually denied access to guns.[33] The irony, then, of critiquing gun ownership as a gendered issue lies in the historic relationship of guns to the state: the American government has in fact consistently controlled the means of force, as in colonial America. This has been one way of perpetuating the patriarchal institutions that traditionally defined gun ownership as a solely masculine prerogative.

Though several of the women I interviewed perceived that guns and gun ownership are about power, and managing and deploying violence, such knowledge did not always sit comfortably with them. It was the relationship between guns and power (precisely why some women are *drawn* to guns) that made several female shooters uneasy. I discussed this issue with Jane and Louise, both shooting instructors:

> AK: And the last question: What do guns symbolize for you?
>
> Louise: It is terrible. My first reaction to that is power. Isn't that terrible?
>
> Jane: The first word that came into my head was freedom.
>
> Louise: Yeah, I thought of that too, power and freedom. To me those are kind of synonymous words.

Although she didn't dwell on it, Louise did articulate a certain discomfort with the idea that guns symbolize power and freedom. In our conversations about what guns are for and how they should be used, she frequently discussed being uncomfortable with the fact that guns are relatively easily acquired in the United States, and that so many people have access to such powerful and dangerous items without "proving" that they can handle that power. She felt that as a shooting instructor, she is in a position to see that many people do not understand the power of guns and are careless with them, and her observations made her uneasy about the ways some gun owners handle themselves around such dangerous items.

Louise expressed ambivalence about these issues to me on several occasions. At one point after one of our lessons, Louise and I stood in the gun shop that was attached to the range where she taught, and we studied the bumper stickers that the range had on display. One of them said simply, "What if Nicole Simpson had a gun?" Looking at the sticker, Louise shook her head in annoyance and said, "Well, then she'd probably have been dead sooner because O. J. would have shot her with it." Louise viewed that kind of sentiment as gun-related machismo on the part of male gun owners, and it frustrated her. She attributed the sentiment embodied in the bumper sticker to a certain naïve belief that guns solve everything, or confer a simple, straightforward protection for their owners, regardless of the context or situation in which they are used.

In this way, despite her committed belief in the protective value of gun ownership, Louise echoed the skepticism of critics who argue that most gun owners do not understand the "inherent dangerousness" of guns. Louise and her business partner, Jane, do not always agree on these issues, particularly because Jane feels that most gun owners do understand these issues, female shooters in particular. Jane voiced the feelings that all of my instructors, including Louise, raised with me: women make better students than men. Instructors feel this way because they believe women tend to listen more attentively to instructors and do not have any macho "I already know what I'm doing" investment in their initial handling of guns. However, Jane and Louise disagree about whether guns should be available to people without training and skill testing. Although Jane supports training and testing, she does not feel that outside authorities have the right to force people to behave in certain ways with their firearms.

Having taken several classes with Louise, I also noticed her discomfort with the possibility that her symbolic association between guns and power could reveal something unacceptable about herself, something that she feels is unfeminine, wrong, or offensive. Her discomfort presumably centers on the idea that she would appear hungry for or interested in power in a way that makes her unhealthy or "abnormal," even eager to hurt or kill someone. Louise expressed the idea that engaging in a sport that is "traditionally a male thing" is pleasurable to her, but I suspect that she isn't always so confident that engaging in behavior defined as traditionally masculine is acceptable for a woman. Her ambivalence demonstrates that some female shooters, despite their commitment to a pro-gun ideology, wear the mantle of their toughness with uneasiness and are sensitive to what it might say about them as women and as human beings.

Whereas the larger paradigm of toughness is a powerful tool for understanding and integrating a series of American core values, toughness as an embodied concept also brings with it several of its own ideological problems and binds. The most prominent of these binds is this: If shooters aren't vigilant, prepared, defensive, and yet they are still victimized, how are they to make sense of their victimization?

This point was forcefully brought home when I attended a women's self-defense class, entitled "Refuse to Be a Victim," sponsored by the NRA and run by Joanne, a forcefully friendly woman who is well-versed in the wide array of options available to women who want to feel safer in their everyday environment. The course was taught at a local shooting range and ran for about three hours. Though the class was not about guns or gun use for self-defense, Joanne did mention that she was an NRA member and would be happy to discuss membership with anyone attending the workshop. At one point during the seminar, in the middle of a discussion about car safety and car-jacking prevention, an attendee said that she'd heard about a woman in the area who had been dragged out of her car in the early evening, while it was still light, and murdered. The story was particularly gruesome, and the class visibly reacted with horror and upset, murmuring and shaking their heads.

Joanne was clearly upset by the story: she shook her head and repeated "No, no" several times. Over and over, she said, "She must have done something wrong, she obviously wasn't careful enough." For Joanne, "doing it right" or being self-protective by exhibiting the kinds of defensive habits that she advocates should serve as a guarantee of her own and other women's safety. Because a woman should take responsibility to make herself safer, if she's victimized, then clearly she did not do enough to prevent her own victimization. Joanne believed that by working to control her own behavior as well as her environment, she was directly reducing the possibility of harm from the criminal other. She did not question the fundamental assumption that women are always going to be vulnerable to being attacked by criminals. For Joanne, the pertinent questions are, What can a woman do about it? and How can she responsibly make herself safe? Sometimes it's difficult to know how tough is "tough enough." Perhaps sometimes safety measures just aren't enough; crimes can still occur, and when it comes down to a single woman being confronted by an attacker, sometimes there is very little a woman can do about her own vulnerability.

This example illustrates another way that the ideology of constant toughness presents inherent challenges to shooters, both male and female. Sometimes events and circumstances that endanger people are larger than any particular individual's ability to make reality conform to his or her expectations. When toughness fails to achieve the desired results and keep everyone safe, shooters find themselves in the awkward position of blaming themselves for their own victimization. This was a long-standing tension not simply for female shooters vis-à-vis toughness, but in shooters' rhetoric regarding gun ownership as crime control more generally. If being tough and vigilant can and should protect you from being victimized, what do you do when it happens anyway?

You've Only Got Yourself to Blame

For the most part, male shooters are only too willing to accept responsibility for themselves and their family, but the weight of this responsibility apparently takes its toll on their peace of mind. The question of what it means to be victimized lurks behind some of the rhetoric offered by some male shooters, just as it does for women. The answer is ambivalent: although shooters have found a way to understand how to attend to their immediate concerns about crime, their vigilance and toughness do not guarantee safety, and can actually incur a good deal of mental and physical stress.

For some shooters, their disquiet manifests itself as a concern with being caught unaware, of not being sufficiently prepared for some future untold disaster. For Manuel, this anxiety takes the form of nightmares in which he cannot effectively protect his family. For other shooters, it emerges more subtly in a form of self-blame about the failure entailed in relaxing one's guard. John briefly mentioned to me that he "had it coming" when he was robbed. In response to my question about whether he uses a gun for self-defense, he said, "I do. I also use a dog, locks, and stuff like that. I've never been burglarized, other than some idiot coming in my garage and taking a tool box, which I kind of asked for 'cause I left the garage open all night."

Although aware that this was a small violation, John took personal responsibility for the robbery, believing that if he is to prevent himself from being robbed, he needs to ensure that he is vigilant about preventing such crimes from happening. Because he failed to do so, he had only himself to blame. Like Joanne, John did not think to blame the robber. By definition, that person wasn't going to change; he was doing what robbers do—rob people. John feels he has a duty to protect his own, and because he failed to do so, he got what he deserved. Both Manuel and John recognize on some level that there are limits to vigilance, and they feel the consequences for failing to maintain it to the standards they have set for themselves. Both men recognize that their position on defense still can leave them vulnerable, not only to crime but to the self-recrimination that comes with failing to "see it through."

Victimization (even in its most minor form) does not sit well with shooters, who are hard on themselves when it comes down to the question of responsibility in terms of safety, their own and their family's. Their anxiety illustrates that the concept of American tough rests on the principle that a defensive stance, both its literal and symbolic manifestations, should be substantial enough to prevent disaster from striking. But likewise, any relaxation of the victim's guard means that the responsibility for victimization should sit squarely on the shoulders of the victim himself. An ideology of toughness and defensiveness highlights a concern about appearing (and feeling) weak and vulnerable, or of being victimized in any respect. This tension in the defensive paradigm may help to illuminate one of the reasons that discussions and disagreements over gun control become so heated and vituperative in popular forums.

Guns represent the most concrete manifestations of safety, physical integrity, and control, be it control of self (shooters argue consistently that handling guns demands skill and self-control) or control of one's environment. Feeling safe and controlling one's environment is becoming more and more difficult. Thus, buying a gun can seem like the only antidote to chronic concerns about being the safest citizen soldier one can possibly be. Policies that stress community safety by making guns harder to get, or making certain guns illegal altogether, spell disaster for shooters because they view gun ownership as one of the most concrete ways they can assert control over their immediate environment.

The ideology of toughness, though at times attending to a sense of community and social collective, is predominantly about individual self-protection. Maintaining physical integrity (controlling their bodies and keeping them "whole") is a primary moral concern for many Americans, a point that has been illustrated in American concerns with illness and disease that disrupt the normalcy of a healthy, intact body.[34] That Americans should choose to keep their bodies safe with a gun, an item of rich cultural meaning and value, shouldn't be that surprising.

Gun ownership is also said to confer protection from the dangerous state. However, I would argue this is largely an issue of symbolic importance. Although criminologists debate the question of whether an armed citizenry confers actual protection from the state, or on behalf of it, I am not convinced that the shooters interviewed here view this is as a primary concern.[35] Few shooters stated they saw their gun ownership as important because it protected them from the state. For most shooters I talked to, concern with protecting the social body is largely about criminal violence: gun ownership for personal protection *within* a dangerous state.

The surge of interest in guns after 9/11 demonstrated this point particularly well: citizens were arming themselves not because they thought that American society would be taken over by terrorists, but because terrorists had already clearly infiltrated American society.[36] Some pro-gun advocates are indeed concerned about government oppression, but the shooters I interviewed were mainly concerned with more local and immediate concerns. Their pro-gun ideology fits into a larger ideological paradigm of toughness: being strong, vigilant, and ready for any possible disaster, which ostensibly means "stay armed."

On the other hand, toughness is also about moral character and a willingness to act on your own convictions. For shooters, that means taking responsibility for yourself and your family even when you've been victimized. As such, toughness puts shooters in a double bind by forcing them to attempt to wrestle with issues that are exceedingly difficult to control, such as having one's house broken into or being mugged. Maintaining complete control over one's surroundings every minute of the day and becoming invulnerable to crime are unrealistic expectations. This point underscores how double binds inherent in an system like American tough can trap its adherents. It addresses the local concerns at the expense of those long-term projects that might in fact make neighborhoods safer, and thus might give whole communities, even communities of shooters, a little more peace of mind. My point is not that focus should turn to long-term concerns at the expense of the short-term ones, only that consistent attention to the short term has seriously undercut any attention (as well as time and energy resources) to reducing crime in the long run.

Toughness as National Character

At no time was the American emphasis on toughness more apparent than in the wake of September 11, 2001. Immediately after the terrorist attacks, and in the months that followed, President George W. Bush sought to rally the American public, not only to support the War on Terrorism but also to prepare for the possibility of future attacks. He first championed the firemen, rescue workers, public health workers, and police who labored during and after the attacks. These were the new American heroes. Then he repeatedly highlighted a vision of national character that Americans found both comforting and appealing. Bush stated, "We have much to do and much to ask of the American people. You will be asked for your patience. . . . You will be asked for your resolve. . . . You will be asked for your strength."[37] His description of the American national character in the aftermath of the attacks emphasized physical and moral strength, vigilance, preparedness, defensiveness, and a particular form of patriotic citizenship, all of which resonate profoundly as celebrated characteristics in American society.

Though other cultures and societies have embraced toughness as definitively masculine, Americans traditionally and currently use toughness to define their national character. Emphasis on the supposed ubiquitous nature of this national character has perhaps allowed the quality of American tough to transcend gender boundaries: as I've mentioned, toughness is not exclusive to men. Women can also demonstrate a form of toughness that is gender-appropriate, although their doing so has evinced a certain ambivalent quality to toughness itself.[38] But ultimately, the paradigm of American tough embraces a variety of values and characteristics, including self-reliance, mental and physical strength, and readiness to take action, all of which are apparent in a variety of cultural and social formulations in American social and cultural arenas.

While 9/11 may have awakened latent fears or vigilant defensiveness in previously complacent segments of the American public, the principles and values inherent in American tough were a familiar paradigm for shooters long before the events of September 11. In our discussions on and off the range, shooters consistently framed their gun enthusiasm, and pro-gun ideology itself, as ways to demonstrate strength of body and character, moral courage, and a vigilant, prepared defensive stance.

These are the themes and values that emerged so strongly in post-9/11 American society, and one of the reasons that these values were trumpeted so quickly and with such sweeping resonance is because they have such profound and rich roots in American history and society. In times of crisis, Americans reach for those values and ideologies that are both comfortable and comforting, and insisting on the toughness of the American citizenry assures that citizenry that it will survive and thrive after such damaging attacks. The need to be prepared, well-defended, vigilant, and strong just seems to make sense. That Americans should look to the heroic actions of so many of the key figures that emerged in that moment is also not surprising: those firefighters, rescue workers, police, and citizens who sacrificed themselves to save lives did serve as primary examples of the best and most celebrated characteristics in the American national character. That guns should be linked to these values is also not surprising, as guns have long been associated with all of those characteristics in American history, and its contemporary mythic rendering.

Conclusions

In the past several years, some scholars as well as gun control advocates have begun to recognize that gun enthusiasts are alienated by or disgusted with the gun debate.[1] These scholars have begun to call not for more empirical evidence to support one position or another, but for creative ways by which *both* sides can begin an honest, working dialogue over the basic issue of how to reduce gun-related violence in the United States. This is obviously no small task because both sides think the other engages in lying, obfuscation, and manipulation of data to mislead the voting public.

Leaving aside those accusations for the moment, there are good reasons to push forward with the gun debate. The current stalemate means that energy and resources are poured into fighting over the relatively inconsequential minutiae of trigger locks and storage techniques, but doing very little that addresses the material circumstances in which violence occurs. In fact, what debaters are actually doing is wasting time arguing about intractable ideological differences and what constitutes the "true" moral good in American society. These are the actual issues that underlie the gun debate. They may bear some relation to the actual circumstances in which gun-related violence occurs, but debating them only moves the debate further from finding concrete solutions to reducing violence.

There are solutions to America's violence problem that do not compromise law-abiding citizens' right to own guns. The real goal of the gun debate should be to find proactive, effective solutions that take into account the reasons behind common forms of gun violence and ways to reduce that violence. With these points in mind, I offer several suggestions for advancing the gun debate.

First, I discuss how the gun control movement has latched onto the public health field to make its case for stronger gun controls. I discuss the strengths and limitations of this connection, paying particular attention to the underlying narrative messages that underscore contemporary gun control ideology. I then offer some assessments of what both gun control supporters and gun enthusiasts assume when they enter into the gun debate. Although it may seem counterproductive to suggest how both sides can advance their position, I do so because both positions offer constructive suggestions that can break the gun control stalemate. Moving the debate forward will potentially produce better violence-reducing public policy.

Gun Control and Public Health

Since the late 1980s and early 1990s, gun control advocates have joined forces with public health researchers to promote a particular vision of gun ownership and its relationship to gun violence.[2] This joint effort should not be surprising: the public health field has increasingly focused on gun violence, arguing that it is a public health problem (as opposed to a criminal justice problem). Gun-related violence does indeed affect huge numbers of Americans every year. For example, guns were used in approximately 10,000 homicides and 16,500 suicides in the year 2000.[3] From the beginning, public health researchers have supported stronger gun control measures, which they argue will lower gun-related violence rates.

In fact, public health officials argue that gun violence is not just a public health problem but an epidemic.[4] In keeping with the broader medicalization of lifestyle choices and social behavior, officials have set their sites on the ownership and usage of guns. They argue that all gun owners run a substantial risk of killing themselves or a family member with their guns, either by accident or in a fit of rage.[5] Guns kept for self-defense are especially dangerous. According to high-profile public health officials, guns kept in the home are far more likely to kill or injure owners or their family members than they are to be used in self-defense.[6] Gun owners become angry, frightened, or simply careless, grab for the gun kept handy in the bedside drawer, and suddenly a friend or family member is dead.[7] Thus, according to one well-known public health researcher, "gun violence . . . is overwhelmingly dependent on a single factor: easy access to a weapon."[8] Simply put, these researchers equate gun ownership to gun violence. *No one* can be trusted to own or use guns safely, and thus all responsible citizens should get rid of their guns.[9]

In this public health model, what shooters (as well as most criminologists and sociologists) usually think of as violent, criminal behavior is instead simply viewed as behavior born of ignorance: gun violence occurs when otherwise well-meaning people don't recognize the inherent risks of bringing guns into their home. Because everyone is thus a potential victim of gun violence, public health officials urge doctors and medical professionals to inform their patients about the ubiquitous dangers of owning guns.[10] According to this rationale, directing moral opprobrium at gun owners is appropriate and necessary because all gun owners are ostensibly engaging in "risky" behavior by virtue of simply owning a gun. These gun owners have only themselves to blame when disaster occurs. This last point strongly resonates with the gun control movement, which has long argued that high rates of gun-related violence are the fault of the NRA, gun owners, and those gun rights advocates who supposedly value their guns over basic human life.

In general, public health researchers have advocated the (allegedly) straightforward link between gun ownership and gun violence not only because they believe it exists, but also because they believe doing so will bring about change in public policy. Their reasoning seems logical: encouraging people to think about gun violence as a health problem will help depoliticize the gun issue, refocus public attention on reducing gun violence, and eventually increase public support for gun control. As the burden of gun owners' carnage falls predominantly on the state (and thus taxpayers), society would be well-served by stronger restrictions on gun ownership. Gun control improves the health and safety of the entire community. Responsible people support it.[11]

The public health field is not without its critics. Medical anthropologists and sociologists have long critiqued public health's particular tendency to moralize about individual behavior as "healthy" (good) or "unhealthy" (bad).[12] Public health literature in general promotes the message that good citizens are individuals who shun all forms of "risky" behavior (e.g., smoking cigarettes, eating fatty foods, not exercising, buying a gun) because risky behavior endangers health. These "health messages" are usually clear: it's better to live risk-free and stay safe because being healthy means better productivity and extending one's life span. In a capitalist society, better health increases productivity and benefits the economy, which is one of the underlying reasons that improving the public's health is so frequently advocated by social and political elites, as well as the state itself.[13] Despite the scathing critiques of these studies offered by a number of social scientists, public health findings are continually disseminated in medical journals, newspaper articles, editorials, popular health magazines, and radio and TV sound bites.[14]

Ultimately, in fact, public health rhetoric serves first and foremost the state and political elites. Rather than recognize the extent to which many Americans are too poor to afford high-quality foods, regular and preventive health care, or even homes with elaborate security systems located in safe neighborhoods, public health officials suggest that people simply *choose* to eat too much fat, shun their doctors, or rely on cheap guns for home defense—all of which endangers their health. According to public health officials, these things are easily preventable—people just have to be informed of their poor health choices and encouraged to make better decisions accordingly.[15] These health issues are viewed less as endemic structural problems within American society than as poor choices that Americans make on an individual basis. In other words, if your health is poor, the question has become, What have you been doing to make yourself so sick? Or, in relation to gun violence, Don't you realize that the gun you own is actually likely to kill you?

Public Health and Liberal Support for Gun Control

Gun control advocates have recognized a strong ally in public health researchers and have smoothly adopted much of the public health rhetoric about gun ownership and gun violence. Public health rhetoric provides the aura of scientific fact to the political agenda of gun control. It avoids the more obvious and politically fraught good guy/bad guy dichotomies, rests moral authority on medical science, and presents antigun ideology as logical reasoning and empirical fact. Within the public health paradigm, there are no overt bad guys, only average people who engage in risky, dangerous behavior. If foolish gun owners knew better, if they had the *facts*, then they'd get rid of their guns. They only need to be educated about their foolish ways.

In these respects, public health messages are appealing to people who care deeply about the high rates of violence but see little value in owning guns. Liberal gun control supporters believe strongly that having guns around just causes more violence. Public health advocacy provides "scientific evidence" for what they have believed for years. At this point, they *know* that guns cause crime.

Having these beliefs legitimated by public health advocacy also provides liberal supporters of gun control with certain material benefits. They don't need to pay more taxes or radically rework operational social welfare programs to help reduce gun violence. All they need to do is vote for tighter gun restrictions or bans on certain kinds of guns. Subscribing to the public health model of gun violence affirms for liberal gun controllers not only that they've been right all along on the gun issue, but they also don't need to alter their lifestyle at all to reduce gun violence.[16] They give up nothing, yet still feel they are getting "tough on crime." Gun control is safe, humane, and, Republican cowardice in the face of the NRA notwithstanding, the most politically expedient way to reduce gun violence. Who could disagree with that?

No part of this paradigm has any resonance for gun enthusiasts. Shooters know there is criminological evidence that contradicts the public health literature on guns, and they are highly skeptical of the gun control advocacy that relies on public health studies.[17] In fact, they find it offensive. As far as shooters are concerned, this kind of gun control advocacy exists not only to inform them of their own ignorance and naïveté, but also to convince them that owning a gun will transform them into murderers or suicide victims.

These messages run so contrary to what shooters know about guns, and what shooters know about *themselves*, that they reject these messages outright as ludicrous and insulting.[18] Shooters *know* that guns are used defensively. They use guns defensively themselves, they read constantly about other individuals who also do so, and they have their own experiences empirically validated by criminological studies and criminologists who have researched the issue extensively.[19] Shooters also do not accept the basic liberal position that "violence just breeds more violence"; as far as they are concerned, defensive gun use *prevents* the escalation of violence. If someone is attacking you but runs away when you pull out a gun, how does that encourage violence? Shooters do not equate threats of violence (e.g., brandishing a gun that is never fired) with actual violence, and they do not accept the proposition that violence would be reduced if victims did not defend themselves. They do not accept the liberal proposition that a well-armed citizenry encourages violent crime.

These are the reasons that shooters interpret gun control in such highly personal terms. When control advocates promote the ubiquitous dangerousness of guns, gun enthusiasts hear ad hominem attacks. Their ideas and concerns about citizenship, core values, and defense of self and common good are ignored. Their arguments that guns confer protection and can counter aggression are disdained. To have the protective value of guns so cavalierly dismissed, especially when gun control advocates purport to want to reduce violence effectively, leads many shooters to simply conclude that gun control advocates are hypocrites. When they hear sarcasm from liberal commentators about the ridiculousness of defensive gun use, shooters hear the arrogant elitism of those who live in exclusive neighborhoods and have the police and liberal politicians in their back pockets. They hear the voices of privilege and ignorance, of elites who don't care about everyday people who are vulnerable to crime.[20]

The real problem, as gun enthusiasts see it, is that criminals get guns and use them against good citizens. They believe gun control laws and antigun politicians have done very little to prevent this problem. Shooters do not believe that gun control will transform criminals into law-abiding citizens because it will be harder to get guns. Over and over shooters repeated to me the old cliché, "If guns are outlawed, then only outlaws will have guns." Gun control laws will *exacerbate* gun violence, not reduce it, because gun control tips the balance away from crime-controlling citizens and toward dangerous, aggressive criminals. For shooters, gun control literally and figuratively destroys the social and moral order. Because gun control advocates and their political sympathizers don't seem to comprehend what is so obvious to shooters (or worse, don't care), shooters are convinced that any more power in the hands of gun controllers will signify a literal and symbolic deterioration of contemporary American society.

The ideological intractability of both sides is why the gun debate is currently at a standstill. This intractability is also why the debate will remain a staple of the political and sociocultural landscape. It will not get any less impassioned or vitriolic unless debaters begin to unpack their ideological assumptions. This is important, because just as gun enthusiasts are not going to give up their guns, liberal politicians and gun control advocates are not going to give up their support for gun control. That being said, if control supporters expect that they can *persuade* gun owners to give up their guns or embrace new legislation because it's for their own good, they are very much mistaken.

What Gun Control Supporters Must Give Up

To move the gun debate forward, advocates on both sides must recognize those aspects of their position that are simply untenable. I begin with those assumptions and ideological beliefs that gun control supporters need to give up if they want to make their position more palatable to gun owners.

The Belief That It's Possible to Dismantle or Destroy the Gun Culture

In the late 1990s, a number of high-profile gun control supporters argued that the only way to pass stringent gun control laws is to destroy the gun culture, or rid the United States of the NRA. These individuals, including such popular intellectuals as Garry Wills and celebrities like Rosie O'Donnell, argued that with the NRA in the driver's seat, the gun culture is killing Americans, particularly American children. Implicit in these assertions are the ideas that the gun culture is a homogeneous "thing," a beastly entity that can destroyed or slain, and that getting rid of the NRA will rid the gun culture of its main support structure and general political impetus. Both ideas are naïve and demonstrate that some gun control supporters apparently have no idea what they are dealing with in terms of the nature and scope of the gun culture.

First, there are more than 250 million guns currently in public circulation.[21] No amount of wishing those guns away is going to substantially alter that fact. Even if the American government was able to call a complete halt to all gun manufacturing, gun importation, and illegal gun smuggling, and then enact a complete ban on all forms of gun ownership (legal and illegal), the government would still need to confiscate the 250 million guns currently owned legally (and illegally) by the general public. As doing so would invariably constitute some form of violation of most individuals' Fourth Amendment rights (which basically protects the right to freedom from searches without probable cause), the likelihood of getting rid of guns in the United States is practically nonexistent.[22]

Then there is the issue of all those people who actually own all those guns. As I've pointed out, the gun culture is a multilayered, multifaceted institution made up of diverse, complex gun subcultures. Examples of gun-owning subcultures include the police, the military, farmers and ranchers, hunters, sport shooters, gun collectors, some right-wing militia groups, some white supremacist groups, some feminist groups, some gay groups, and some black civil rights groups. Obviously, not every gun owner is a member of the NRA. In fact, many gun owners are *not* members of the NRA. However, *many of these groups and individuals have thoroughly integrated guns into their lives.*

Each of these groups has its own reasons and rationale for owning guns. These groups are not necessarily demographically similar in any respect except that they own guns and they accept some basic form of pro-gun ideology. This fact illustrates several important things. First, pro-gun ideology is so accommodating, and so profoundly intertwined with deeply held cultural beliefs and values, that diverse groups of Americans embrace it as fundamentally American even when they come from opposite ends of the political spectrum. What do white supremacists and pro-gun black civil rights groups have in common ideologically, except a belief in the right and necessity of being armed? Groups that work at ideological cross-purposes can share a basic support for gun rights.

Pro-gun ideology works as a kind of glue for the gun culture: it provides a shared rationale and common discursive elements that allow diverse sets of individuals to come together to celebrate their gun rights. While discrediting or disproving pro-gun ideology would go a long way toward advancing the gun control cause, truly discrediting pro-gun ideology would be exceedingly difficult if not impossible. Pro-gun ideology makes a lot of sense to gun-owning Americans whether they consider themselves gun enthusiasts or not. Pro-gun adherents believe that they are simply recognizing the reality of guns and crime, not subscribing to some radical political position. They hear antigun arguments as naïve, misinformed, elitist, or dangerously wrong.

Gun control supporters need to recognize that America's gun culture has deep roots in American history, and pro-gun ideology has deep roots in the country's political culture. No matter where one marks the origins of these intertwined phenomena, they are both fundamental parts of American culture as a whole. Members of the gun culture are not all menacing warrior-wannabes in camouflage gear, potential terrorists, or unemployed skinheads hanging out at gun shows. Most of the shooters I met were average members of society: they have regular jobs, they go to neighborhood picnics and PTA meetings, they have children and grandchildren. They interact with their coworkers, their bosses, their employees, their neighbors, friends, and families in socially positive ways. Even if the NRA were to magically disappear tomorrow, the gun culture would remain. The people who compose it are simply not interested in giving up their guns, no matter what gun control advocates or health experts have to say about the matter.

Guns and the gun culture are so thoroughly intertwined with American culture that at this point, many Americans perceive guns as utterly, unremarkably normal. Most gun owners have unexciting, if not entirely banal, experiences with guns all the time. Claiming that all gun owners are mentally ill or that the gun culture is really a "cult" will not change the fact that most gun owners are relatively ordinary people.[23] But arguing that all gun owners (or even enthusiasts) are just plain crazy only makes them angry. Gun enthusiasts are not going to relinquish their basic belief in gun rights or their belief that guns signify their Americanness just because gun control supporters hate them. Gun control supporters can get angry about that fact, but they are not going to change it. Put simply, members of the American gun culture are members of American society as a whole. Remembering this basic point might go a long way toward defusing the vitriol of the gun debate as it currently stands.

The Belief That Gun Control Can Bring About
Fundamental Change in American Culture

Gun control advocates and pro-gun advocates alike tend to make facile comparisons between the United States and other nations, particularly with regard to gun ownership and homicide rates. Pro-gun advocates typically compare the United States to Switzerland or Israel, both of which have high rates of private gun ownership but low civilian homicide rates. The pro-gun point is that more guns equal less crime. On the other side, gun control advocates usually cite Great Britain or Australia to illustrate that low rates of private gun ownership (i.e., tight gun control) produce low homicide rates. Their point: gun control equals low gun crime. Gun control advocates argue that the United States needs gun controls that resemble controls in other Western democracies, which will lower American gun crime rates to the point where the the country resembles Britain or Australia. If those countries can do it, why can't the United States?[24]

What is illustrated by both positions is a profoundly limited notion of culture itself. Rarely does either side discuss what constitutes culture, how it operates, or how to think about cultural difference versus cultural similarity.[25] At the heart of this matter for gun control supporters is the belief that gun control can bring about cultural change. Stringent gun control will curb access to guns, which will eventually wean Americans of the desire to own guns. Gun control will reduce children's access to guns, and with fewer guns around, children are less likely to be interested in them. Eventually, Americans will lose interest in guns altogether, reducing their capacity for and tendency toward violent behavior. Americans will then be more like the citizens of Western democracies where gun control helped curb the basic desire to have guns.

This position is flawed on several basic levels. First, Western democracies are not all the same, or even particularly similar. The United States has a government, legal system, economy, frontier history, immigration history, indigenous population, and history of slavery and ethnic conflict, to name but a few factors, that substantially differentiate it from all other Western nations, even Australia.[26] All of these different factors have influenced how Americans think about guns and how they use guns, again differentiating the United States from all other Western democracies.

In the past decade, high-profile shootings have occurred in both Britain and Australia. The governments of those nations reacted swiftly to enact highly restrictive gun control laws, complementing their already fairly restrictive gun control policies.[27] Although both Britain and Australia have pro-gun lobbying organizations, those nations never had the widespread structural manifestations of the gun culture, nor the widespread cultural acceptance of pro-gun ideology, that currently exists in the United States. The widespread public support that would have been needed to seriously challenge the proposed gun control legislation never materialized substantially enough to defeat it. Also, there is no Second Amendment in either Britain or Australia to raise the question of the constitutionality of this new legislation.

The larger point to make about Britain and Australia, however, is that gun control did not reduce the desire to have guns in these nations. It was the other way around. The lack of desire to have guns facilitated the passage of stronger gun control laws. Shock and horror at various shooting massacres, widespread lack of interest in guns by the voting public, and politicians conceding to the public's demands all brought about swift calls for legislation and swift enforcement of that legislation once passed.[28]

The bottom line is that Americans feel very differently about guns than do citizens of other Western democracies. A very strong contingent of the American voting public wants to hold onto its guns, and this pro-gun contingent is able to mobilize political support far more effectively than can the gun control lobby. Related to this point, remember that gun control is about regulating access to guns, *not* eradicating the desire to own them. Gun ownership articulates some deeply held sociocultural and political convictions for many Americans. Some of these Americans have made guns a single voting issue, as supporters for rigorous gun controls continue to discover at the polls.

Gun control alone will not alter the cultural attitudes and behaviors of gun-owning Americans. In a nation as fixated on guns as the United States, outlawing guns will not wean Americans of their interest in guns. This tactic didn't work with alcohol or drugs. It certainly won't work with guns. So although it is not unreasonable to work toward lowering American homicide rates so that they someday compare with Britain's or Australia's, believing that gun control is the best way to do that radically *over*estimates the power of gun control to change wider American culture.

These cultural comparisons may also be designed simply to shame or humiliate American gun owners for being less "civilized" than the British or Australians. This is what some shooters believe is intended with these comparisons, hence their disgust and annoyance with this line of argument. If this is in fact the case, then gun control supporters who are using the gun debate to articulate what disgusts them about their fellow Americans should recognize that they lower the potential productivity of the gun debate.

The Belief That Guns Have No Intrinsic Social or Political Worth

Gun control ideologues have made it very clear that they see little value in owning guns. As they see it, the point to owning guns is to kill people. Because killing people is illegal, there is really no point to owning guns. Such (often vociferous) critics of gun ownership are certainly entitled to their opinion, but unfortunately they have also tended to assume that everybody else should share that opinion. They basically argue that because guns have no intrinsic value for them, guns have no intrinsic value, period.

But in fact, such arguments do not take into account what American history has to say about guns, gun ownership, and the variety of values attached to guns in different periods. The power of the state to confer the mantle of citizenship has loomed large in discussions about guns in American history because citizenship has often hinged on the ability to "keep and bear arms" on behalf of oneself or the state. This is the concrete social reality lurking underneath discussions of freedom, equality, and personhood on both sides of the debate, not only in terms of history but also in terms of contemporary reality. Some Americans who identity themselves as feminists, people of color, sexual minorities, and fellow travelers in effect argue that banning guns dismantles the patriarchy. They see guns linked to a long history of oppression, violence, and fear, often at the hands of gun-wielding white men who could more easily consolidate their power because they wielded force. Modern-day antigun coalitions want that history of oppression and violence to end, and end now. Not surprisingly, they see promise in the formation of social and political collectives that effectively lobby the state to protect them, and they see safety and freedom from gun violence as their right.

These coalitions have chosen gun control as the main mode to accomplish this change because guns are the thread that ostensibly weaves elements of the patriarchy together. Brutality, abusive masculinity, nationalism, violent conflict resolution, domestic violence, hate crimes—all of these facets of the patriarchy are made more deadly by guns. Guns now symbolize these phenomena for those Americans who dislike and distrust guns. Gun control promises to attack all these phenomena, leaving their perpetrators literally and symbolically disarmed. This is a powerful vision of a less violent, more free America, made manifest in a very strongly held ideological position. Adherents are no more likely to relinquish this basic moral and political frame-work as pro-gun ideologues are to relinquish theirs.

But the formula equating gun ownership to the patriarchy does not tell the whole story. Feelings about identity, either group or individual, do not necessarily predict ideological inclination.[29] Just as some people believe that their group identity and the past experiences of their social group legitimate their protest against the gun culture, equally legitimate are the groups who believe that because of their group identity, they should encourage gun *own-ership*, not gun control. This point is made clear by the emergent groups of feminists, ethnic minorities, and sexual minorities who view their own his-tory of harm and oppression by the state, and therefore predominantly by white men, as good reason to distrust the state and its (limited) ability to protect their rights and safety.

As I've discussed, the state has historically denied minority groups the right to be counted as full persons and citizens. Citizenship and status was reserved for white, propertied men (a point that liberal gun controllers usu-ally recognize). The ability to own guns and membership in the institutions that use force to maintain power (e.g., the military and the police) are ex-amples of how guns have been linked literally and symbolically to power in American society. In a contemporary setting, these historical formulas for determining citizenship, status, and power still have tremendous signifi-cance for many Americans, whether they choose to own guns or not.

Is it really so surprising, then, that some Americans, including women, blacks, and gays, draw links between their sense of personhood, citizenship, and social power to owning guns? The history of oppression that these groups have endured historically is *exactly* what provides their sense of moral authority in owning guns *now*. And because gender has in large part been the historical and even current arbiter of who wields this power appropri-ately and who does not, these debates are still relevant to the social con-structions of masculinity and femininity in American culture, and how the construction of gender either preserves or destroys the patriarchal order.

The point to make most resoundingly on this issue is that whereas patri-archy has indeed been sustained in part because of guns, even in the mod-ern register, it is *equally true* that the patriarchy is sustained in part because of gun control. Certain forms of gun control (e.g., bans on cheap guns) still effectively prevent some Americans (largely the poor and disenfranchised) from choosing a gun for self-defense (or defining their own parameters for personal safety) in the same ways wealthier people do. On the presumption of common good, gun control prohibits some individuals from getting guns.

Ironically, those individuals are often the very people most vulnerable to crime: women, gays, the poor, and people of color. Stringent gun controls force these groups to rely on the state to keep them safe, simply by effectively reducing their own ability to keep themselves safe. Invariably, because of who they are, gun control ensures that these individuals have fewer rights (of several kinds) than their predominantly white, middle-class, pro-gun counterparts.

Some of these groups find this situation intolerable. They want access to guns, not more gun control. And their collective histories of oppression and denial at the hands of the (patriarchal) state, as well as their knowledge of the ways the state has failed to protect them, fuel the moral authority and legitimacy of their arguments. Historically, the state bolstered its own power by giving access to guns to some and restricting others. This process continues today through "discretionary" laws that give local police or state officials the power to decide who shall receive a handgun license and who shall not, or by banning certain kinds of guns, like ones that only the poor can afford (e.g., Saturday Night Specials). These laws curb the ability of some to be armed without affecting the abilities of others. In this way, the state once again confers rights and powers to some but limits the rights and powers of others. This is one of the reasons the NRA takes such a hard-line, "unreasonable" stance on these kinds of gun controls. Although she does not make this argument on behalf of the NRA, Elaine Scarry articulates the underlying rationale for why fewer restrictions are ultimately more egalitarian than more restrictions: "*If* as a nation-state we are to have injuring power, the authorization over the action of injuring (as well as over the risk of receiving injury in return) must be dispersed throughout the population in the widest possible way. . . . However much injuring power we have, like all other forms of political access, it must be spread throughout our entire numerical expanse."[30]

The logical response to this argument is, of course, that the risks of receiving injury in return are not shared equally.[31] Victims of gun violence are typically not the NRA members making this argument, which is why some social critics have been quick to point out what appears to be hypocrisy from the NRA. And in fact, I largely agree that the majority of gun enthusiasts discussed in this book are not at risk of being murdered (by their own guns or someone else's). Their collective safety is not due primarily to being armed, but rather from the benefits that come from being middle class (and white). They are able to rely largely on the insulating factors of safe neighborhoods, security systems, and the presence of community police who will respond to their complaints (if not always in a timely fashion) to keep them safe. These factors, in keeping with their guns, are most likely to keep them safe. But while critics may distrust the sincerity of the NRA's position against most forms of gun control, the bottom line is that the NRA's position appears far more egalitarian than arguments supporting gun control laws that entail discretionary licensing procedures and bans on cheap guns.

In sum, the ability of both individuals and social collectives to wield force has been one of the traditional ways that these individuals and social collectives have measured their equality in the eyes of the state. By that same token, those without access to the means of force (the force that others can deploy) are not politically equal in the eyes of the state. For this reason, noting which groups are prevented access to guns makes a statement about how those groups are viewed by the state and society more generally. The statement being made usually centers around perceived dangerousness, lesser status or personhood, or perceived vulnerability or incompetence. However discomforting it is to recognize that political status has been, and can be, denoted by the ability to deploy or defend against violence (through access to guns), this was one of the primary principles on which American government was founded. On some level, Americans have been struggling with that issue ever since. This is one of the ways that liberal ideology vis-à-vis gun ownership has been confused and contradictory, in part due to its limited understanding of both the meanings of gun ownership and the political uses of gun control.

Contemporary debates about history and guns—whether guns have served moral or immoral purposes, whether gun ownership denotes the patriarchy or its demise, and whether gun owners have always been the good guys or the bad—are actually competing ideological representations of American history itself. Both pro- and antigun debaters seem to believe that if we could figure out which "side" owned more guns (the good guys or the bad), then we would understand more concretely what guns mean now. But such assumptions are naïve; ultimately, how individuals and social collectives read the past is very much like how they read the present: through the prism of such factors as their ethnicity, their social class, their sex, and their individual, familial, community, and national experience. There is no easy or "correct" way to interpret what the past means to people now. History itself, just like the present, is rich with moral ambiguity.[32]

Likewise, there is no single, correct way to understand what a gun is or what it does. Like any object and symbol of great cultural significance, guns are polysemic: they have various meanings and signify a multitude of things.

What they mean at any given time and place depends on the context in which they are owned and used, and on the intentions of their users. Just like the historical events that provide them context, guns themselves are subjective by their very nature. Until more Americans recognize this fundamental point, they will forever be using the gun debate not to discuss guns, but to ostensibly offer differing visions and ideological notions of what constitutes moral behavior and moral order in contemporary American society.

The bottom line is that groups with guns have power. Individuals who wield guns have power. This is concrete, literal power, and it is symbolic, figurative power. Sometimes these notions of power are intertwined, sometimes they are mutually exclusive. Gun control supporters must understand this point on some level, or they would not build so much of their case on the idea that guns have the power to wreak havoc through society, and permitting guns to violent racists and potential terrorists gives those dangerous people power. If guns give power to criminals and terrorists, then guns give power to "ordinary" citizens, too. This point is common sense, and negates the idea that guns have no social or political worth.

The Belief That Empirical Evidence Will Prove Gun Controllers Right

Americans, like Westerners in general, tend to place their confidence in scientific paradigms, in rational and clear logic that assists in bringing their social reality into focus and under control.[33] In keeping with that paradigm, Americans seek to attach numerical values to things, to quantify and concretize social value even when the topic defies such categories. This is one of the reasons that the public health paradigm, which links statistics and empirical facts to the "social deficits" of guns, has such rhetorical power for gun control supporters. In fact, the gun debate is often discussed in these terms because both sides believe that if they arrive at the right statistics and place them in the most persuasive political context, those statistics will present the most convincing evidence for the moral superiority of their ideological position.

I've discussed the ways that gun control supporters use the facts and figures of gun violence to argue their case to policymakers and receptive politicians. But I've also pointed out how and why shooters are not persuaded by gun control supporters' interpretations of those numbers (or even the numbers themselves), because those statistics can often mean something entirely different to gun enthusiasts. Shooters have their own statistics that are meaningful to them. This begs the questions: Whose statistics are right? Are there statistics that could settle the gun debate? Are there statistics that are uncontested, unambiguous, and verifiable in relation to the gun debate?

Even if there were such (magical) statistics, arriving at them will not necessarily settle the gun debate. The constant battle over statistics is yet another example of the subjectivity of meaning and experience in relation to guns. Different people arrive at different conclusions about what they value more or value less. Advocates on both sides apparently believe that their preferred statistics have great meaning and power that extends beyond the context of the gun debate. A pro-gun advocate may see some gun-related fatality statistics as positive because they include "justifiable homicides": a woman who kills the man trying to rape her, or a store owner who kills a burglar trying to rob him. These numbers demonstrate the "social benefit" of gun ownership. But to a gun control supporter, even these justifiable homicides are problematic because they point to the horror and violence of living in the United States and the ways that different kinds of citizens must engage in hand-to-hand combat simply to stay alive. Guns don't improve this situation, even in the "right" hands, because violent problems will never be solved with violent solutions. Thus, gun-related statistics really just demonstrate something horrible about the American people as a whole.

These contrasting positions demonstrate a deep divide in the ideological and moral frameworks of debaters.[34] The gun debate is often discussed in terms of who has correctly interpreted history, or who has accurately assembled the "real facts," or even whose voice speaks most accurately for the kinds of people Americans have been in the past and who they'll be in the future. This is the ferocious debate about citizenship and identity that lies just beneath the surface of the gun debate but is no more likely to be easily resolved. Gun control advocates are not going to convince gun owners that guns *don't* represent the triumph of freedom any more than gun owners are going to convince gun controllers that guns *do*. These are obviously deeply subjective issues that don't really have right answers.

I mentioned earlier that the gun debate is not really about guns. The gun debate is about core American values and how Americans choose to articulate those values in the practices of their everyday lives. The gun debate is fundamentally about how individuals and social collectives choose to express their values in relation to three intertwined concepts: citizenship, safety, and moral order within American society. The gun debate asks of Americans, What makes a good citizen? How can Americans keep themselves safe? and How should Americans work toward the common good? Shooters answer these questions by stating that their gun ownership makes them good citizens. Guns protect them personally and safeguard their families, their communities, and the nation. For shooters, guns embody freedom and responsibility, individualism and equality. Actually, guns not only embody these values but protect them as well. The common good in American society balances freedom and safety, but *both* are secured by a well-armed citizenry.

In fact, debaters on both sides are using different mythological and ideological visions of the nation's past and present to make their case.[35] These competing myths and ideological visions are not about facts and statistics. They are about subjective interpretation, fantasy, imagining how things used to be, and understanding how things are right now. Gun control advocates can continue to argue that gun enthusiasts should pay more attention to the death and destruction caused by guns, but they need to recognize that gun enthusiasts have their own facts and figures that they find just as inherently convincing. Gun enthusiasts *do* pay attention to the statistics that illustrate the high levels of violence in American society. Those statistics are *exactly* why shooters own guns. In a violent world, sometimes guns can feel like the most concrete kind of protection. Richard Slotkin puts it well: "A violent history begets an expectation of future violence."[36] Cold, hard numbers can be persuasive, but in the context of the gun debate, they only preach to the already converted.

What Gun Enthusiasts Must Give Up

It's important to state at the outset that shooters need to stop using the gun debate to articulate what they find so intolerable about American society, or what they dislike or distrust about liberal political ideology and politics. Though they are certainly entitled to their opinion, and their ability to express it openly in public forums, when their dislike of liberals and liberal positions becomes intertwined with the gun debate, they weave their concerns about guns and gun ownership into larger issues that they will never be able to resolve. These are ways that shooters make themselves even more vulnerable in the context of the gun debate, and there's no real reason to do so.

I've discussed some of the underlying assumptions that guide gun control supporters in the debate, and what they need to realize will not make their case. Now it's important to recognize that gun enthusiasts too must revise their thinking and also be willing to make some compromises in relation to the gun debate. In order for gun enthusiasts to really talk to their political opponents, they also need to relinquish some of their assumptions of what can be accomplished in this debate. The following assumptions are hindering shooters from articulating their legitimate and understandable concerns.

The Belief That Gun Control Is Completely Useless for Reducing Crime

One of the casualties of the gun debate has been nuance of argument and subtlety of terminology. The term "gun control" is one such casualty. The term is now overtly politicized and ideological, by which I mean that it is no longer an agreed-upon set of practical, applicable laws grounded in the material reality of the criminal justice system. It is now an abstract set of political beliefs and cultural values, even a worldview. But what is embraced by those beliefs, values, and worldview is radically different for the opposing sides of the gun debate. Hence, for an average gun enthusiast, the term gun control usually means laws created by ignorant people designed to control me and my personal behavior; laws that help criminals who want to hurt or rob me; laws that hinder me from effectively protecting myself; and laws that trash the Constitution and degrade the core values that signify being a good American. Because these things are all anathema to gun enthusiasts, they are infuriated by the very concept of gun control.

Not surprisingly, gun control supporters take a different position. For an average gun control supporter, gun control has come to mean necessary and purposeful laws that reduce criminals' access to gun; laws that force gun owners to be more responsible and accountable to the state and society; laws that prevent children and other vulnerable people from having unnecessary accidents or being murdered; laws that reflect the will of the people but are thwarted by the NRA; laws that would break the gun culture's thrall over Congress and/or the American people; and laws that bring the United States in line with the rest of the civilized world. Because these concepts reflect values and ideals that resonate deeply with gun control supporters, particularly liberals, they support the concept of gun control and cannot understand why gun owners and the NRA are being so constantly unreasonable.

When gun control remains an ideological concept, it only reflects whatever any given speaker thinks it reflects, no more or less. To a certain extent, I've been guilty of using the term this way myself (in certain parts of this book) because I've wanted to reflect how shooters think and feel about the concept of gun control and why shooters are so resistant to the idea of it. Because of their perceptions of gun control, it has become a target for their anger and frustration.

But if shooters are interested in advancing the gun debate to their own advantage, they need to recognize that gun control can be connected to some concrete, grounded laws that are not necessarily designed to control or inconvenience them, trash what they believe in, or force them to submit to the will of criminals or gun controllers. It is in shooters' best interests to wrest the term from the abstract and attach it to something concrete that they can live with.

One way they can begin to do so is to recognize that the term is already connected to some concrete and positive laws that work to shooters' advantage. For example, laws that prohibit felons from legally purchasing guns are, in fact, gun control laws. Laws that prohibit children from purchasing handguns are gun control laws, as are laws that prohibit people who are addicted to drugs or alcohol from purchasing guns. Some of these laws are not well enforced, or easily enforced. Shooters know this is true, which is frustrating. But the point is that some gun control laws do produce positive balances among rights, freedoms, and public safety, and should be acknowledged to do so.

Shooters might want to begin thinking concretely and realistically about what kinds of gun control laws they can accept and what kinds of laws they find unacceptable. Doing so might clarify for their critics and themselves that they are willing to make compromises and are willing to work with legislators to refine and improve the kinds of laws that would concretely address crime reduction. Taking positive steps in that direction may also enable shooters to proactively take control of the debate and define the parameters for themselves. Shooters thus far have taken a largely defensive position in the gun debate, always waiting for gun control supporters to advance the next step and come up with yet another piece of legislation that shooters invariably find completely unacceptable.

Instead of taking such a defensive position, shooters could assert themselves more positively, taking public stands to support new gun control laws that are designed not to address legal gun purchasing by law-abiding citizens but rather illegal markets: straw purchasing, nonprofessional gun transfers, and programs that address illegal behavior with guns by persons who are also most vulnerable to victimization by gun violence. These are the kinds of laws that shooters should recognize do not harm them either directly or indirectly. Supporting these kinds of legislation will help to demonstrate to gun control supporters that gun enthusiasts are indeed interested in reducing gun crime. Unless shooters can actively persuade gun control supporters to give up the entire paradigm of gun control (which is unlikely, to say the least), shooters can assertively work within this paradigm to effectuate change that ultimately benefits everyone, while simultaneously demonstrating their willingness to compromise. I discuss these specific kinds of gun controls later in the chapter.

The Belief That They Can Convince Liberal Gun Control
Supporters That Bad Guys Are Inherently Bad

One of the most consistent features of shooters' discourse in relation to gun violence and gun crime is their reference to "bad guys." I've discussed this tendency at various points in the book, discussed why this term is used and the extent to which it also has become an ideological category in much the same vein as "gun control." Bad guys are the ultimate criminal others. But the question now becomes whether the term bad guys has cachet for Americans outside of gun enthusiasts' circles, or if it is meaningful only to gun enthusiasts. Put another way, are pro-gun clichés like "There are no bad guns, only bad guys" and "If guns are outlawed, only outlaws will have them" resonant with cultural values that Americans hold more generally?

There is evidence from some criminological studies that wide swaths of American society hold ideas about crime and criminality that jibe with the belief that the country is full of people who are simply immoral or amoral, people who purposefully set out to harm and victimize average or "good" people.[37] Inherent in American beliefs about crime more generally are ideas about how some people are just born bad, a belief that is usually labeled somewhat politically conservative in relation to crime.

But liberals have tended to be more cagey about these issues and usually tend to look for what they consider environmental or social reasons for why some individuals turn to crime. Although much of the discussion about gun control as crime control has redirected liberals away from the more structural, root causes of crime (which has weakened liberal ideology vis-à-vis crime considerably), the remnants of the root causes argument can be found in liberal gun control supporters' dislike and distrust of the gun enthusiasts' insistence that bad guys will always get guns. It's not that these gun control supporters don't believe that there are indeed individuals who are determined to maim and kill, it's just that gun control will help stop them and is more humane and civilized than arguing "Just buy a gun and shoot at the bastards." Thus, liberal gun control supporters like Katha Pollitt remain disgusted with the NRA's stance against gun control, and Garry Wills becomes enraged after gun enthusiasts protest the gun control initiatives that are proposed after yet another high-profile shooting incident.

But identity politics have encouraged a particular way of thinking about crime for some more leftist progressives. I've mentioned that the topic of gun enthusiasm generated angry and passionate responses from some of my friends and colleagues, to the point that I realized the very words I used to describe both gun enthusiasts (i.e., "law-abiding people," "legal gun own-ers") and people usually implicated in gun violence scenarios (i.e., "illegal gun users," "criminals," "people who misuse guns") played right into the frustration and distrust my colleagues were expressing. I assumed that I was using more neutral terminology and making the point that gun ownership does not inherently denote criminality. However, I subsequently figured out that my remarks were being interpreted differently from how I thought. At the risk of being presumptuous, I believe my colleagues were interpreting my remarks as follows:

> You keep describing these gun enthusiasts. What you're really describing are rich white people who have the social, material, and political power to buy guns and damn the consequences. These are the people who create a "climate of violence" because they own, use, and recreate with guns. The fact that these gun enthusiasts block gun control demonstrates how selfish and uncaring they are: they want what they want whenever they want it. They clearly don't care that people are dying. They clearly don't care that guns kill people. These are the people that you apparently think are the "good guys."
>
> On the other side, we have the poor, the disenfranchised, the people of color, all the people who suffer disproportionately from gun violence because your so-called good guys want guns and won't pass reasonable gun controls. These are the unfortunate individuals who "misuse" guns. But guns are made to kill, period! So how can you say that people who kill with guns are misusing them? In any case, people who do commit crimes with guns probably only do so only because they are poor, disadvantaged, and generally disenfranchised from American society. If the poor and disenfranchised have to get guns illegally, it's because they are shut out of society anyway. They are victims. And then there are yet more victims, the people who got in the way of a bullet, the people in the wrong place at the wrong time. These are all the people who you apparently think are the "bad guys." The *real* crime is not that people get guns illegally, it's that *any* person can get guns *at all*, legal or otherwise.

This interpretation is certainly speculative, but it fits with the kind of asser-tions that friends and colleagues made to me during the course of my re-search. Here again, then, is why gun enthusiasts and the NRA are so often accused of making racist, punitive arguments about gun crime. The NRA is creating and maintaining an environment in which the poor and disenfranchised are being murdered, usually with guns that white, middle-class, male NRA members think everybody should be able to own.

The question of how liberal thinkers address the issues of violence and personal responsibility has become increasingly contentious in relation to both domestic and international issues. Although my interpretation of the liberal position on guns may seem extreme, there is evidence that this is how some liberal thinkers do indeed think about these issues. Consider the writings of British reporter Robert Fisk, who was beaten by a group of Afghans during his coverage of the War in Afghanistan in November 2001. He managed to escape with his life because he fought back against his attackers and because he stumbled upon an Afghan man who assisted him to safety. Of the attack and his self-defensive, violent response, he has written:

> I was back in the middle of the road but could not see. I brought my hands to my eyes and they were full of blood and with my fingers I tried to scrape the gooey stuff out. . . . I began to see again and realised that I was crying and weeping and that the tears were cleaning my eyes of blood. "What had I done," I kept asking myself? I had been punching and attacking Afghan refugees, the very people I had been writing about for so long, the very dispossessed, mutilated people whom my own country—among others—was killing, along with the Taliban, just across the border. "God spare me," I thought. I think I actually said it. The men whose families our bombers were killing were now my enemies too.[38]

It's worth pointing out the obvious: in that particular moment, Fisk was not particularly powerful, and his Afghan attackers *did* have some measure of power (the power to beat him to death, if nothing else). But to Fisk, this point is apparently completely immaterial. Those Afghans did not have the kind of power that really matters. In fact, on some level, they are not really capable of acting—they only *react*, to outsiders or those who have "always" controlled their destiny.[39]

This example illustrates a form of extreme identity politics—group or national identity over individual identity, to the point where individual actions are ostensibly erased from the paradigm. But in this way the example is instructive in relation to the liberal distrust of self-defensive gun use. Liberal supporters of gun control view support for self-defensive gun use, particularly when it's advocated by high-profile NRA members, as just another example of "the strong" further abusing "the weak." Not surprisingly, the root of the issue is power and what kind of power really matters. For Robert Fisk and his fellow travelers, individual physical power is always less important than collective social, political, and economic power. Real power is the power imbued in socioeconomic background, in the historical and geopolitical interweaving of race and privilege that has rendered whites more powerful than blacks, the West more powerful than the non-West, et cetera.

Thus, some of the shooters who make the argument that they need guns for self-defense should be aware that they may be discredited not just because of what they say, but because of *who they are*. Because so many liberal supporters of gun control sincerely believe that guns are only about violence and punishment, and that the majority of the American white middle class are inherently privileged and (as a consequence) inherently racist, such liberal supporters of gun control hear gun enthusiasts making arguments about the legitimacy of the alleged good guys (i.e., rich whites) using their guns against the alleged bad guys (i.e., poor blacks). To liberal supporters of gun control, this was never a fair fight and it never will be, regardless of particular circumstances. The specifics of any given event are far less important than its presumed sociopolitical dimensions.

For this reason, self-defensive gun ownership is unlikely ever to have much appeal for liberal supporters of gun control. This is especially true when the most vocal proponent of self-defensive gun ownership is the NRA. Even while gun control supporters usually argue that guns are generally *not* used for self-defense (citing the supposed lack of reputable proof for widespread defensive gun use), what some gun control supporters are really saying is that guns *shouldn't* be used for self-defense. Truly civilized people living in a truly civilized society shouldn't need to do that. To boot, the "average" self-defense scenario is really just about the rich middle class shooting at the disenfranchised poor, who really engage in crime only because they're socioeconomically disadvantaged. No matter how shooters try to argue the point, they are unlikely to convince liberal gun control supporters otherwise. Pro- and antigun discourses obviously employ very different ideological models for self-defense and criminality, and finding a common model for what is shared by various ideologically opposed groups is unlikely to happen within the context of the gun debate.

But at the end of the day, a simple glance at statistical tables on who is most greatly affected by gun violence in the United States demonstrates that those who are most victimized *are* usually poor and disenfranchised, and are often young people of color.[40] These are quantifiable facts that accurately reflect the nature of gun violence in American society, facts that neither shooters nor the NRA have seriously contested. The question, then, to put to shooters and the NRA is this: If guns are not responsible for this situation, what is?

Here again is where mythic history provides the subtle, unspoken answer: stories about guns in the hands of "good colonists and frontiersmen" who used their guns righteously against Indians and outlaws have metamorphosed into modern-day law-and-order ideologies that are ostensibly used to similar effect. Yesterday's Indians and horse thieves are today's ubiquitous bad guys, the two-legged predators, monsters, and psychos that lurk behind shooters' discourse about why they need to keep guns in their homes and in their lives. Unfortunately, most of the shooters I interviewed were disinterested in thinking about who these bad guys really are, or why they got that way.

I believe it is a cop-out to argue that people who perpetuate the majority of gun violence do so because they suffer from a lack of moral character from birth, or they've made unfortunate "lifestyle choices," or they're simply "bad people." I'm not doubting that some shooters are actively endangered in their daily lives or live under dangerous circumstances. But the way shooters describe the individuals who threaten them does demonstrate the extent to which they are disinterested in who these so-called bad guys are, why they engage in crime, or what Americans can do about them, either individually or as a larger social collective.

The fact of the matter is that no one *chooses* to be born poor or grow up in a decaying inner-city environment. These are two important factors that contribute seriously to the extreme violence in the United States. But violence in the United States is an enormously complex issue. The good guy/bad guy dichotomy fails utterly to capture its nuances, regardless of who is designated good or bad. And shooters' usual solution to the violence problem—citizen armament for the good guys and the occasional "get tough" laws that increase sentencing for various crimes—concentrates solely on short-term, individually based solutions to complex, deeply entrenched socioeconomic conditions that are profoundly interwoven with the American violent crime problem. Although there may be truth to shooters' arguments that widespread citizen armament is more egalitarian than reliance on gun controls like discretionary licensing or bans on "junk guns," eventually shooters' arguments do little toward finding adequate solutions to why American society is plagued by violent gun crime. When shooters fail to seriously consider how and why violence is really occurring, and dismiss the problem as not their concern, they affirm for their critics that they don't really care about violence in American society. If shooters really are going to continue to argue that "Guns don't kill people, people kill people," then shooters need to start thinking about and investing in *people*.

As I mentioned, gun control supporters often talk about how many people are shot with guns and how many people die by gunshot. These statistics and figures are indeed one of the concrete realities of guns in the United States, and they are the tragic and horrible evidence of the power of guns. But these figures tell only one part of the story. On the other side are the individuals who use guns to defend themselves. There are numbers attached to this concept as well, but this is a social reality that is far more difficult to measure and concretize. Most incidents of defensive gun use leave no material trace (i.e., no body count to total) because those who use guns for self-defense rarely need to fire those guns, much less kill or even wound their attackers.[41]

When respected criminologists Gary Kleck and Mark Gertz quantified the number of defensive gun uses per year, gun enthusiasts felt their arguments had finally been validated. Finally, they were vindicated! Kleck and Gertz's figure of 2.5 million defensive gun uses per year made plain to gun enthusiasts that there was indeed a way for them to prove the social value of guns and prove that guns are used regularly to thwart crime and save lives.[42]

I do not want to quarrel with the ways this research has validated the subjective experiences of gun owners; however, arguing that there is indeed a right number of defensive gun uses per year no more advances the gun debate than does the gun controllers' argument about gun-related fatalities. The idea that there is an actual number of times that Americans use guns defensively is discussed by both criminologists and public health researchers as if discovering what that number might be would either prove that there is indeed some social benefit to private gun ownership, or alternatively, prove there is no such benefit (and thus there is only the social deficit of injury and fatality). But how many times must Americans use guns defensively before such benefit is illustrated? Would 100,000 times illustrate a benefit, or must the number reach 1 or 2 million? If the exact number of defensive gun uses is far lower than any of the estimates thus far (leaving the data on injury and fatality the only "true" gun-related statistics), would gun ownership in private hands constitute a social deficit? How should researchers, much less gun owners, think about the "positive" or "beneficial" versus the "negative" or "detrimental" aspects of this debate?[43]

This is a particularly important issue when one realizes that there is no reliable way to quantify how guns are valued as a symbol. If we focus only on the material value of guns, and how many people are saved or killed by guns, does that mean that the symbolic value of guns does not matter? Criminologists and social scientists have tended not to focus on the symbolic value of guns (perhaps because there is no reliable way to quantify that value), but gun control supporters (especially public health advocates) pretend that the symbolic value of guns simply doesn't exist. Or worse, that this symbolic value is of negligible consequence. This is downright silly. At the risk of stating the obvious, guns have enormous symbolic value to gun enthusiasts. Pretending that this value is nonexistent, meaningless, or inconsequential is a mistake that only gun control supporters make, usually to their serious political detriment.

The number of 2.5 million defensive gun uses a year is a powerful one, and if correct would illustrate that guns are used on an everyday basis to ward off crime. But not surprisingly, this number is criticized by other respected criminologists as an overestimate, as evidence predominantly of how people may report "false positives." False positives are instances in which people report that they used a gun defensively but didn't, or report instances in which they imagine that their guns were useful, but in fact they overestimate the danger they were in to begin with.[44] Although Cook and Ludwig make these arguments while acknowledging that Kleck and Gertz have provided some form of quantification of defensive gun use, they are ostensibly arguing that in the absence of material evidence that these events occurred, there is good reason to be skeptical about researchers' ability to accurately measure the subjective experience of gun owners. Cook and Ludwig are not necessarily intending to slight gun owners, they are simply arguing that people more generally tend to exaggerate, misconstrue, misunderstand, or generally misrepresent the nature of their subjective experience.[45]

While Cook and Ludwig offer a reasonable critique of Kleck and Gertz's figure, Kleck and Gertz offer just as persuasive a rebuttal.[46] In any case, no part of this argument really addresses the issue for shooters (except insofar as it confirms their belief that some academics are politically compromised). The reason is simple. Shooters are very aware of events in which "real" defensive gun use takes place. They reaffirm what they already know through a variety of sources. NRA publications like *American Hunter* and *American Rifleman* run the column "The Armed Citizen" every month. Small, local (mostly conservative) newspapers run stories about individuals who use guns to thwart robberies or break-ins all the time. Down at the shooting range or at the local gun store, shooters tell stories among themselves about crimes that were prevented by defensive gun use. The national news might not be interested in defensive gun use by citizens, but these stories are regular fodder for more local venues, and as such they get around one way or another.

But these stories of actual defensive gun use are not the only important factor here. Shooters also tell stories about crimes that *almost* happened, crimes that *could* have happened, and crimes that *might* occur in the future. These stories are told in everyday settings: at the dinner table, at a local picnic, or at the range. They are in effect cautionary tales with very obvious moral ramifications. These stories tell of *potential* crimes, would-be happenings that illustrate the necessity of being armed just as powerfully as stories of crimes that have actually occurred. Would-be crimes are also ones that demand of shooters not only foresight, vigilance, and toughness, but a willingness to literally and figuratively be on guard, ready to defend themselves and their gun rights. This is true because despite the fact that would-be crimes have not occurred, they help project shooters into a possible future (or an alternative past) where guns are always helpful, always necessary. In these ways, guns are tools for fantasy and imagination. By envisioning pasts or futures in which guns were or could be important and helpful, shooters affirm for themselves the "real" value of their guns.

As I've discussed, a good deal of the gun debate revolves around subjectivity of experience. Guns are valued (or hated) in ways that can never really have a number or a statistic attached. But the subjectivity of the gun debate does not make the horrors of guns or the value of them any less real or important to the people who are so deeply, emotionally invested in this debate. Gun control supporters' disregard for the question of defensive gun use demonstrates that they're not interested in the numbers of times that guns are used defensively. For gun control supporters, defensive gun use denotes an attempt to prevent violence with violence, or threats of violence, which is a morally unacceptable tactic for fighting crime. For that reason, even if criminologists and gun enthusiasts could find a way to confirm without a doubt that guns are effectively used to prevent crime and violence, real antigun liberals are never going to find this an acceptable reason to not restrict guns.

How Gun Control Supporters Can Advance the Gun Debate

Many of the attacks on gun ownership that are published by gun control supporters are remarkably counterproductive to the gun control cause. This is largely because insulting, ridiculing, or attempting to shame and humiliate gun owners alienates gun owners, who only end up even more disgusted by the idea of gun control. Of course, it's possible that gun owners or their sympathizers are not the target audience of gun control advocates. If control advocates are only trying to reach people who already support gun control, and the point of such tactics is to amuse or rouse the passions of this already established constituency, then presumably these tactics are accomplishing their goal. These control supporters probably know that hardcore pro-gun ideologues are a lost cause anyway. But presumably there is an audience sitting on the fence, open to being persuaded by a reasonable point of view toward new gun controls. If that's the audience gun controllers are trying to reach, then I suggest that gun control supporters are underestimating the way their rhetoric alienates this reachable group of people.

Stop Demonizing Gun Owners

Current debate tactics—subjecting gun owners to belittlement and allusions to their inadequacies as human beings—are not advancing the gun debate. If nothing else, they are just proving to shooters that gun control supporters have no respect for gun owners. Shooters get this point loud and clear. So, they reason, if these gun controllers and their favored politicians had any more power, *of course* they'd take our guns away, *of course* they'd make our lives a living hell. They've already demonstrated that they don't give a damn about what we think or feel. And shooters proceed to block any new gun control legislation and lobby long and hard against pro-control politicians. One criminologist calls this entire social process "poisoning the well for gun control."[47] When gun control supporters make their arguments in such virulent terms or treat gun owners like pariahs, why evince surprise when gun enthusiasts don't trust them to be honest or respectful should they obtain enough political power to enact new gun controls?

Discontinuing these tactics of public ridicule would go a long way toward establishing better faith with gun owners more generally. What would happen if a liberal politician actually publicly stated that he or she realized that gun owners owned their guns legitimately, and did so in a long and well-established tradition of American citizenship and civic pride? That gun owners too want to reduce gun violence, and that his or her administration welcomed an opportunity to meet and speak with gun owners to hear their suggestions about making the legal gun market safer and more rigorously defended against illegal buying and selling? I realize how unlikely it is that liberal politicians would be willing to concede the basic framework that provides them with the benefits of a certain hardcore antigun constituency, and who argue that compromise in the gun debate means selling out to dirty, ugly, dangerous people. I also realize that gun owners are not going to trust "no-good liberals" and gun control–oriented politicians that easily. It's not difficult to understand why they feel that way. But in the next section, I argue that another tactic is to actually converse with gun owners, which I believe will pave the way for good faith efforts.

Use Local and Neighborhood Gun Owners as Resources in the Gun Debate

Americans own over 250 million guns.[48] But it's not just that Americans own a lot of guns. A lot of Americans own them. Chances are there are at least a few gun owners, or gun-owning families, in every town, city, and county in the United States. Chances are that most supporters of gun control are well-acquainted with at least one person who owns a gun and considers himself or herself a gun enthusiast. Instead of relying on letters to the editor in the national media or sound bites from the NRA to explain what constitutes gun enthusiasm or pro-gun ideology, perhaps gun control supporters should simply ask their friends and neighbors. If people begin honest dialogues with others they are predisposed to trust, then they also might be less interested in taking a hard-line position with regard to the entire gun debate.

Many people (especially children) are fascinated with or frightened by guns because they don't know anything about guns. In the absence of parents introducing their children to guns safely and in a controlled environment, asking neighborhood police or firearms experts to give children and young adults a rundown about what guns do, how they work, and why children shouldn't touch them unless under controlled circumstances might go a long way to dispelling the myths and fantasies that are attached to such seductive, powerful things. The absence of real, constructive information does not promote lack of interest in guns, only ignorance about their dangerousness.

Reconnect Gun Control to Measures That Do Not Simply Penalize Gun Owners

This last point is troublesome because many gun enthusiasts make the argument that there is no such thing as gun control that doesn't radically inconvenience or penalize them. But to a large extent, this is an unreasonable argument, and moderates on both sides should recognize and reject it. One way to begin to separate the quality from the dross in new gun control proposals is to think about what each piece of legislation aims to accomplish and whether it can conceivably achieve its goals. Gun control supporters should make a real effort to research the gun control policies they support because some policies are more well-designed than others, and some are designed simply to disarm the poor and most vulnerable. Despite the fact that many gun control supporters undoubtedly think general disarmament is a good idea, are they really interested in policies that basically selectively disarm people like poor blacks, battered women, and gay activists?

I was in the San Francisco Bay Area for the first Million Mom March, and I went to the Oakland site to watch and listen to marchers and activists speak publicly and among themselves about gun control. Clearly, people cared deeply about the issue of violence in their community, and the extent to which many individuals were grieving lost relatives or friends to gun-related violence made the march that much more poignant and meaningful. I met a woman who carried a poster of a daughter who had been shot, and everywhere someone had a story about an incident or a "near miss" involving a shooting. People were grieving together. In this sense, the gathering was enormously positive, a very constructive way to enable people to collectively mourn, empathize, and comfort each other in the wake of ongoing violence in the community and nation.

But I was also struck by the extent to which people were using the notion of gun crime to describe such a diversity of happenings in the community. Gun crime was a gang shooting, a shocking suicide, a store robbery that someone heard about, and the horrifying murder of a teenage daughter. Gun crime was a totalizing phenomenon, anything and everything involving guns, regardless of context. In this sense, the term gun crime has become a kind of metaphor for tragic losses in people's lives, their fear of violence and chaos in their communities. Because those anxious feelings ultimately generate rage and grief, gun crime has become the target for that rage and grief. This isn't surprising: the concept of gun crime is just flexible enough, just abstract enough, to embrace a host of diverse and painful emotions. Blaming gun crime means *not* blaming a particular person (in some cases, there is no specific person to blame), but rather something that would otherwise seem too large and incomprehensible to grasp or address directly. Terms like gun crime make abstract and diverse phenomena concrete, identifiable, a "thing" that can be contained and eventually eradicated.

In this vein, the concept of gun crime is similar to the concept of gun control. Gun control is also broad and flexible enough to complement the equally broad concept of gun crime. In this sense, gun control has become a kind of panacea for the pain, anger, and grief that is generated by gun crime. I've alluded to this issue before, and nowhere was it more apparent than at the Million Mom March. As an event that empowered people to come together to express their grief and anger over the chaotic and incomprehensible, the Million Mom March was a brilliant and powerful phenomenon. But when the talk got more specific about gun control, things started to unravel.

I asked several people what they considered to be sensible gun controls that would help reduce gun crime and gun violence. Most said licensing and registration of handguns. When I asked why this would help reduce gun crime, more often than not I encountered blank faces and a few halting replies that touched on the literature and pamphlets that organizers had provided. People informed me that licensing and registration keeps track of the guns that go into the community and allows the police to more effectively do their job. These explanations generally exhausted people's answers for why this kind of gun control would reduce gun crime and violence. It's possible that people (and organizers) at the march had other, more concrete answers for why licensing and registration would reduce gun violence, but I wasn't privy to those answers. I was struck by the extent to which these notions of gun control were making people feel quite positive and empowered, but *how* these proposed gun control laws were going to produce change was apparently not terribly important, even to those who loudly expressed support for these laws.

In fact, a number of criminologists do support licensing and registration of guns, particularly handguns, for several reasons.[49] One is that licensing and registration would facilitate identification of consistent straw buyers, those individuals who purchase guns legally but then resell them illegally to prohibited buyers. Another is that registration would help identify those dealers who knowingly and consistently sell in bulk to straw buyers. Law enforcement officials would be able to see patterns emerging that would indicate who buys in bulk, who sells in bulk, and where those guns end up before and after crimes are committed with those guns. Although licensing and registration is relatively politically untenable on a federal level, supporters have made strong cases for how and why such tactics could effectively reduce the amount of illegal firearms that flow to dangerous individuals and into vulnerable communities.[50]

However, criminologists have also noted that the gun control movement, which has traditionally supported licensing and registration, has never matched the power and grassroots support of the gun lobby, which does not support it. One reason that this kind of gun control does not have the necessary public support is that control advocates send confused and conflicting messages about what it can accomplish, and control advocates have not effectively persuaded substantial numbers of voters that their proposed policies will concretely reduce criminal activity with guns.[51]

Also, gun control policies that were supposed to address criminal gun use have also been used to confiscate legally purchased, registered guns from noncriminal gun owners. Gun enthusiasts are aware that in some cases, registration has indeed led to confiscation, primarily because the guns that were legally purchased and registered were subsequently made illegal, and then confiscated by officials who used registration lists to track the guns.[52] Some gun control supporters have then argued, Well, too bad if that happens. But those control supporters are really only exemplifying why gun enthusiasts have good reason not to trust them or trust gun control policies involving registration. What's unfortunate about this entire issue is that there is a lot of time wasted on suggested policy that isn't likely to pass, and little time spent addressing some of the already working projects that could be adopted (both entirely and in part) on larger scales than they already are. I discuss these options below.

How Gun Enthusiasts Can Advance the Gun Debate

Recently, gun enthusiasts and pro-gun advocates have been handed enormous victories in the gun debate from a wide variety of corners. The election of pro-gun president George W. Bush and his appointment of John Ashcroft to attorney general (a pro-gun politician who has made his support for the NRA flagrantly clear) have ensured that gun control will not be high on the list of priorities for that administration.[53] The various lawsuits against the gun industry, touted as gun control's Great White Hope because they would presumably hold the industry accountable for guns that fall into dangerous or criminal hands, have not been meeting with great success in the courts. A number of the cities, counties, and special interests groups that have lodged those suits have already lost their cases.[54]

There is also the ongoing problem that a substantial number of Americans do not consider gun control (however it is construed) to be an issue important enough to sway their vote to politicians who build a platform on the issue.[55] So, while there will always be a fairly substantial number of Americans who consider preserving their gun rights to be a single voting issue, the same cannot be said to the same extent about gun control. All of these things bolster gun enthusiasts' position to prevent more gun control from being enacted in the near future.

Recognize the Power of the Emerson Decision to Preserve
Basic Gun Rights and Accept the Win Graciously

One of the most powerful weapons in shooters' arsenal is the *Emerson* decision, which could potentially have enormous impact on the future of gun
control politics on a national scale. The facts of this case are as follows: Dr.
Timothy Joe Emerson was indicted in 1998 for possessing guns while under
a restraining order to not threaten his wife, who was in the process of di-
vorcing him.[56] He moved to dismiss the indictment on the basis that the restraining order violated his Second Amendment rights to own a gun, including a handgun. In 1999, a federal judge in Lubbock, Texas asserted that
Emerson's Second Amendment rights had indeed been violated. However,
the government appealed the decision. The appeal was heard in New Or-
leans by the United States Court of Appeals for the 5th Circuit, and the majority decision stated that the Second Amendment did indeed confer an
individual right to own a gun. The court's ruling, which sets law only for
Mississippi, Louisiana, and Texas, also said that although this is indeed an
individual right, that right is not absolute. The ruling stated that Second
Amendment rights are subject to certain restrictions and limitations, including a domestic restraining order, which effectively allowed the courts to
disarm Dr. Emerson. Constitutional scholar Lawrence H. Tribe argues that
the decision would likely both please and displease activists on either side
of the debate, but the decision was a rational one.[57]

This is an important court decision, one with several ramifications for the
gun debate. A powerful federal court has now decreed that Americans have
a constitutionally protected individual right to own a gun. Although this ruling does not preclude the passing of gun control measures, the decision was
undoubtedly a great disappointment to gun control supporters, although
some are cleverly pointing out the strengths in the ruling for their position
vis-à-vis the gun debate.[58] In any case, the broader ramification of this decision is that Americans now have a recognized individual right to own guns,
clearly asserted by an important federal court. This Second Amendment
right is not absolute, but it never has been, as most gun enthusiasts (and pro-
gun advocates) already widely recognize. Gun rights do not need to be absolute in order to provide a wide variety of Americans with the ability to
legally own a variety of guns with a relative minimum of paperwork and restrictions.

But what the *Emerson* decision also means is that gun enthusiasts, and in particular the NRA, no longer need to argue an absolutist stance against any and all new forms of gun control legislation. The NRA has traditionally argued that most (if not all) gun control is dangerous because it will lead the United States down the "slippery slope" to eventual gun confiscation.[59] But because of the *Emerson* decision, future confiscation by local or federal authorities is highly unlikely.[60] Again, a significant federal court has now recognized that Americans have an unambiguous Second Amendment right to own guns. This is the kind of legal protection that would effectively prevent what gun enthusiasts foresee as the "worst-case scenarios" of gun control, which are that gun ownership is made entirely illegal (through incrementally passed bans or restrictions), or that authorities are able to confiscate all currently held guns (by making use of registration lists and confiscating guns that are suddenly made illegal).[61]

With the *Emerson* decision in place, gun control policies that could effectively reduce or prevent gun trafficking, as well as policies that provide law enforcement officials with the means to track "crime guns," are *not* necessarily policies that endanger legal gun owners. For example, if and when gun dealers on a national scale were forced to keep records of sales that could be made available to law enforcement authorities (as they are in California), and authorities tried to confiscate legally owned guns without adequate legal cause, then gun owners would theoretically be able to argue that their Second Amendment rights were being violated. There is now case law that protects them.

There are now undoubtedly activists and advocates who are seeking to overturn certain kinds of controls already in place that do indeed violate individuals' Second Amendment rights. But an equally constructive project would be for gun enthusiasts and pro-gun advocacy groups like the NRA and Gun Owners of America to think constructively about how they can contribute to a body of law that continues to sanctify the rights of gun owners, but also more effectively prohibits dangerous and criminal gun use, which is particularly rampant in areas of the nation that are extraordinarily underserved anyway. I address this issue below.

Recognize That the *Emerson* Ruling Allows for the Existence of Beneficial Gun Control Policies

In fact, there are a number of firearms researchers who are sympathetic to gun owners and the notion of defensive gun use, but who also support certain kinds of gun control legislation. These researchers believe that some gun control policies can effectively reduce or help prevent gun-related crime.

These researchers notably include Gary Kleck, who has offered several important and realistic suggestions, including more rigorous and effective laws that regulate the private sales of guns among nonprofessional dealers.[62] Hardened pro-gun advocates argue that these laws are a hassle for otherwise law-abiding gun owners, who just want to sell or trade guns among themselves. But there has to be a point at which gun owners concede that guns that are in the wrong hands are dangerous, and they would therefore be willing to put up with some hassles to help reduce gun-related crimes and violence.

The example of unregulated private gun sales is a good one. This is a serious problem in relation to gun crime; there is strong evidence that crime guns are purchased through informal, third-party channels.[63] This problem could be addressed by regulating nonprofessional gun transfers and penalizing people who circumvent professional dealers. Several criminologists have discussed and outlined how such laws could operate, as have other academics and policymakers interested in reducing illegal gun possession.[64] If trustworthy academics and researchers support such efforts, shooters would be well-served to also recognize their value. These are gun control laws that do not eradicate shooters' ability to purchase firearms. These laws would not attack basic gun rights.[65] Although they do limit avenues for gun purchasing slightly, they do so only by requiring that sellers and purchasers go through a professional dealer and pay a nominal fee. The bottom line is that if gun owners are indeed good citizens who uphold the rule of law, then they'll be willing to assist law enforcement efforts that ensure everyone does the same.

Local shooting communities are often familiar with dealers and gun stores that are not always scrupulously honest in their dealings with the public. Many of the shooters I met knew which dealers were engaged in the illegal practice of selling guns to straw buyers. I was constantly surprised that people I knew and dealt with on a regular basis either knew or had suspicions about dealers in the community who were engaged in illegal practice. If such dirty dealing was public knowledge (or quasi-public knowledge), why were shooters not more proactive about notifying local or state authorities?

Shooters may be so distrustful of the government organizations that regulate guns, or have so little faith in organizations like local or national BATF (Bureau of Alcohol, Tobacco, and Firearms) offices more generally, that they don't want to have any contact with those organizations. Alternatively, shooters may not want to call attention to their own gun ownership practices by reporting the unscrupulous business practices of others, fearing that the general climate of distrust would mean that they make themselves targets of law enforcement unnecessarily. If this is the case, it's unfortunate, because dealers and individuals who engage in illegally buying and selling guns damage the *entire* gun-owning community. This is yet another area where it's in shooters' best interests to attempt to halt such practices in their community. Perhaps open, honest, "good faith" outreach by local and state BATF offices to the gun-owning community more generally (not just with dealers and store owners, but also sports people and general enthusiasts) would facilitate the community's working more closely to prevent illegal gun activities.

Finally, there have been a number of projects developed in the past several years that are enormously promising in their capacity to reduce youth violence, gang violence, and gun crime more generally. One of the most impressive and sophisticated of these is the Boston Gun Project, also knows as Operation Cease Fire.[66] The Boston Gun Project is the invention of Harvard professor of public policy David Kennedy, who began in the mid-1990s to work in concert with the Boston Police Department, youth outreach coordinators, and community activists who work with inner-city youth and gang members. Kennedy's approach was to unite the efforts of all of these agencies and individuals and disrupt the patterns of violent gun crime that was substantially contributing to Boston's homicide rates. After working extensively with the police and local BATF, Kennedy was able to learn that there were several particular dealers who regularly sold guns to straw buyers (thereby contributing vastly to the guns illegally bought and sold on the street). This was one method by which the project was able to identify and disrupt the availability of guns that were quickly finding their way into dangerous hands.

Kennedy also advocated the "pulling levers" approach to addressing the youth violence issue. Working with community activists and gang specialists, he held meetings with local gang members and youth considered at risk for committing violent crime. Community activists and outreach workers discussed with youth how their dangerous behavior was hurting them, hurting their families and friends, and damaging the community, physically and in terms of morale. Also important, the project members discussed with these youth the ramifications of the highly dangerous behavior that only some of them were engaged in: all the participants were informed that homicidal behavior would not be tolerated, it would be federally criminalized, and all of the project's separate agencies (the police, the BATF, and community services organizations) were going to throw their weight behind making those offenders' lives uncomfortable until the violent behavior stopped. Individuals who were engaging in the most violent behavior were identified by the coordinating agencies, and swift intervention and adjudication followed the most violent, dangerous acts. All of the youth involved in the program (and in the community) witnessed what happened to those individuals who were engaged in the most violent behavior, which acted as a substantial deterrent to further violence and eventually lower-level activities as well.[67]

The Boston Gun Project has been enormously successful in helping to reduce homicide in Boston: since its inception, the program is credited with helping reduce homicide rates by 70 percent in that city.[68] It has been supported by the NRA, particularly because the project does not address the question of gun rights or argue for broad-scale gun control policies targeting a wide variety of people in order to net a few.[69] The project is now spawning similar programs in other cities as well.[70]

One of the strongest aspects of this program is that it combines the best and most empirically supported aspects of both liberal and conservative ideology in terms of addressing violent behavior. The program combined the efforts of a number of government and community agencies, and illustrated that those agencies could work together effectively to address the concerns of both. The program thereby made use of local and more regional information sources and knowledge bases to address a local problem with regional significance. The project leaders and coordinators dealt with young people in the community with dignity, respect, and foresight, ostensibly pointing out to these young people that their conduct was contributing to the pain and deterioration of not only the community but their families and themselves. The project coordinators communicated the point that these young people have options and violent behavior has consequences, which would be felt in all areas of their lives. The youth involved were not punished unduly nor as a social collective. Nor were they assumed as a collective to be evil or stupid because of the violent behavior of a few in their midst. This program is grounded in basic concepts of assistance and guidance for troubled youth, but it also provides models for action and consequences for behavior.

These are the kinds of programs that shooters in communities across the country should be actively seeking out and supporting, for a host of reasons. This kind of program falls right in line with the best and more idealistic kinds of arguments that shooters shared with me about reducing violence: better law enforcement, recognition that it's not "only about guns," programs targeting the people most at risk for eventually harming themselves and others, and working with individuals who have grounded and specific areas of expertise for reducing crime in a community. But this program could easily be considered part of effective gun control: the project discovered dealers who were engaged in illegal practice, attempted to disrupt gun trafficking, and attempted to slow or stop the activities associated with eventual gun violence.

What these kinds of programs are also doing, without making a big deal about it, is addressing a very needs-hungry community on the inner-city landscape. It is unnecessary and even foolish for shooters to deny that gun violence is a serious problem in America's inner cities, where the majority of the residents are poor and black and cannot rely on safe neighborhoods, security systems, and responsive police to keep them safe. Guns may help protect some of these residents, but not all of them. Why should these particular Americans suffer unduly? When shooters argue that guns are not the problem but then disregard basic issues of lack of jobs, lack of resources, and fairly obvious structural inequalities for the inner-city poor, all in favor of "failed moral character" arguments for why crime occurs, shooters confirm the worst fears of their critics. Shooters are basically arguing that inner-city residents suffer higher rates of gun violence because they live in neighborhoods full of "bad people." This is not an empirical argument but an ideological one, and a bigoted one at that.

This is a point that gun rights advocates could recognize and confront openly, for several reasons. It allows them to effectively beat gun control supporters at their own game by arguing that the best and most effective gun control strategies are the ones that most effectively address violence in the community. Not only that, but these kinds of strategies make use of the law effectively while radically reducing the numbers of guns on the streets, but without being overly punitive or harsh to young people in inner-city neighborhoods more generally.

The best criminological evidence about American violence more generally comes from scholars whom many shooters may hear as liberal, but in fact these scholars have no real beef with guns.[71] These issues include the widening gap between the rich and the poor, structural collapse stemming from unequal distribution of resources (e.g., cutting funding for hospitals, schools, afterschool programs, and job-training programs in already poverty-stricken areas), alcohol and drug abuse, and decay in inner-city urban environments overall.

These are issues that respected criminologists like Gary Kleck, Don Kates, and David Kopel consistently argue lie at the basis of high rates of gun crime. Shooters owe it to themselves and the civil rights movement on which they rest many of their arguments to recognize that punitive social and public policies aimed at the vulnerable urban poor and minority communities work *against* them in the gun debate. Many of the shooters I met and worked with were people who did care about violence in American society, and were invested in trying to understand why that violence occurrs. Thus, when the shooting community votes for politicians who promise to preserve gun rights but also to eradicate social welfare programs or resources for inner-city school districts, shooters are doing themselves *no* favors in relation to their gun rights. Some shooters recognize that fact and are starting to vote accordingly.

Throughout this book I've emphasized the ways that guns are embedded in American society and culture, and discussed the ways that shooters understand that fact. It is therefore time for shooters to work harder to understand why violence occurs as well. Clearly, guns are not the only reason, or perhaps even the "real" reason. But figuring out how to solve the real problems means that the work is just beginning. Shooters should lead the way in this good fight. That is the best way for them to win the gun debate.

Appendix

Gun Enthusiasm: Questions for Semistructured Interview

1. Do you consider yourself a gun enthusiast? How do you define "gun enthusiast"?
2. Do you own guns? If yes, how long have you owned them?
3. How did you become interested in guns?
4. Why do you like guns?
5. What does owning a gun mean to you?
6. Do you associate a certain lifestyle or way of living with owning a gun?
7. Do you think that there is a certain "culture" (define however you like) with owning or using handguns?
8. Do you associate a certain political affiliation with gun ownership? Please describe.
9. Do you use a gun for home protection?
10. If yes, why is this gun appropriate for home protection?
11. Please describe the kinds of situations in which you would actively use your gun and why you'd do so.
12. Have you ever taken any classes to learn how to use your gun safely? How did you learn safe gun usage?
13. Have you ever attended a gun show? If yes, what did you think of it? If no, why not?
14. Are you currently able to purchase the kinds of guns you are interested in shooting?
15. What do you think about our current gun laws?
16. Where do you enjoy practicing to shoot your gun (private or public shooting range; other)?
17. Do you think that men and women use guns differently? How so?

18. Do you think that some guns are more appropriate for women than others?
19. Tell me about all the ways that you express your interest in guns (joining clubs, etc.).
20. What do guns symbolize for you?

Notes

Preface

1. Editorials and opinion pieces employing these terms are numerous. See, for examples, Denis Horgan, "Forget Gun Control: Ban Them Altogether," *Hartford Courant,* 14 May 1999, A2; "NRA Shoots Itself in Both Feet," editorial, *New York Daily News,* 1 May 1999, 20; Robert Scheer, "Pete Wilson's Twisted Logic on Handguns," *Los Angeles Times,* 30 September 1997, B7; Bob Ewegan, "Liar, Liar, Pants on Fire," *Denver Post,* 7 August 2000, B10; "Mothers Know Best," editorial, *New York Daily News,* 13 May 2000, 16; Michael Kramer, "Pataki and Guns: The DNA Solution," *New York Daily News,* 19 March 2000, 49; Amy Pagnozzi, "Gun-Control Plan Is an Empty Shell," *Hartford Courant,* 28 April 1999, A12; Eric Sharpe, "Outdoorsmen Can't Ignore Gun Control," *Los Angeles Daily News,* 11 June 1995, S11. Sharpe is expressing contempt for the idea that civilian gun ownership is a protection against foreign invasion. His exact words are "Maybe the most obvious answer is to point out that if the combined might of the United States Army, Air Force, Coast Guard, Marine Corps and Navy can't preserve our government, a handful of middle-aged fat guys with popguns aren't going to impress an invader much, either." The Media Research Center, a conservative media watchdog, conducted a study analyzing 653 news stories on guns on ABC, CBS, NBC, and CNN from June 1, 1997 to June 30, 1999. The study found that 60 percent of the stories moved beyond reporting to advocacy of a pro-control stance. A description of the study by the Associated Press appeared on January 5, 2000 entitled "Media Accused of Gun Control Bias." See the Media Research Center's Web site, http://www.mediaresearch.org/, specifically its study on guns in the media at http://secure.mediaresearch.org/specialreports/news/sr20000105.html. See also Michael Bane, "Targeting the Media's Anti-Gun Bias," *American Journalism Review* 23 (July/Aug 2001): 18. For the best analysis to date on the negative tone of the media coverage of the NRA, and that tone's effect on the gun rights movement, see Brian Anse Patrick, *The National Rifle Association and the Media: The Motivating Force of Negative Coverage* (New York: Peter Lang, 2003). For examples of negative coverage, see "The Scourge of Guns," editorial, *New York Times,* 5 Septem-

ber 2000, A30; Bob Herbert, "Addicted to Guns," *New York Times,* 1 January 2001, A17; Richard Cohen, "Good Parents, Bad Kids: And Far Too Many Handguns," op-ed, *Washington Post,* 8 March 2001, A21; "Illegal Guns and the District," editorial, *Washington Post,* 3 June 2001, A18.

2. Mark Morford, "Pistol-Packin' Polyester," *San Francisco Gate,* 21 March 2001, http://sfgate.com/cgi-bin/article.cgi?file=/gate/archive/2001/03/21/notes032101.DTL, accessed May 15, 2003; Mark Simon, "Gun Control/Myth of a 'Well-Regulated Militia'/Second Amendment: A Loaded Question," *San Francisco Chronicle,* 1 July 2001, D3.

3. Historian Jackson Lears writing for *Newsday* describes the NRA as a cult that worships and fetishizes guns and masculinity: "Guns' Mystique Clouds Debate," *Newsday,* 27 March 2001, A36. For similar sentiments, see Thomas J. McCarthy, "Whatever I Want: The Freedom to Wield a Gun Symbolizes Our Twisted National Desideratum," *America* 181 (25 September 1999): 6. See Bryant Gumbel, *The Early Show,* CBS, 1 April 2000; Media Research Center, "Notable Quotables" 13, no. 7, http://www.mediaresearch.org/news/nq/2000/nq20000401.html, accessed 3 February 2004; Garry Wills, "Murderers at One Remove," *Baltimore Sun,* 6 September 1994, 11A.

4. This is the underlying theme in most of the publications cited here. This position is articulated particularly clearly by Jann S. Wenner, writing in the *Los Angeles Times,* who lists and dismisses all other factors for motivating violent behavior except gun availability: "If You're Looking for a Scapegoat, Try NRA," *Los Angeles Times,* 21 May 1999, B7.

5. See, for examples, Peter Cummings and Thomas Koepsell, "Does Owning a Firearm Increase or Decrease the Risk of Death?" *Journal of the American Medical Association* 280, no. 5 (1998): 471–473; Arthur L. Kellermann and Donald T. Reay, "Protection or Peril? An Analysis of Firearms-Related Deaths in the Home," *New England Journal of Medicine* 314 (1986): 1557–1560; Arthur L. Kellermann, F. P. Rivara, N. B. Rushforth, et al., "Gun Ownership as a Risk Factor for Homicide in the Home," *New England Journal of Medicine* 329, no. 15 (1993): 1084–1091. See Amitai Etzioni, "Are Liberal Scholars Acting Irresponsibly on Gun Control?" *Chronicle of Higher Education,* 6 April 2001, B14. Interestingly, Etzioni apparently assumes that conservative scholars are inherently irresponsible about gun control by virtue of their presumed stance against it. Garry Wills penned a scathing critique of the work of "Standard Modelers," those scholars who see an individual right in the Second Amendment: "To Keep and Bear Arms," *New York Times Review of Books* 42 (21 September 1995): 62–73. The scholars who take an individual rights position on the Second Amendment (the position called the Standard Model) and are the target of Wills's attack include Stephen P. Halbrook, *A Right to Bear Arms* (Westport, CT: Greenwood Press, 1989); Don B. Kates Jr., "The Second Amendment and the Ideology of Self-Protection," *Constitutional Commentary* 9 (1992): 87–104; Glenn Harlan Reynolds, "A Critical Guide to the Second Amendment," *Tennessee Law Review* 62, no. 3 (1995): 461–512. See Wendy Brown, "Guns, Cowboys, Philadelphia Mayors, and

Civic Republicanism: On Sanford Levinson's 'The Embarrassing Second Amendment,'" *Yale Law Review* 99 (1989): 661–667; Lauren Snider, "Toward Safer Societies: Punishment, Masculinities and Violence against Women," *British Journal of Criminology* 38, no. 1 (1998): 1–39; Andrew Herz, "Gun Crazy: Constitutional False Consciousness and the Dereliction of Dialogic Responsibility," *Boston University Law Review* 75 (1995): 57–153.

6. However, my advisors and dissertation committee members did not express any prejudice against gun owners. They were outspokenly open-minded, and I appreciated their fairness and support throughout my research.

7. See, for example, Bane, "Targeting the Media's Anti-Gun Bias"; Bernard Goldberg, "On Media Bias, Network Stars Are Rather Clueless," *Wall Street Journal,* 24 May 2001, A22; Thomas McIntyre, "Attacking Gun Owners," *Sports Afield* 224 (December 2000/January 2001): 28–29.

8. Quoted in Richard Cohen, "Heaven Help the Gun Nuts," *Washington Post,* 23 March 2000, A29.

9. Ibid.

10. Don B. Kates, introduction to *Armed: New Perspectives on Gun Control,* G. Kleck and D. B. Kates, eds. (Amherst, NY: Prometheus, 2001), 13–30.

11. Historians and scholars who make this point include Robert Cottrol, "The Second Amendment: Invitation to a Multi-Dimensional Debate," in *Gun Control and the Constitution: Sources and Explorations on the Second Amendment,* R. J. Cottrol, ed. (New York: Garland, 1994), ix–xviii; Leonard Williams Levy, *Origins of the Bill of Rights* (New Haven, CT: Yale University Press, 1999); Joyce Lee Malcolm, *To Keep and Bear Arms: The Origins of an Anglo-American Right* (Cambridge, MA: Harvard University Press, 1994). It's important to point out, however, that there is hardly a consensus within the discipline of history about the meaning of the Second Amendment. For a strong volume offering perspectives on both sides of the issue, see S. Cornell and R. E. Shalhope, eds., *Whose Right to Bear Arms Did the Second Amendment Protect?* (Bedford, NY: St. Martin's, 2000), and for a fair-minded consideration of several important issues in the debate, see Robert E. Shalhope, "To Keep and Bear Arms in the Early Republic," *Constitutional Commentary* 16 (1999): 269–281.

12. See Gary Kleck, *Targeting Guns: Firearms and Their Control* (Hawthorne, NY: Aldine de Gruyter, 1997), 70–72; James D. Wright, "Ten Essential Observations on Guns in America," in *Guns in America: A Reader,* J. E. Dizard, R. M. Muth, and S. P. Andrews Jr., eds. (New York: New York University Press, 1999), 500–507; Gary Kleck and Marc Gertz, "Armed Resistance to Crime: The Prevalence and Nature of Self-defense with a Gun," *Journal of Criminal Law and Criminology* 86 (1995): 150–187.

13. See James Wright, Peter Rossi, and Kathleen Daly, *Under the Gun: Weapons, Crime, and Violence in America* (Hawthorne, NY: Aldine de Gruyter, 1983); James D. Wright, "Second Thoughts about Gun Control," in *The Gun Control Debate: You Decide,* L. Nisbet, ed. (Buffalo, NY: Prometheus, 1990), 93–107. For a rigorous and sophisticated discussion of the efficacy (or lack thereof, in some cases) of various forms

of gun control, see James B. Jacobs, *Can Gun Control Work?* (New York: Oxford University Press, 2002).

14. It's important to point out that some academics and researchers are also unabashedly pro-gun advocates. Examples include Robert Cottrol, Don B. Kates, and David Kopel. I do not mean to suggest, however, that their pro-gun stance compromises their scholarly integrity. Many scholars who take positions on this issue are able to maintain high standards of scholarship, as do the preceding three scholars. For the positions of various pro- and antigun academics, activists, and social critics, see Marjolijn Bijlefeld, *People For and Against Gun Control: A Biographical Reference* (Westport, CT: Greenwood Press, 1999).

15. I realize there's a certain irony to making this statement after the publication of Michael Bellesiles's highly controversial *Arming America: The Origins of the National Gun Culture* (New York: Knopf, 2000). However, this work was enormously contested, and critic after critic has managed to demonstrate empirically that colonial and frontier Americans did own guns in substantial numbers. Thus, it's fair to say that guns were an integral part of early American history. For analyses of and rebuttals to Bellesiles's work, see Robert Churchill, "Guns and the Politics of History," *Reviews in American History* 29 (2001): 329–337; James D. Lindgren and Justin Heather, "Counting Guns in Early America," *William and Mary Law Review* 43 (2002): 1777–1842; Gloria L. Main, "Many Things Forgotten: The Use of Probate Records in Arming America," *William and Mary Quarterly*, 3 ser. 59 (January 2002): 211–216; Randolph Roth, "Guns, Gun Culture, and Homicide: The Relationship between Firearms, the Uses of Firearms, and Interpersonal Violence," *William and Mary Quarterly*, 3 ser. 59 (January 2002): 223–240.

Chapter 1. Introduction: Guns in America

1. To protect the confidentiality of the individuals I met and interviewed, I use pseudonyms for all of the people and places I describe.

2. There is a vast and rich literature on the issue of socialization into gun ownership and the geographic regions in which individuals are inducted into cultures with pro-gun values. For example, Lizotte and colleagues have documented evidence of subcultural explanations of gun ownership for sport: Alan Lizotte, David J. Bordua, and Carolyn S. White, "Firearms Ownership for Sport and Protection: Two Not So Divergent Models," *American Sociological Review* 46 (1981): 499–503. Jo Dixon and Alan Lizotte found evidence that males living in and raised in the South are more likely to own guns than those raised or living outside the South: "Gun Ownership and the 'Southern Subculture of Violence,'" *American Journal of Sociology* 93, no. 2 (1987): 383–405. Gary Kleck sums up the literature by stating that "the pattern of evidence as a whole is fully compatible with the thesis that gun ownership is a product of socialization into a rural hunting culture. The findings support a simple explanation of the high level of gun ownership in the United States" (*Targeting Guns*, 85).

3. Kleck, *Targeting Guns*, 82–85.

4. Ibid.

5. An excellent description of ethnography as method comes from Michael H. Agar, *The Professional Stranger: An Informal Introduction to Ethnography* (San Diego, CA: Academic Press, 1980).

6. J. P. Spradley, *The Ethnographic Interview* (New York: Holt, Rinehart & Winston, 1979), cited in Janice M. Morse and Peggy Ann Field, "An Overview of Qualitative Methods," in *Qualitative Research Methods for Health Professionals* (Thousand Oaks, CA: Sage, 1995), 21–41.

7. See Jack Katz, "Ethnography's Warrants," *Sociological Methods and Research* 25, no. 4 (1997): 391–423.

8. Gary Kleck's *Targeting Guns* provides an encyclopedic review of the extensive criminological literature on firearms and their ownership.

9. Katz, "Ethnography's Warrants."

10. Ibid. For further discussions on the legitimacy and relevance of ethnography to social science research more generally, see Robert A. Stebbins and William Shaffir, *Experiencing Fieldwork: An Insider View of Qualitative Research* (Thousand Oaks, CA: Sage, 1991), especially 1–23.

11. Because of the variation and diversity of what has been described as America's gun culture, it's important to recognize that this book contributes to the social science research on guns by considering *one aspect* of America's gun culture and by discussing *one subgroup* of American gun owners: those predominantly white, middle-class individuals who self-identify as gun enthusiasts, live in a largely urban environment in the West, own guns legally and recreationally, and form meaningful social collectives around their interests in guns. The individuals interviewed here were contacted as part of an ethnographic study, which means that I did not attempt to contact and interview individuals who would collectively provide a representative sample of gun owners from across the United States.

12. Part of my efforts to understand gun enthusiasm included reading NRA magazines and other publications. However, it's important to keep several caveats in mind with regard to using NRA materials as data. One is that although NRA publications and gun magazines do provide insight into what pro-gun writers, publishers, and the NRA see as the key issues in the gun debate, how shooters read these publications and think about the issues is another matter. I am skeptical that the NRA speaks for all gun enthusiasts on a number of issues. For example, the NRA has taken a very hard line on opposing such things as mandatory trigger locks to be included with all new firearms sold, and has spent a good deal of money to block initiatives in Colorado to close "the gun show loophole" (which ostensibly allows individuals purchasing firearms at a gun show to be exempt from background checks). The individuals with whom I spoke had varying opinions about these kinds of issues, and because there is no gun show loophole in the state of California, this issue was irrelevant for the shooters I interviewed. My point is that al-

though the NRA takes certain stances on some policy issues and makes its opinions known in its publications, it would be unwise to rely on the NRA to provide a unified voice for gun enthusiasts. Shooters are obviously capable of speaking for themselves.

13. Agar, *The Professional Stranger*.

14. Ibid., 11.

15. I see these conflicts as cultural as opposed to sociopolitical because they center on ethical and moral dilemmas, as opposed to ideological differences that have roots in differing visions of history and society. These conflicts point to fundamental differences in the ways Americans interpret their own history, society, moral choices, and culture itself.

16. California has fairly strict firearms laws, particularly compared to neighboring states like Arizona and Nevada. For example, dealers are required to keep records of sales that serve as de facto registration records. There are bans on assault weapons as well as the small, cheap handguns known as Saturday Night Specials. See http://caag.state.ca.us/firearms/ for detailed information about California's firearm laws. For a discussion of the process by which certain firearm laws were enacted in California, see Marcia L. Godwin and Jean Reith Schroedel, "Gun Control Politics in California," in *The Changing Politics of Gun Control*, J. M. Bruce and C. Wilcox, eds. (Lanham, MD: Rowman and Littlefield, 1998), 88–110.

17. See the Web site for this organization, www.bellcampaign.org. The national office is located at San Francisco General Hospital.

18. Janine DeFao, "Mom's March in Oakland Draws 5,000 People," *San Francisco Chronicle,* 15 May 2000, A15.

19. Sociologist William R. Tonso has discussed how the gun culture coexists alongside an "adversary culture," which is hostile to gun ownership. See the introduction to *The Gun Culture and Its Enemies* (Bellevue, WA: Second Amendment Foundation, 1990), 1–5.

20. Donna Horowitz, "East Bay Cities Fight Guns," *San Francisco Examiner,* 9 July 1996, A-3; Carl Ingram and Mark Gladstone, "Davis Urges Timeout on New Gun Bills," *Los Angeles Times,* 1 October 1999), A3. But interestingly, several of the more popular gun shops in the area found their business booming and saw soon-to-be-banned guns practically leaping off the shelves, a point told to me personally by a manager in one of the more well-stocked and well-respected gun shops in the Bay Area.

21. For a discussion of how and why the designation of gun enthusiasts as a pariah group can provide cohesion and group solidarity, see F. Fred Hawley's "Culture Conflict and the Ideology of Pariah Groups: The Weltanschauung of Gun Owners, Southerners and Cockfighters," in Tonso, *The Gun Culture and Its Enemies,* 109–125.

22. I found many interviewees through the process of "snowball sampling," meaning that through participant observation, I met shooters who introduced me to other shooters, and so on. It's possible that there is a subsection of shooters in the area who were not as sociable as the people I met, individuals who prefer to shoot

on private lands instead of at more public sites, and who would be suspicious of being interviewed by a social scientist. Those individuals are obviously not included here. The shooters here were self-selected for the study and necessarily represent the more public face of shooting in the area.

23. I met all of these individuals because they worked on a range, taught a class, or were introduced to me by other shooters.

24. At the time of fieldwork, only one black cowboy shooter regularly participated in the sport in the area.

25. I interviewed only men in this category because I came to know only male shooters in that group. However, I met several women who shot with these men on occasion.

26. I did not observe this event, but it was described to me extensively in interviews and casual conversation.

27. These portraits come from Gary Kleck, *Targeting Guns*, and James Wright et al., *Under the Gun*.

28. However, I did not collect extensive information about income level and degree of educational and professional achievement, the criteria often used by social scientists to denote socioeconomic class. I did not want to ask prying questions about issues not relating to guns. I made educated assumptions about shooters' class status based on what they said they did for a living, how they lived, and how they described themselves in terms of socioeconomic class.

29. Kleck, *Targeting Guns*, 70–72.

30. Kleck reviews the statistics on who owns guns and asserts that conservatives are more likely to own guns than liberals (*Targeting Guns*, 71). In terms of how I assessed shooters' politics, I went about this in a somewhat roundabout fashion. Rather than pointedly asking shooters how they vote and what their political affiliations are, which could be interpreted as rude or invasive, I asked if shooters believed one particular political tradition over another better supported gun rights. This question often led to a shooter's discussion of his or her own politics and many would volunteer a characterization of their political leanings vis-à-vis gun ownership.

31. I may have netted a higher number of liberal shooters because the Bay Area skews liberal.

32. Because I was not trying to measure the extent to which victimization occurred among this population, the efficacy of armed response, or even whether or not their experiences "transformed" them into gun enthusiasts, I did not press shooters to describe these situations or their feelings about them.

33. Interestingly, during only one of these events did the shooter in question actually fire the gun he was using for self-defense. In almost all of the scenarios mentioned, brandishing or verbally threatening to fire the weapon was enough to ward off aggressors or end the attack. For the one shooter who did fire his weapon, he did so fending off an acquaintance who was running at him with a meat cleaver. Some of the shooters stated that they felt their lives had been endangered; others stated that

they were preventing themselves from being mugged or robbed. These incidents do beg the question of the efficacy of self-defensive gun use in the sense that having and brandishing an accessible weapon prevented the intended victim from being further jeopardized. However, for me to assess the *actual* danger that each individual faced would have been impossible. Every individual has a particular take on what constitutes an actual threat, how he or she feels about that threat, what to do about it, and what actually happened from start to finish. Not only would I have offended people had I tried to question whether they were truly in danger, but how does one legitimately assess the question of objective danger from subjective experience? That being said, convincing people that they don't *really* need guns to defend themselves, particularly after they've already done so, would have been an exercise in futility anyway. The shooters who had used their guns defensively were quite certain that those guns had prevented their injury or even death. I would not have felt comfortable trying to convince them otherwise, even if I had felt that way about their experiences. For these reasons, I do not explore whether or not guns are "objectively" useful for defending against crime. In fact, this issue is one that criminologists have explored extensively, so I leave the question of the efficacy of defensive gun use to them. See Kleck, *Targeting Guns*, 147–190, for an extensive discussion of these issues.

34. Mihaly Csikszentmihalyi and Eugene Rochberg-Halton, *The Meaning of Things: Domestic Symbols and the Self* (New York: Cambridge University Press, 1995).

35. Ibid., 84.

36. Don B. Kates also points out that loading and firing modern ammunition can severely damage an older, fragile gun. Collectors who prize not only new, pristine collectors' items may also not want their older, antique guns fired either, but for different reasons (Don B. Kates, personal e-mail communication with the author, 8 April 2003).

37. For a discussion of the sensual pleasures of transgression on a broader scale, see Jack Katz, *Seductions of Crime: A Chilling Exploration of the Criminal Mind— From Juvenile Delinquency to Cold Blooded Murder* (New York: Basic Books, 1990).

38. Barry Bruce-Briggs comments on the use of the cliché and argues that it's a facile one to make because it seems "self-evident." However, he points out that it is never backed with any scholarly data or studies because none exist. See "The Great American Gun War," *Public Interest* 45 (1976): 37–62. Kleck makes the same point in *Targeting Guns*, 81–82.

39. For several examples of this interpretation of gun ownership, see Emmanuel Tanay, "Neurotic Attachment to Guns," which is discussed in Don B. Kates Jr. and Nicole Varzos, "Aspects of the Priapic Theory of Gun Ownership," in Tonso, *The Gun Culture and Its Enemies*, 93–107; and Margo Jefferson, "The Lethal Icon That Is Turning Upon Its Worshippers," *New York Times*, 9 August 1999, B2. Jefferson's comment on this topic is brief, but her distaste for what she considers the dubious masculinity of gun owners is clear.

40. The interest in or eroticization of guns could represent a latent and/or repressed homoeroticism on a larger sociocultural level. However, this point seems

somewhat uninformative, except to note that roughly 73 million Americans, mostly men but a sizable number of women, could therefore be expressing latent homosexuality through their gun ownership.

41. James William Gibson argues that in the 1970s and 1980s, images appeared in popular films and posters depicting "dangerous-looking" women holding guns or knives. In several high-profile films, Gibson argues, soldiers were depicted as loving and fondling their guns, which were likened to "deadly women." Gibson argues that the point was that guns were more trustworthy than actual women, yet both were deadly. Gibson suggests that the point was to celebrate guns and killing while simultaneously disparaging women. See *Warrior Dreams: Violence and Manhood in Post-Vietnam America* (New York: Hill and Wang, 1994), 97–100.

42. As I mentioned, Kleck reviews the literature on the supposed psychopathology of gun owners and finds the contention unsupported in the scholarly literature. See *Targeting Guns*, 81–82.

43. Take, for example, local legislation introduced in the summer of 1999 in Northern California to bar gun shows and anything "associated with gun culture" from being conducted on county property. Alameda County passed such legislation and it was upheld in the courts after the sponsors of a traveling gun show sued the county. See Henry Weinstein, "Federal Court Backs County Ban on Guns," *Los Angeles Times,* 19 February 2003, part 2, p. 6. California also maintains legislation banning so-called Saturday Night Specials. See http://caag.state.ca.us/firearms/ for detailed information about California's firearm laws.

44. See Kleck, *Targeting Guns*, 74–86 for discussion of this issue. Kleck references a survey by Hal Quinley, *Memorandum Reporting Results from Time/CNN Poll of Gun Owners*, 6 February 1990, Yankelovich Clancy Shulman Survey Organization.

45. See David Wagner, *The New Temperance: The American Obsession with Sin and Vice* (Boulder, CO: Westview Press, 1997), 151–165 for a discussion of the politics of pleasure.

46. Hans Toch and Alan J. Lizotte, "Research and Policy: The Case of Gun Control," in *Psychology and Social Policy*, P. Suedfeld and P. E. Tetlock, eds. (New York: Hemisphere, 1992), 235.

47. Gun control advocates like Garry Wills have argued that eradicating the gun culture is an important goal that would reduce gun violence in the United States. See Wills, "Do Not let the Gun Nuts Win," *Las Vegas Review-Journal,* 27 April 1999, 7B. Kleck has argued that one of the implicit goals of the best-known gun control organizations, such as Handgun Control, Inc., has been to eventually prohibit gun ownership altogether, which they see as the strongest way to attack the gun culture. See Gary Kleck, "Absolutist Politics in a Moderate Package: Prohibitionist Intentions of the Gun Control Movement," in *Armed: New Perspectives on Gun Control*, G. Kleck and D. B. Kates Jr., eds. (Amherst, NY: Prometheus, 2003), 129–172.

48. James Wright and Linda Marston, "The Ownership of the Means of Destruction: Weapons in the United States," *Social Problems* 23 (1975): 93–107.

49. Ibid., 99.

50. I state this based on their current gun-related activities, which, taken as a whole, indicate the existence of a self-defined subculture. I did not test whether these shooters were raised in environments with active sporting subcultures, or raised in rural hunting subcultures. Some of them revealed that they were indeed raised in these environments, but I did not ask shooters specific questions about the geographic locales where they were raised, or if they were socialized into gun ownership and use.

51. Of the shooters I interviewed, thirty-five of the thirty-seven stated that they owned guns for protection as well as recreation.

52. Barbara Stenross, "Turning Vices into Virtues: The Dignifying Accounts of Gun Avocationists," in *Marginal Conventions: Popular Culture, Mass Media, and Social Deviance*, C. R. Sanders, ed. (Bowling Green, OH: Bowling Green State University Popular Press, 1990), 56–64.

53. Ibid.

54. See Emile Durkheim, *The Division of Labor in Society*, G. Simpson, trans. (Glencoe, IL: Free Press, 1960); Kai T. Erikson, *Wayward Puritans: A Study in the Sociology of Deviance* (New York: Wiley, 1966); Erich Goode and Nachman Ben-Yehuda, *Moral Panics: The Social Construction of Deviance* (Cambridge, MA: Blackwell, 1994).

55. Although these terms are used in popular discourse and sometimes in the scholarly literature on guns, they usually lack concrete definition or even empirical content, particularly when they are not connected to behavior or context. In terms of the actual behavior of the individuals interviewed in this book, to my knowledge they have not and do not engage in illegal behavior with their guns.

56. This position is held by a number of gun control proponents and public health researchers. See Kellermann and Reay, "Protection or Peril?"; Kellermann et al., "Gun Ownership as a Risk Factor for Homicide in the Home"; Arthur L. Kellermann, F. P. Rivara, G. Somes, et al., "Suicide in the Home in Relationship to Gun Ownership," *New England Journal of Medicine* 327 (1992): 467–472. A number of gun control advocates also articulate this position in a well-balanced article by Gary Rosen, "Yes and No to Gun Control," *Commentary* 110 (September 2000): 47–53.

Chapter 2. The World of Gun Enthusiasm

1. Parts of this chapter were published previously. See Abigail Kohn, "Their Aim Is True," *Reason* 33 (May 2001): 26–32.

2. The thoughts and opinions of John and other gun enthusiasts are discussed in detail in a paper I cowrote with Jesse A. Dizard, "Individual versus Social Responsibility for Gun Crime: Shooters Talk Back," presented by Dizard at the 1999 annual meeting of the American Society of Criminology in November in Toronto, Canada.

3. In 2002, the range started with a new fee schedule. There is now a one-time joining fee of $40 and annual dues thereafter of $60.

4. Tom Diaz, *Making a Killing: The Business of Guns in America* (New York: New
Press, 1999), 181. Such a statement does beg the question: Unsafe compared to where?
To make his claim, Diaz simply lists newspaper articles gathered mostly from local
and regional papers in California that reported suicides, accidents, or alleged murders at shooting ranges. Although he does demonstrate that such incidents do occur
at shooting ranges, this is not a rigorous empirical examination of safety at shooting
ranges. Nor does this method make distinctions among different ranges, or question
how safety standards are implemented or enforced at different ranges. Suicides and
murders are tragic, but a lack of safety implies sloppiness or high rates of accidents.
Suicides and murders are not necessarily accidents, and are not likely to endanger all
range visitors equally. Nor does the occurrence of suicide or murder at ranges imply
that range visitors lack competence with firearms. Diaz does not question whether
suicides and murders occur more frequently at ranges than they do in other locales
(homes for suicide, for example, or parking lots for murder), which would be important to investigate if one were to argue that ranges are "particularly" unsafe. Diaz
does not pursue any of these issues in his analysis.

5. For example, one shooter who is a former police officer told me that he knew
that employees at this particular shop regularly sold guns to straw purchasers, that
is, buyers in good legal standing who turn around and sell guns illegally to purchasers with criminal records. This practice is illegal but very difficult to prevent.
The shooter stated that employees at this shop knew that their clients were making
straw purchases, and the shop did little to prevent it. On the issue of sexism, several
female shooters mentioned that the store employees were rude and patronizing to
women. Note, however, that this is not the same store that Jane and Louise mentioned—unfortunately, more than one gun store in the Bay Area has a reputation
for employing sexist store clerks.

6. For a discussion of the ways local government was targeting gun sellers, see
Donna Horowitz, "East Bay Cities Fight Guns," *San Francisco Examiner*, 9 July 1996,
A3.

7. It's possible that some shooters purchased guns over the Internet, but this was
not an activity that I heard much about from the shooters I interviewed. Although
it's possible to purchase guns on-line, my sense is that most interviewees would be
unlikely to do so simply because they would want to see, handle, and check the guns
they're interested in purchasing.

8. Subsequent to writing this description, California implemented a variety of new
laws, including the "one gun a month" law and an "assault weapons" ban. Although
these kinds of laws may affect purchasing, I do not believe they negate the
basic information about buying a gun described here. See http://caag.state.ca.us/
firearms/, accessed May 2003, for detailed information about California's firearm
laws.

9. Apparently, this style of shooting course had fallen out of favor by the time of this book's publication. I was told by international shooters who shot IPSC in the United States that shooting competitions were no longer attempting to so closely mimic a home invasion scenario.

10. It is true that some of the people I encountered and interviewed had been in the military, but it is important to note that criminologists have not found that veterans are more likely to own guns because of their military background. See Lizotte et al., "Firearms Ownership for Sport and Protection."

Chapter 3. Cowboy Action Shooting

1. This is a quote by the actor David Landry appearing as a guest star on "Space Ghost." It was played on the San Francisco radio station Alice@97.3 FM in 1998.

2. Linda Kintz, *Between Jesus and the Market: The Emotions That Matter in Right-Wing America* (Durham, NC: Duke University Press, 1997).

3. This description is an amalgam of several different shoots I attended. I merged several shoots to preserve the anonymity of shoot organizers, and I have not quoted Wild Phil verbatim for the same reason.

4. See the SASS Web site, http://www.sassnet.com/pages/briefhistory.html, accessed May 2002. The membership numbers are as of May 2002.

5. I use the term "cowboy" here to describe both men and women who engage in the activity of cowboy action shooting. I am conscious that the term is not gender-neutral, but I have not heard women on the range make an issue of using the term to describe either male or female shooters. For the sake of linguistic economy, I also make the choice to use the term to describe shooters of both sexes.

6. Journalist Susan Laws documented the history of SASS in her article "On the Trail with the Single Action Shooting Society," *Gun News Digest* 3, no. 2 (1998): 26–32.

7. Ibid.

8. I never officially became a member of SASS because it was not necessary to do so to participate in the shoots, membership seemed relatively expensive for a graduate student, and other members shared with me the materials that members are sent by the organization.

9. A berm in this context is a long bank of packed earth anywhere from 8 to 15 feet high that serves as a buffer between shooting areas and behind targets, absorbing fired bullets.

10. My understanding is that the official paperwork is always completed before these guns are awarded to winners.

11. Sherry Ortner, *Sherpas through Their Rituals* (Cambridge, UK: Cambridge University Press, 1990), 3.

12. Ibid.

Chapter 4. Citizen Soldiers

1. This quote is from James Burgh, an English writer of importance to American revolutionaries. His work is *Political Disquisitions: Or, An Enquiry into Public Errors, Defects, and Abuses, 1774–75*. I use this quote from Linda Kerber, *No Constitutional Right to Be Ladies: Women and Obligations of Citizenship* (New York: Hill and Wang, 1998), 238–239, and she in turn takes it from James G. A. Pocock, *The Machiavellian Moment: Florentine Political Thought and the Atlantic Republican Tradition* (Princeton, NJ: Princeton University Press, 1975), 84, 90.

2. According to the Movie Times Database, *The Patriot* grossed a respectable US$215,300,000 worldwide and spent sixteen weeks in the top 60 movies in terms of gross. See the the Movie Times Web site for *The Patriot*, http://www.the-movie-times.com/thrsdir/top60dir/top60Search.mv?The%20Patriot, accessed 17 May 2003.

3. Bernard Bailyn, *The Ideological Origins of the American Revolution* (Cambridge, MA: Harvard University Press, 1967); Gordon S. Wood, *The Radicalism of the American Revolution* (New York: Vintage Books, 1991).

4. Wood, *The Radicalism of the American Revolution*.

5. Bailyn, *The Ideological Origins of the American Revolution*; Wood, *The Radicalism of the American Revolution*.

6. Richard H. Kohn, *Eagle and Sword: The Federalists and the Creation of the Military Establishment in America, 1783–1802* (New York: Free Press, 1975).

7. Ibid.

8. Lee Kennett and James LaVerne Anderson, *The Gun in America: The Origins of a National Dilemma* (Westport, CT: Greenwood Press, 1975).

9. Malcolm, *To Keep and Bear Arms*, chap. 8.

10. A number of historians and scholars have made this point. They include Saul Cornell, "'To Keep and Bear Arms': The Militia, the People, and the Problem of Rights in Revolutionary America," in Cornell and Shalhope, *Whose Right to Bear Arms Did the Second Amendment Protect?* 9–16; Robert Cottrol and Raymond Diamond, "The Second Amendment: Toward an Afro-Americanist Reconsideration," in *Gun Control and the Constitution: Sources and Explorations on the Second Amendment*, R. J. Cottrol, ed. (New York: Garland, 1994), 375–428; and Kennett and Anderson, *The Gun in America*.

11. Kennett and Anderson, *The Gun in America*, chap. 2.

12. Kohn, *Eagle and Sword*, 4.

13. Historians who make this point include Cottrol and Diamond, "The Second Amendment"; Alexander DeConde, *Gun Violence in America: The Struggle for Control* (Boston: Northeastern University Press, 2001); and Malcolm, *To Keep and Bear Arms*.

14. Cottrol and Diamond, "The Second Amendment"; Kennett and Anderson, *The Gun in America*.

15. See DeConde, *Gun Violence in America*, 20–25, for a good summary.

16. Kennett and Anderson, *The Gun in America*, 50.

17. Cottrol and Diamond, "The Second Amendment."

18. Ibid.

19. Malcolm, *To Keep and Bear Arms*, 141.

20. Ibid.

21. Ibid.

22. Several social scientists have argued that republican ideology still resonates with Americans. Two of the most persuasive works on this topic are Robert N. Bellah, Richard Madsen, William M. Sullivan, Ann Swidler, and Steven M. Tipton, *Habits of the Heart: Individualism and Commitment in American Life* (Berkeley: University of California Press, 1985), and Nancy L. Rosenblum, *Membership and Morals: The Personal Uses of Pluralism in America* (Princeton, NJ: Princeton University Press, 1998).

23. Please note that I am *not* asserting that these shooters are modern incarnations of the archetypal citizen soldier. I am suggesting that the archetype of the citizen soldier provides a model for understanding the thoughts, beliefs, and ideological concerns of these shooters.

24. Bellah et al., *Habits of the Heart*, 23.

25. Seymour Martin Lipset discusses the American Creed, its components, and the way it is deployed with complexity to mark American exceptionalism in *American Exceptionalism: A Double-Edged Sword* (New York: Norton, 1997); see chap. 1 in particular.

26. Bellah et al., *Habits of the Heart*, 25.

27. Harold edited himself in this quote.

28. For a discussion of the passing of the assault weapons legislation in California, see Godwin and Schroebel, "Gun Control Politics in California."

29. Louise raises some concerns in this quote, including the idea that shooting can be frightening to her, which are analyzed in chap. 6.

30. Thomas C. Heller and David E. Wellbery, introduction to *Reconstructing Individualism: Autonomy, Individuality, and the Self in Western Thought* (Stanford: Stanford University Press, 1986), 1.

31. Although this belief holds true for many shooters, sociologists and criminologists have pointed out that, in general, the demographic portrait of gun owners suggests that most are white, male, and middle class.

32. Anthony Giddens, *Modernity and Self-Identity: Self and Society in the Late Modern Age* (Stanford: Stanford University, 1991).

33. The literature on rights and the Constitution is indeed vast. For examples from two respected scholars, see Akhil Reed Amar, *The Bill of Rights: Creation and Reconstruction* (New Haven: Yale University Press, 2000), and Levy, *Origin of the Bill of Rights*.

34. Carl Wellman, "Rights," in the *Cambridge Dictionary of Philosophy*, R. Audi, ed. (Cambridge, UK: Cambridge University Press, 1995).

35. In fact, few citizens in Germany in the 1930s owned firearms or were legally entitled to own them. These gun control laws had been established by the Weimar Republic, and the Third Reich rigorously enforced them against Jews. Hitler then exempted the Nazis and military officers in the Third Reich from following these laws, which in effect armed the Nazis when few others had legal access to guns. See Daniel D. Polsby and Don B. Kates Jr., "Of Holocausts and Gun Control," *Washington University Law Quarterly* 75, no. 3 (1997): 1237–1275, for further discussion.

36. Such counterfactual arguments are problematic because they reinvent the past to imagine a possible future. In fact, Jews were not well-armed and were not able to adequately defend themselves against Nazi aggression. Thus, reimagining a past in which they were and did does not provide a legitimate basis for arguments about what might have followed.

37. See "Gun Rights are a Myth," *USA Today,* 28 December 1994, 8A; Denis Horgan, "Let's Get Rid of the Guns," *Las Vegas Review-Journal,* 18 May 1999, 7B; Robin West, "Gun Rights," *Tikkun,* 1 September 1999, 25.

38. David Kopel explores this issue at length: "Children and Guns," in *Guns: Who Should Have Them?* D. Kopel, ed. (Amherst, NY: Prometheus, 1995), 309–406.

39. Among the scholars who make this point are Cottrol and Diamond, "The Second Amendment"; Kerber, *No Constitutional Right to be Ladies;* Rosenblum, *Membership and Morals;* and Richard Slotkin, "The Fall into Guns," *Atlantic Monthly* 286 (November 2000): 114–118.

40. The correct term for midget is "little person," and the indignities to which this sport subjects little people are obvious.

Chapter 5. Cowboy Lawmen

1. Richard White, *"It's Your Misfortune and None of My Own": A New History of the American West* (Norman: University of Oklahoma Press, 1991), 618.

2. This point is emphasized by William Hosley, a biographer of Samuel Colt: *Colt: The Making of an American Legend* (Amherst: University of Massachusetts Press, 1996).

3. Ibid., 51.

4. Ibid. Colt never actually served in the military. The title of colonel was an affectation.

5. This point is made succinctly by Rupert Wilkinson, *American Tough: The Tough-Guy Tradition and American Character* (Westport, CT: Greenwood Press, 1984).

6. David T. Courtwright, "The Cowboy Subculture," in *Violent Land: Single Men and Social Disorder from the Frontier to the Inner City* (Cambridge, MA: Harvard University Press, 1996), reprinted in *Guns in America: A Reader,* J. Dizard, R. M. Muth, and S. P. Andrews, eds. (New York: New York University Press, 1999), 86–104.

7. Ibid., 89–93.

8. Ibid., 87.

9. Ibid., 93–95.

10. Richard Maxwell Brown, "The American Vigilante Tradition," in *The History of Violence in America: Historical and Comparative Perspectives*, H. D. Graham and T. R. Gurr, eds. (New York: Bantam, 1969), 184.

11. *Lonesome Dove* began as a novel by Larry McMurtry and was eventually turned into a television miniseries.

12. Richard Slotkin, *Gunfighter Nation: The Myth of the Frontier in Twentieth-Century America* (New York: HarperPerennial, 1992).

13. James Oliver Robertson, *American Myth, American Reality* (New York: Hill and Wang, 1980), 158–165.

14. Bellah et al., *Habits of the Heart,* 145–146.

15. Peter A. French, *Cowboy Metaphysics: Ethics and Death in Westerns* (Lanham, MD: Rowman and Littlefield, 1997).

16. James R. Grossman, introduction to *The Frontier in American Culture: An Exhibition at the Newberry Library, August 26, 1994–January 7, 1995*, J. R. Grossman, ed. (Berkeley: University of California Press, 1994), 1–5.

17. Richard White, "Frederick Jackson Turner and Buffalo Bill," in Grossman, *The Frontier in American Culture,* 7–66; Kintz, *Between Jesus and the Market.*

18. Anne M. Butler, "Selling the Popular Myth," in *The Oxford History of the American West,* C. A. Milner II, C. A. O'Connor, and M. A. Sandweiss, eds. (New York: Oxford University Press, 1996), 771–802.

19. Paul Reddin, *Wild West Shows* (Champaign: University of Illinois Press, 1999), 76.

20. Butler, "Selling the Popular Myth," 781.

21. Robert G. Athearn, *The Mythic West in Twentieth-Century America* (Lawrence: University Press of Kansas, 1986).

22. Kintz, *Between Jesus and the Market.*

23. I am referring to school plays, themes at parties and celebrations, and in countless cultural productions such as plays, novels, television shows, and films.

24. A number of shooters spoke to me about how they enjoy the cowboy action shooting because they knew they were shooting alongside active or retired members of local police forces, or in some cases retired members of the armed services. Shooters who are in the local police or armed services have a certain cachet among other shooters, in part because they are thought to need their guns in a professional capacity and are therefore considered to be more skilled. Whether these shooters are necessarily more skilled (in terms of speed, accuracy, and general proficiency with their firearms) was not something I tried to measure or question people about, except in the most general terms. I took this tack in part because I did not want to offend those I was asking about their skill level, and because for the most part cowboy shooters are not a terribly competitive group.

25. Attorney Jeffrey Snyder remarks on the fact that U.S. courts have repeatedly

held that the police cannot be held legally responsible for preventing crimes or for saving lives during the commission of crimes. See Jeffrey Snyder, "A Nation of Cowards," in *Guns in America: A Reader*, J. Dizard, R. M. Muth, and S. P. Andrews, eds. (New York: New York University Press, 1999), 182–193.

26. This is a complex issue, and a number of researchers have commented. For a broad overview from a social critic, see Wendy Kaminer, *It's All the Rage: Crime and Culture* (Reading, MA: Addison-Wesley, 1995), 226–239. For a more criminological analysis, see Kleck, *Targeting Guns*, 130–135. Kleck also provides the best summarization of the evidence (130–135). Other discussion can be found in Steven Brill, *Firearm Abuse: A Research and Policy Report* (Washington, DC: Police Foundation, 1977) and James D. Wright and Peter H. Rossi, *Armed and Considered Dangerous: A Survey of Felons and Their Firearms* (Hawthorne, NY: Aldine de Gruyter, 1986), 219–220.

27. T. Marcus Funk, "Gun Control in America: A History of Discrimination against the Poor and Minorities," in *Guns in America: A Reader*, J. Dizard, R. M. Muth, and S. P. Andrews, eds. (New York: New York University Press, 1999), 390–402, provides a more detailed discussion of this argument.

28. See Kaminer's *Its All the Rage*, 226–239, for a discussion.

29. This point has been made most persuasively by Richard Slotkin in his triology, *Regeneration through Violence: The Mythology of the American Frontier, 1600–1860* (Middletown, CT: Wesleyan University Press, 1973); *The Fatal Environment: The Myth of the Frontier in the Age of Industrialization, 1800–1890* (Middletown, CT: Wesleyan University Press, 1986); and *Gunfighter Nation*.

30. Snyder, "A Nation of Cowards," 184, 187.

31. Fred Pfeil also argues that these are the sentiments that underlie white, working-class, male anger over gun control, though Pfeil also suggests that there is a strong core of antifederalism that runs through this discourse as well: "Sympathy for the Devils: Notes on Some White Guys in the Ridiculous Class War," In *Whiteness: A Critical Reader*, M. Hill, ed. (New York: New York University Press, 1997), 21–34.

32. A number of researchers have made this point. Some of the more articulate examples include Robert Cottrol, "Submission Is Not the Answer: Lethal Violence, Microcultures of Criminal Violence and the Right to Self-Defence," *University of Colorado Law Review* 69, no. 4 (1998): 1029–1080; Cottrol and Diamond, "The Second Amendment"; Funk, "Gun Control in America"; and Rosenblum, *Membership and Morals*.

33. Rosenblum, *Membership and Morals*, 295.

34. The social scientists who make this point most persuasively are Cottrol and Diamond, "The Second Amendment."

35. The phrase "regeneration through violence" is Richard Slotkin's from *Regeneration through Violence*.

36. My point is that the sport of cowboy action shooting may not see too many black shooters not because blacks are necessarily antigun, but because they do not

relate to the predominantly white, middle-class values and history that are integrated into the sport.

37. I thank my professor Philippe Bourgois for making this specific point clear in our various conversations about cowboy action shooting.

38. Slotkin, *Regeneration through Violence*.

Chapter 6. Tough Americans

1. Wilkinson, *American Tough*.

2. Dana Nelson, *National Manhood: Capitalist Citizenship and the Imagined Fraternity of White Men* (Durham, NC: Duke University Press, 1998).

3. Cited in Anthony Rotundo, *American Manhood: Transformations in Masculinity from the Revolution to the Modern Era* (New York: Basic Books, 1993), 16.

4. George Custer in 1874, quoted in *In Their Own Words: Warriors and Pioneers*, T. J. Stiles, ed. (New York: Perigee, 1996), 131.

5. Wilkinson, *American Tough*.

6. For the argument that in polite, politically correct, middle-class America, the idea that teaching a child to shoot (or just engaging in shooting or hunting in general) is considered dangerous or repulsive, see Mary Zeiss Stange, "Teach Proper Gun Use is Schools?" *USA Today,* 23 August 1999, 15A; Charles Eisendrath, "So Shoot Me, I'm a Hunter," *Chronicle of Higher Education* 47 (24 November 2000), B5. For an example of a social critic who finds the notion of children being exposed to guns appalling, see Mitch Albom, "Gun Violence Ends When Guns Are Gone," *Los Angeles Business Journal,* 19 March 2001, 65.

7. I use the term gun ownership/enthusiasm to indicate that within this particular discourse, rarely is there a distinction made between owning a gun and being a gun enthusiast. To my knowledge, the study documented in this book is the only one that has tried to parse out the social practices and ideological positions supported by gun enthusiasts, who can be differentiated from gun owners by their level of interest in guns. Critics, however, have rarely made this distinction.

8. Wilkinson, *American Tough*, 113.

9. White, *"It's Your Misfortune and None of My Own,"* 621.

10. Wilkinson, *American Tough*.

11. Abigail Adams to John Adams, Sept. 20, 177[6], Adams Family Correspondence, II, 129, quoted in Linda Kerber, *Women of the Republic: Intellect and Ideology in Revolutionary America* (Chapel Hill: University of North Carolina, 1980), 67.

12. Reddin, *Wild West Shows*, 142.

13. Patricia Nelson Limerick, *The Legacy of Conquest: The Unbroken Past of the American West* (New York: Norton, 1987). See chap. 1 in particular.

14. See the work of the following feminist scholars: Martha McCaughey, *Real Knockouts: The Physical Feminism of Women's Self-Defense* (New York: New York University Press, 1997); M. Z. Stange and C. Oyster, eds., *Gun Women: Firearms and*

Feminism in Contemporary America (New York: New York University Press, 2000). Stange and Oyster penned most of this volume but have included short pieces by other gun-owning women, feminists, and scholars.

15. D. A. Clarke, "A Woman with a Sword: Some Thoughts on Women, Feminism, and Violence," in *Transforming a Rape Culture*, E. Buchwald, P. Fletcher, and M. Roth, eds. (Minneapolis: Milkweed Editions, 1993), 399; emphasis added.

16. Stange and Oyster, *Gun Women*.

17. Stange and Oyster, *Gun Women*, 34, state that Audre Lorde is invoked to make this point, and I concur. Lorde's argument can be found in "The Master's Tools Will Never Dismantle the Master's House," in *This Bridge Called My Back: Writings of Radical Women of Color*, C. Moraga and Gloria Anzaldúa, eds. (Latham, NY: Kitchen Table Press, 1983), 98–101. Stange and Oyster note that Lorde's overall argument does not refer to firearms in any way, but her theoretical point can be found in various feminist arguments. For example, Susan Caufield argues, "As I noted in my reflexive statement, I am both a feminist and a peace activist. From this viewpoint, the greatest difficulties with the current criminal justice process center on the use of violence in an attack against violence. *When one goes to war against crime or violence, and uses a military model to do so, what gets modeled is that violence is acceptable, so long as it is done by those in positions of relative power.* This is at the center of why people support war. As long as they are the 'good guys,' war is a necessary and acceptable evil. While we may curse the enemy who kills our child, we simultaneously cheer our soldier who kills someone else's son" (emphasis added). Caufield also cites feminist bell hooks to make the same point: violence just encourages more violence. See Caufield, "Transforming the Criminological Dialogue: A Feminist Perspective on the Impact of Militarism," *Journal of Political and Military Sociology* 27, no. 2 (1999): 303.

18. Sheley et al. argue that although the popular media played up the theme of increasing numbers of armed women, their own study demonstrates that there is no empirical evidence that the numbers are increasing. See Joseph F. Sheley, Charles J. Brody, and James D. Wright, "Women and Handguns: Evidence from National Surveys, 1973–1991," *Social Science Research* 23 (1994): 219–235.

19. Tom W. Smith and Robert J. Smith, "Changes in Firearms Ownership among Women, 1980–1994," *Journal of Criminal Law and Criminology* 86 (1995); Smith and Wesson survey cited on 133–149.

20. Stange and Oyster, *Gun Women*.

21. Ibid.

22. Don B. Kates in his introduction to *Armed*, 26, n. 9 discusses the position of gun control advocates on the issue of how individuals should respond when attacked, using material published by former leader of Handgun Control, Inc., Nelson Shields, in *Guns Don't Die, People Do* (New York: Arbor House, 1981), 124–125, and pro-control academics Franklin Zimring and Gordon Hawkins, *The Citizen's Guide to Gun Control* (New York: Macmillan, 1987), 32.

23. Kates discusses this issue in "'Poisoning the Well' for Gun Control," in Kleck and Kates, *Armed*, specifically 126–127, nn. 41, 45, 46.

24. A review of several of the Web sites for the most well-known gun control organizations does not yield information about these organizations' position on what to do if a would-be victim is attacked. Most organizations do, however, state emphatically that guns are not an effective tool for self defense. See the Brady Campaign to Prevent Gun Violence at http://www.bradycampaign.org/. Another organization is JoinTogether Online (http://www.jointogether.org/home/), which also does not mention the question of how to respond to an attack. However, JoinTogether does reference the policies of another gun control organization, the Violence Policy Center (VPC), on the question of using guns for self-defense. The VPC argues that women are far more likely to be murdered by handguns than use them for self-defense, an argument the VPC bases on a 1986 study by public health researchers Arthur Kellermann and Donald Reay, "Protection or Peril? An Analysis of Firearms-Related Deaths in the Home." This study has long been critiqued by criminologists for a series of methodological flaws, not the least of which is that it measures the effecitveness of using a handgun in self-defense only by whether or not the potential victim killed his or her attacker, not whether or not simply brandishing a gun was enough to stop the attack itself. The VPC, and consequently JoinTogether, effectively reiterate this position (that because so few attackers are actually killed by would-be victims, as oppsosed to simply frightened off, guns are not an effective tool for self-defense) by citing the Kellermann and Reay study and related statistics to "prove" that guns are not an effective means of self-defense. See the Web site for the Violence Policy Center, http://www.vpc.org/. All Web sites accessed May 2003.

25. McCaughey, *Real Knockouts*; Mary Zeiss Stange, "Arms and the Woman: A Feminist Reappraisal," in *Guns: Who Should Have Them?*, D. B. Kopel, ed. (Amherst, NY: Prometheus, 1995), 15–52; and Stange and Oyster, *Gun Women*.

26. McCaughey, *Real Knockouts*; Stange, "Arms and the Woman"; Stange and Oyster, *Gun Women*.

27. See Dawn McCaffrey's review of McCaughey's book: "Real Knockouts: The Physical Feminism of Women's Self-Defense," book review, in *Violence Against Women* 5, no. 7 (1999): 829–833.

28. McCaughey, *Real Knockouts*, 95.

29. See, for example, Demie Kurz, "*Real Knockouts: The Physical Feminism of Women's Self-Defense*, by Martha McCaughey," book review, in *Gender and Society* 13, no. 1 (1999): 145–147; and McCaffrey, "*Real Knockouts: The Physical Feminism of Women's Self-Defense*."

30. Stange and Oyster, *Gun Women*, chap. 2.

31. See the following Web sites: the Pink Pistols at http://www.pinkpistols.org/index2.html; the Second Amendment Sisters at http://www.sas-aim.org/; and the Tenth Cavalry Gun Club at http://www.tenthcavalrygunclub.org/. All accessed July 2003.

32. See Janis Cortese's Web site dedicated to third-wave feminism at http://www.io.com/~wwwave/self-defense/self-def.html, accessed April 2002.

33. Cottrol and Diamond, "The Second Amendment"; Cottrol, "Submission Is Not the Answer."

34. Gay Becker, *Disrupted Lives: How People Create Meaning in a Chaotic World* (Berkeley: University of California Press, 1997).

35. See, for example, Polsby and Kates, "Of Holocausts and Gun Control."

36. "Sept. 11 Convinces Many New Jerseyans to Buy Guns," Associated Press state and local wire, 18 November 2001; Tina Dirmann and Timothy Hughes, "More Residents Taking Up Arms," *Los Angeles Times,* 14 October 2001, part 2, p. 1; Dante Chinni and Tim Vanderpool, "More in U.S. Carry Guns," *Christian Science Monitor,* 6 December 2001, 1.

37. President George W. Bush, radio address from Camp David, 15 September 2001, reported in *The Times of London,* 17 September 2001, 12.

38. Wilkinson, *American Tough.*

Chapter 7. Conclusions

1. Scholars who have recognized that the violence statistics that are frequently used to support gun control are not convincing to gun enthusiasts include Donald Braman and Dan M. Kahan, *More Statistics, Less Persuasion: A Cultural Theory of Gun-Risk Perceptions*, Working Paper No. 5, Public Law and Legal Theory Working Paper Series, Yale Law School, 2001; and Katz, "Ethnography's Warrants." A gun control advocate who recognizes the limited appeal of models being used by control advocates, much less the tactics of insult and humiliation, is Roger Rosenblatt, "Get Rid of the Damned Things," *Time* 154, no. 6 (9 August 1999): 38–39.

2. A number of gun control advocacy organizations use public health models and frameworks for promoting their control agenda, based on the idea that the public health literature has demonstrated a sound scientific and empirical basis for limiting the availability of guns to the general public. For what could be read as a mission statement for the health care professional on the topic, see an article signed by nineteen high-level medical professionals advocating tougher federal gun control: Karl P. Adler et al., "Firearm Violence and Public Health: Limiting the Availability of Guns," *Journal of the American Medical Association* 271, no. 16 (27 April 1994): 1281–1283. See also the Web site for the Brady Campaign to Stop Gun Violence and the Million Mom March, which have combined: http://www.millionmommarch.com, in particular the Issue Brief "Facts: Guns in the Home," at http://www.millionmommarch.org/facts/issuebriefs/gunhome.asp, which relies heavily on the study by Kellermann, Rivera, and Rushforth, "Gun Ownership as a Risk Factor for Homicide in the Home," as well as others by Kellermann. Material accessed 19 May 2003. The scholars who have noted the increasing reliance of the gun control movement on public health studies include Peter Squires, *Gun Culture or Gun Control?* (Lon-

don: Routledge, 2000), 90–92; William J. Vizzard, *Shots in the Dark: The Policy, Politics, and Symbolism of Gun Control* (Lanham, MD: Rowman and Littlefield, 2000).

3. For homicide statistics, see the U.S. Department of Justice's Bureau of Justice Statistics Web site, http://www.ojp.usdoj.gov/bjs/homicide/tables/weaponstab.htm. For suicide statistics, see the Web site for the American Association for Suicidology, http://www.iusb.edu/~jmcintos/SuicideStats.html.

4. See A. Colburn, "Gunshots as an Epidemic: Some Doctors call Firearms a 'Toxin' in the Environment," *Washington Post,* Health section, 1 November 1988, Z6; Mike Ellis, "Conference Will Consider Gun Violence as Health Issue," *Indianapolis Star,* 25 September 2000, 1A; Sameh Fahmy, "Doctors Debate Whether Firearms Are a Health Issue," *News-Star* (Monroe, LA), 22 March 2002, 1B; Mark L. Rosenberg, Patrick W. O'Carroll, and Kenneth E. Powell, "Let's Be Clear: Violence Is a Public Health Problem," *Journal of the American Medical Association* 267, no. 22 (1992): 3071–3072; Sarah Webster, "Violence: A Hidden Health Epidemic," *Detroit News,* 27 November 2000, 7A.

5. The public health field as a whole has promoted the message that gun ownership is statistically potentially injurious to self and family, and therefore poses inherent danger to anyone who owns a gun. For the high-profile studies that argue this point empirically, see Kellermann and Reay, "Protection or Peril?"; Kellermann et al., "Gun Ownership as a Risk Factor for Homicide in the Home"; Kellermann et al., "Suicide in the Home in Relationship to Gun Ownership."

6. Kellermann and Reay, "Protection or Peril?"; Kellermann et al., "Gun Ownership as a Risk Factor for Homicide in the Home."

7. Arthur Kellermann, a high-profile public health researcher and author of a number of gun-related studies, made this point in David Johnston, "It May Not Feel True, but Gunshot Deaths Are Down," *New York Times,* 29 August 1999, 5. This summarizes the material that is used by the Million Mom March and the Brady Campaign to Stop Gun Violence in their issue brief, "Guns in the Home," which can be found at http://www.millionmommarch.com/-Guns in the Home, accessed 19 May 2003.

8. This quote is from Arthur Kellermann interviewed by David Johnston, "It May Not Feel True, but Gunshot Deaths Are Down." Dr. Kellermann also states in the same article that "On average, the gun that represents the greatest threat is the one that is kept loaded and readily available in a bedside drawer."

9. For a longer discussion of the way this message is formulated and promoted, see Abigail Kohn, "Shooters: The Moral World of Gun Enthusiasts" (Ph.D. diss., University of California, Berkeley and San Francisco, 2000).

10. See, for example, Cummings and Koepsell, "Does Owning a Firearm Increase or Decrease the Risk of Death?" The authors argue that based on the public health evidence, doctors should advise their patients not to own guns.

11. On the basis of the previously mentioned studies and others, public health researchers have tended to argue in an advocacy capacity that gun ownership serves

little or no positive social or political benefit and therefore should be far more restricted. See Adler et al., "Firearm Violence and Public Health"; C. Everett Koop and George D. Lundberg, "Violence in America: A Public Health Emergency," *Journal of the American Medical Association* 267 (1992): 3075–3076; Lawrence J. Purdy, "Knife and Gun Clubs of America," *Journal of the American Medical Association* 267 (1992): 3086. Several scholars now also make the argument that guns place an undue burden on the state in financial terms, which further emphasizes the need for better regulation. See Philip J. Cook and Jens Ludwig, *Gun Violence: The Real Costs* (New York: Oxford University Press, 2000).

12. See Deborah Lupton, "Risk as Moral Danger: The Social and Political Functions of Risk in Public Health," *International Journal of Health Services* 23, no. 3 (1993): 425–435; Alan Petersen and Deborah Lupton, *The New Public Health: Health and Self in the Age of Risk* (London: Sage, 1996); Wagner, *The New Temperance,* which provides an excellent popular overview.

13. Medical anthropologists have long critiqued the underlying moral discourse of public health as a discipline. For good overviews, see Lupton, "Risk as Moral Danger," and Petersen and Lupton, *The New Public Health.* In terms of the criminological response to the public health literature on guns, a number of criminologists have offered damning critiques of flawed methodology, confusion about the causal relationship between gun ownership and gun violence, and the tendency of public health professionals to vastly overgeneralize about their study conclusions. See, for example, Don. B. Kates Jr., Henry E. Schaffer, John K. Lattimer, George B. Murray, and Edwin H. Cassem, "Bad Medicine: Doctors and Guns," in Kopel, *Guns: Who Should Have Them?*, 233–308; Kleck, *Targeting Guns,* 56–62.

14. See Wagner, *The New Temperance.*

15. Public health officials have frequently made rather naïve statements (that bespeak their middle-class backgrounds) about how most people should buy a home security system or get a dog, rather than rely on guns for home defense. See a lay discussion of these issues in Ann Japenga, "Would I Be Safer with a Gun?" *Health* 8, no. 2 (1994): 52–64. Stange also discusses the issue in "Arms and the Woman: A Feminist Reappraisal."

16. Deborah Homsher also makes this point about liberal supporters of gun control: *Women and Guns: Politics and the Culture of Firearms in America* (Armonk, NY: M.E. Sharpe, 2001), 197–238.

17. There are a number of criminological works that illustrate the flawed methodology and erroneous conclusions of many of the high-profile public health studies on guns. See, for example, Kates et al., "Bad Medicine"; Kleck, *Targeting Guns,* 56–62; Stange, "Arms and the Woman." There are a number of Web sites created by and for gun owners discussing the flaws in the public health studies on guns. On the NRA's ILA (Institute for Legislative Action) Web site, several fact sheets discuss the flaws in Kellermann's studies in particular. See http://www.nraila.org/FactSheets.asp?FormMode=Detail&ID=119&T=print, accessed 11 December 2001, and http://

www.nraila.org/FactSheets.asp?FormMode=Detail&ID=117&T=print, accessed 6 November 1999. Public health studies, and Kellermann's work in particular, are also discussed on the GunCite Web site, http://www.guncite.com/gun_control_gcdgaga.html, accessed 16 January 2002.

18. There's little doubt that gun enthusiasts find gun control advocacy unpersuasive, else they would not so frequently ridicule, reject, or protest it almost ubiquitously in NRA magazines, letters to the editor, and public forums that allow for the expression of their opinion on the matter. There are also several criminologists who make the point that these images of gun ownership (as inherently dangerous) and gun owners (as potential murderers) have very little basis in statistical fact. See, for example, Kates, introduction to *Armed*, 13–30, and Kleck, *Targeting Guns*, 63–72.

19. See Kleck and Gertz, "Armed Resistance to Crime"; John R. Lott Jr., *More Guns, Less Crime* (Chicago: University of Chicago Press, 1998). These two studies were frequently raised by shooters in my discussions with them about defensive gun use and are frequently discussed and quoted in pro-gun editorials, letters to the editors, NRA publications, and popular forums for discussing the gun debate. Both Kleck's and Lott's works are controversial because their studies generally confer tremendous empirical validity to the argument that law-abiding citizens use guns capably to deter crime. Though shooters and gun enthusiasts are aware that the research is controversial, they dismiss the critiques and the attacks on Kleck and Lott as politically motivated and therefore invalid. For readers interested in a critique of Kleck's work, see Philip J. Cook, Jens Ludwig, and David Hemenway, "The Gun Debate's Mythical New Number: How Many Defensive Gun Uses per Year?" *Journal of Policy Analysis and Management* 16 (1997): 463–469. For a critique of Lott's work, see Dan Black and Daniel Nagin, "Do 'Right to Carry' Laws Reduce Violent Crime?" *Journal of Legal Studies* 27 (1998): 209–219.

20. For an example of a liberal commentator who is disdainful of defensive gun use, see Molly Ivins, "If Guns Were Outlawed . . . ," *Chicago Sun-Times*, 21 August 1999), 20, and "To the Worried: Arm with Knives, Not Guns," *Salt Lake Tribune*, 7 February 1999, AA1.

21. Jacobs, *Can Gun Control Work?*, viii.

22. David Kopel makes this point in *The Samurai, The Mountie, and the Cowboy: Should America Adopt the Gun Controls of Other Democracies?* (Buffalo, NY: Prometheus, 1992). Jan E. Dizard, Robert Merrill Muth, and Stephen P. Andrews Jr. also make this point in their introduction to *Guns in America: A Reader*, J. Dizard, R. M. Muth, and S. P. Andrews, eds. (New York: New York University Press, 1999), 1–13. Dizard et al. estimate the number of guns at 200 million, however. I use James Jacobs's more current figure from *Can Gun Control Work?*, viii.

23. See, for example, Garry Wills's editorial in which he states, "It is this fragile structure of myth that the gunnies are trying to preserve. They should be fearful for its survival. It crumbles at a touch of real learning or research. I have my own test for hysteria on public issues: The number of intemperate letters I get on any subject.

And for real frothing-at-the-mouth missives, the gunnies are up there with the anti-Semites and the Hillary-haters in their mailing habits. (They will prove this again by sending me more of the stuff for this column—like most fanatics, they do not see that their tactics backfire.) The gun cult is a pathology. It is mental sickness." "Gun Control Debate: More or Less?" *Chicago Sun-Times*, 31 May 1999, 23.

24. Gregg Lee Carter provides a good summary of how pro-gun and antigun advocates structure their arguments using international comparisons: "Dueling Statistics," *Forum for Applied Research and Public Policy* (1 January 2000): 68–75. For examples of advocates engaging in the international comparison argument, see Derrick Z. Jackson, "A Tale of Three Time Lines on Gun Control," *Boston Globe*, 14 May 1999, A23; Steven Riczo, "Guns, America, and the 21st Century," *USA Today*, 1 March 2001, 16–18.

25. There are several notable texts that attempt to address these issues with more complexity, including the thorough work by David B. Kopel, *The Samurai, The Mountie, and the Cowboy*, and Peter Squires, *Gun Culture or Gun Control?* Kopel is a criminologist expressly interested in cross-cultural comparisons of gun control legislation, and he makes similar points to mine. Squires is a social scientist interested in cross-cultural comparisons between the British and U.S. experiences with guns, and uses the gun debate to analyze cultural differences and similarities between the two cultures. Robert Cottrol also explores similar issues about cultural attitudes and beliefs about guns, as well as about violent behavior. See Cottrol, "Submission Is Not the Answer."

26. I single out Australia because it is mythologized to be very similar to the United States in terms of history and culture. Like the United States, Australia is a former British colony and has a frontier history. That being said, it would take a thorough ethnographic study to document and demonstrate the ways in which Australia and the United States are different in some ways and similar in others. Suffice it to say here that Australia is still a monarchy operating with a parliamentary-style governmental system, with democratic procedures. The U.S. government is a republican system with democratic procedures. Australia's frontier history was considerably shorter than America's. Australia's current health and welfare systems are considerably better financed than America's, as demonstrated by the simple fact that all Australians have some basic form of access to health care, whereas millions of Americans are uninsured. Anglo-Australia has yet to reconcile its terribly brutal relationship with its aboriginal population. Although the United States cannot take tremendous pride in its dealings with its own native population, Native American peoples currently have far more sovereignty over their land than do Australian Aborigines and are considerably more enfranchised than Australian Aborigines. The United States has the Second Amendment to its Constitution, which has functioned to protect private gun ownership to a large extent from wholesale restriction by the state. Australian gun owners have never had similar constitutional protection. Last, but importantly, self-defense (and home defense) is rare and ostensibly functionally

illegal in Australia for the following reasons. Since the 1930s, Australian gun owners have had to obtain permits to keep handguns, and while such permits are obtainable, self-defense with guns is not a legitimate, legal reason to own a gun. Australians are required by law to store guns unloaded in locked safes, separate from the ammunition. If an Australian citizen were to use a gun for self-protection, even if that gun was legally owned, that individual would face legal prosecution on the presumption that he or she used excessive force in relation to the situation. All of these issues just touch on the ways the United States and Australia differ. Some of these issues affect the gun issue, others less so, but it is simply untrue that the United States and Australia are entirely similar countries in most, even many, respects.

27. For a very brief overview of the high-profile shooting incidents and the subsequent gun control enactment, see Jackson, "A Tale of Three Time Lines on Gun Control." For an extensive discussion of the impact of the Dunblane, Scotland shooting, see Squires, *Gun Control or Gun Culture?*

28. See Squires, *Gun Control or Gun Culture?*

29. Wendy Kaminer makes this point clear in her discussions of the left's use of identity politics: "Politics of Identity," *American Prospect* 12 (24 September 2001): 32.

30. Scarry is not expressly arguing that everyone in the United States should buy a gun. Nor did she make this point in defense of NRA policy. She is in fact conducting an interpretive analysis of the language of the Constitution and exploring the original intent of the Framers vis-à-vis the right to bear arms. Eventually considering the issue of presidential authority to deploy nuclear arms, she argues that the means of force must be distributed within the widest possible expanse of any given population in which the means of force exist. She logically points out that if arms are selectively restricted, parties without access to arms cannot enter into a binding social contract without inherently begging the question of whether or not they were coerced into doing so. Scarry also suggests through her analysis some of the same conclusions I have drawn regarding access to the means of force (and the ability to bear arms in the militia context) with full rights and citizenship within any given political body. See Elaine Scarry, "War and the Social Contract: Nuclear Policy, Distribution, and the Right to Bear Arms," *University of Pennsylvania Law Review* 139, no. 5 (1991): 1257–1316; this quote comes from 1269–1270.

31. Peter Squires makes this point succinctly in relation to public health arguments for gun control: *Gun Control or Gun Culture?*, 90–92. Katha Pollitt also makes it "Moms to NRA: Grow Up!" *The Nation* (12 June).

32. Limerick, *The Legacy of Conquest.*

33. The Western, and U.S., fixation with science and rationality as a prevailing paradigm for understanding social reality is well-documented by social scientists. See, for example, Richard C. Lewontin, *Biology as Ideology: The Doctrine of DNA* (New York: HarperPerennial, 1993).

34. When gun control supporters make scientific arguments about risks, even when they rely on methodologically sound research, they presume that everyone is

using the same risk framework or that everybody is measuring the same risks in the same way that they do. As social scientists and anthropologists have long demonstrated, different people employ different frameworks for assessing risks. The risk of killing a family member is the most worrisome to gun controllers. The risk of encountering an attacker is the most worrisome to gun owners. This basic difference illustrates that these two groups use different frameworks for conceptualizing "greater" risk. This is yet one more area in which there is unlikely to ever be much agreement. For a discussion of the cultural construction of risk, see Mary Douglas and Aaron Wildavsky, *Risk and Culture* (Berkeley: University of California, 1982); Lupton, "Risk as Moral Danger."

35. See Dizard et al., introduction to *Guns: A Reader*.

36. Personal e-mail communication between Richard Slotkin and the author, 19 September 1999.

37. See, for example, Daniel S. Claster, *Bad Guys and Good Guys: Moral Polarization and Crime* (Westport, CT: Greenwood Press, 1992); and Ester Madriz, *Nothing Bad Happens to Good Girls: Fear of Crime in Women's Lives* (Berkeley: University of California Press, 1997).

38. Robert Fisk, "My Beating by Refugees Is a Symbol of the Hatred and Fury of This Filthy War," *The Independent*, 10 December 2001, 1.

39. Richard Landes describes this kind of left-wing description of social events as "masochistic omnipotence syndrome," which he defines as a "narcissistic focus on the self, to the exclusion of the other." He elaborates: "We are guilty for *everything* wrong, and if we could only make *ourselves* perfect, then *everything* would be alright [*sic*]." Landes also argues, and I concur, that a radical unconscious racism underscores this kind of thinking because ultimately it suggests that victimized "subaltern" peoples should not *and cannot* be held to the same moral standard as their abusers, which renders them as "incapable of moral reasoning as animals." See Landes, "The Question of Rationality: A Response to Joel Kovel," *Tikkun* 18, no. 3 (2003): 54–57.

40. This point has been thoroughly established by social scientists. See, for example, Jeffery Fagan and Deanna L. Wilkinson, "Guns, Youth Violence, and Social Identity in the Inner Cities," *Crime and Justice* 24 (1998): 105–188; David M. Kennedy, Anne M. Piehl, and Anthony A. Braga, "Youth Violence in Boston: Gun Markets, Serious Youth Offenders, and a Use-Reduction Strategy," *Law and Contemporary Problems* 59 (1996): 147–196; Frank E. Zimring, "Kids, Guns, and Homicide: Policy Notes on an Age-Specific Epidemic," *Law and Contemporary Problems* 59 (1996): 25–38.

41. See Kleck and Gertz, "Armed Resistance to Crime."

42. One of the constant charges made by criminologists against the public health literature is that it does not concede any legitimacy or validity to defensive gun use. In some cases, some researchers argue, public health officials deliberately mislead the public about defensive gun use. See Don B. Kates, "Guns and Public Health: Epidemic of Violence, or Pandemic of Propaganda?" in *Armed*, 31–106, for an overview of this assertion.

43. Otis Dudley Duncan raises similar questions and issues in his critique of the statistics war in the defensive gun use debate: "Gun Use Surveys: in Numbers We Trust?" *Criminologist* 25, no. 1 (2000): 1–7.

44. See Cook and Ludwig, *Gun Violence: The Real Costs,* 36–39.

45. In fact, Cook and Ludwig argue that the NCVS, or National Crime Victimization Survey, provides a much lower estimate than what Kleck and Gertz estimate because the NCVS more effectively reduces false positives. However, Kleck provides a convincing rationale for why Kleck's and Gertz's is in fact a more accurate estimate and why the NCVS numbers are too low. One reason is that when gun owners use guns defensively, they often do so under quasi-illegal circumstances: they are carrying a firearm without a permit, or they are unsure if they are legally allowed to carry. They therefore are unwilling to report that experience to NCVS officials, who are government representatives who interview people in their homes to collect data. Thus, the NCVS numbers are too low with respect to defensive gun use. The Kleck and Gertz study was an anonymous survey conducted over the phone and therefore less subject to that particular underreporting problem. As Kleck also points out, the problems of telescoping (believing things that happened years ago actually occurred more recently) and false positives are probably cancelled out by people who have forgotten incidents of defensive gun use as well. Kleck defends the Kleck and Gertz study effectively in "The Frequency of Defensive Gun Use: Evidence and Disinformation," in Kleck and Kates, *Armed,* 213–284.

46. See Kleck, "The Frequency of Defensive Gun Use," 213–284.

47. Kates, "'Poisoning the Well' for Gun Control," 107–128.

48. Jacobs, *Can Gun Control Work?*

49. Supporters for licensing and registration include William J. Vizzard, *Shots in the Dark*; and Cook and Ludwig, *Gun Violence.*

50. See Vizzard, *Shots in the Dark.*

51. Ibid.

52. See David B. Kopel, "Background Checks and Waiting Periods," *In Guns: Who Should Have Them?* D. Kopel, ed. (Amherst, NY: Prometheus, 1995), 53–126, 122 n. 124. Kopel notes several occasions when registration led to confiscation, and how that process occurred.

53. See Cheryl W. Thompson, "Ashcroft Graces NRA Cover," *Washington Post,* 24 July 2001, A19.

54. Chris Mondics, "Attack on Gun Makers Losing Steam," *Philadelphia Inquirer,* 26 August 2001, City-D section, A08. Mondics notes that suits in New York and California were dismissed. Some states are prohibiting the suits wholesale. For example, Missouri courts decided not even to allow the suits against the gun makers to be processed in that state. See an editorial entitled, "A Can-Do-No-Wrong Industry?" *St. Louis Post-Dispatch,* 12 March 2001, C6.

55. Kleck, *Targeting Guns,* 329–334.

56. See William Glaberson, "Court Says Individuals Have a Right to Firearms,"

New York Times, 17 October 2001, 14; Doug Simpson, "Prosecutors Win Second Amendment Appeal over Gun Ownership," Associated Press Newswires, 16 March 2001.

57. Lawrence H. Tribe quoted in Glaberson, "Court Says Individuals Have a Right to Firearms."

58. For example, the Violence Policy Center, a hard-line gun control organization, applauded the decision by saying that the court upheld the gun control restrictions preventing a domestic abuser from getting access to guns. The organization also argued that the NRA advocated that domestic abusers should be allowed to be armed. The VPC's Web site stated, "Mathew Nosanchuk, VPC litigation director and legislative counsel states, 'Today the Fifth Circuit Court of Appeals rejected the sweeping arguments of the gun lobby that the Second Amendment guarantees domestic abusers an individual right to possess a gun. Final score: public safety, one; gun lobby and domestic abusers, zero.'" See http://www.vpc.org/press/0110emer.htm, accessed 16 October 2001.

59. Kleck discusses the slippery slope argument in his chapter "Absolutist Politics in a Moderate Package," 129–172.

60. The caveat to this statement is, of course, unless the gun owner in question violates the law. Individuals who commit a felony (or have a felony record), are mentally ill, or are addicted to an illegal substance could of course find their guns confiscated by legal authorities.

61. A number of scholars who are firmly pro-gun make this argument about the *Emerson* decision as well. For examples, see Glenn Harlan Reynolds, "Gun by Gun," available at legalaffairs.com: http://www.legalaffairs.org/current_issue_scenes02.html, accessed 17 May 2003.

62. Kleck, *Targeting Guns*, 388–390. Other researchers and criminologists who support gun controls from the moderate to the more rigorous include Don B. Kates, Phillip Cook, and William Vizzard. For overviews of the positions of a number of researchers, see Bijlefeld, *People For and Against Gun Control*.

63. Criminologists making this evidence-based argument are Kennedy et al., "Youth Violence in Boston"; Joseph F. Sheley and James D. Wright, *In the Line of Fire: Youth, Guns, and Violence in Urban America* (New York: Aldine de Gruyter, 1995); Wright and Rossi, *Armed and Considered Dangerous*; and Vizzard, *Shots in the Dark*. For an argument that this is a serious crime problem, but one for which the NRA has lobbied to weaken the federal regulation, see Anthony A. Braga, "More Gun Laws or More Gun Law Enforcement?" *Journal of Policy Analysis and Management* 20 (summer 2001): 545–549.

64. Kleck, *Targeting Guns*, 388–390.

65. Undoubtedly, the NRA would not agree. In keeping with the argument that this kind of regulation unnecessarily hinders the harmless trade and/or sale of second-hand firearms and further enables the government to track gun ownership by law-abiding citizens, the NRA would likely oppose rigorous attempts to regulate

the secondary market. However, I believe the benefits of regulating the secondary market outweigh the possible inconvenience of doing so for law-abiding gun owners.

66. Kennedy et al., "Youth Violence in Boston"; see also David M. Kennedy, "Can We Keep Guns Away from Kids?" *American Prospect* 18 (1994): 75–80.

67. Kennedy et al., "Youth Violence in Boston"; see also Edward Epstein, "Boston Speaker Tells Summit How to End Violence," *San Francisco Chronicle,* 8 March 2001, A18.

68. Kennedy et al., "Youth Violence in Boston"; and Epstein, "Boston Speaker Tells Summit How to End Violence." Please note that an anonymous reviewer of this book suggested that strong confidence in the Boston Gun Project is somewhat unwarranted because other factors that came into play at the same time could have also substantially reduced the violent crime rate in Boston. This may in fact be the case, as crime in the mid- to late 1990s was declining in the United States overall. For an overview, see Alfred Blumstein and Joel Wallman, eds., *The Crime Drop in America* (New York: Cambridge University Press, 2000).

69. "Boston Program Wins Ford Award," *American Rifleman* 146, no. 1 (1998): 18.

70. Other cities include San Francisco and Omaha, Nebraska. See Susan Sward, "Stop Killing, Offenders Warned," *San Francisco Chronicle,* 17 December 2001, A1; Tanya Eiserer, "Project Directed at Youths: Omaha Copies Boston Effort in Hopes of Reducing Gun Violence among the Young," *Omaha World-Herald,* 19 December 1999, 1B.

71. Elijah Anderson, *Code of the Street: Decency, Violence, and the Moral Life of the Inner City* (New York: Norton, 2000); James F. Short Jr., *Poverty, Ethnicity, and Violent Crime* (Boulder, CO: Westview, 1997).

Bibliography

Adler, Karl P., et al. 1994. "Firearm Violence and Public Health: Limiting the Availability of Guns." *Journal of the American Medical Association* 271(16): 1281–1283.

Agar, Michael. 1980. *The Professional Stranger: An Informal Introduction to Ethnography*. San Diego, CA: Academic Press.

Amar, Akhil Reed. 2000. *The Bill of Rights: Creation and Reconstruction*. New Haven: Yale University Press.

Anderson, Elijah. 2000. *Code of the Street: Decency, Violence, and the Moral Life of the Inner City*. New York: Norton.

Athearn, Robert G. 1986. *The Mythic West in Twentieth-Century America*. Lawrence: University Press of Kansas.

Bailyn, Bernard. 1967. *The Ideological Origins of the American Revolution*. Cambridge, MA: Harvard University Press.

Bane, Michael. 2001. "Targeting the Media's Anti-Gun Bias." *American Journalism Review* 23 (July/August): 18.

Becker, Gay. 1997. *Disrupted Lives: How People Create Meaning in a Chaotic World*. Berkeley: University of California Press.

Bellah, Robert N., Richard Madsen, William M. Sullivan, Ann Swidler, and Steven M. Tipton. 1985. *Habits of the Heart: Individualism and Commitment in American Life*. Berkeley: University of California Press.

Bellesiles, Michael A. 2000. *Arming America: The Origins of the National Gun Culture*. New York: Knopf.

Bijlefeld, Marjolijn. 1999. *People For and Against Gun Control: A Biographical Reference*. Westport, CT: Greenwood Press.

Black, Dan, and Daniel Nagin. 1998. "Do 'Right to Carry' Laws Reduce Violent Crime?" *Journal of Legal Studies* 27: 209–219.

Blumstein, Alfred, and Joel Wallman, eds. 2000. *The Crime Drop in America*. New York: Cambridge University Press.

"Boston Program Wins Ford Award." 1998. *American Rifleman* 146(1): 18.

Braga, Anthony A. 2001. "More Gun Laws or More Gun Law Enforcement?" *Journal of Policy Analysis and Management* 20 (summer): 545–549.

Braman, Donald, and Dan K. Kahan. 2001. *More Statistics, Less Persuasion: A Cultural Theory of Gun-Risk Perceptions.* Working Paper No. 5, Public Law and Legal Theory Working Paper Series, Yale Law School.

Brill, Steven. 1977. *Firearm Abuse: A Research and Policy Report.* Washington, DC: Police Foundation.

Brown, Richard Maxwell. 1969. "The American Vigilante Tradition." In *Violence in America: Historical and Comparative Perspectives.* H. D. Graham and T. R. Gurr, eds. New York: Bantam, 154–217.

Brown, Wendy. 1989. "Guns, Cowboys, Philadelphia Mayors, and Civic Republicanism: On Sanford Levinson's 'The Embarrassing Second Amendment.'" *Yale Law Journal* 99: 661–667.

Bruce-Briggs, Barry. 1976. "The Great American Gun War." *Public Interest* 45: 37–62.

Butler, Anne M. 1996. "Selling the Popular Myth." In *The Oxford History of the American West.* C. A. Milner II, C. A. O'Connor, and M. A. Sandweiss, eds. New York: Oxford University Press.

Carter, Gregg Lee. 2000. "Dueling Statistics." *Forum for Applied Research and Public Policy* (1 January): 68–75.

Caufield, Susan. 1999. "Transforming the Criminological Dialogue: A Feminist Perspective on the Impact of Militarism." *Journal of Political and Military Sociology* 27(2): 291–306.

Churchill, Robert. 2001. "Guns and the Politics of History." *Reviews in American History* 29: 329–337.

Clarke, D. A. 1993. "A Woman with a Sword: Some Thoughts on Women, Feminism, and Violence." In *Transforming a Rape Culture.* E. Buchwald, P. Fletcher, and M. Roth, eds. Minneapolis: Milkweed Editions, 393–404.

Claster, Daniel S. 1992. *Bad Guys and Good Guys: Moral Polarization and Crime.* Westport, CT: Greenwood Press.

Cook, Philip J., and Jens Ludwig. 2000. *Gun Violence: The Real Costs.* New York: Oxford University Press.

Cook, Philip J., Jens Ludwig, and David Hemenway. 1997. "The Gun Debate's Mythical New Number: How Many Defensive Gun Uses per Year?" *Journal of Policy Analysis and Management* 16: 463–469.

Cornell, Saul. 1999. "'To Keep and Bear Arms': The Militia, the People, and the Problem of Rights in Revolutionary America." In *Whose Right to Bear Arms Did the Second Amendment Protect?* S. Cornell and R. E. Shalhope, eds. New York: Bedford/St. Martin's, 9–16.

Cornell, Saul, and Robert E. Shalhope, eds. 2000. *Whose Right to Bear Arms Did the Second Amendment Protect?* New York: Bedford/St. Martin's.

Cottrol, Robert J. 1994. "The Second Amendment: Invitation to a Multi-Dimensional Debate." In *Introduction to Gun Control and the Constitution:*

Sources and Explorations on the Second Amendment. R. J. Cottrol, ed. New York: Garland, ix–xviii.

————. 1998. "Submission Is Not the Answer: Lethal Violence, Microcultures of Criminal Violence and the Right to Self-Defence." *University of Colorado Law Review* 69(4): 1029–1080.

Cottrol, Robert J., and Raymond T. Diamond. 1991. "The Second Amendment: Toward an Afro-Americanist Reconsideration." *Georgetown Law Journal* 80: 309–361. Reprinted in *Gun Control and the Constitution: Sources and Explorations on the Second Amendment.* R. J. Cottrol, ed. New York: Garland, 1994, 375–427.

Courtwright, David T. 1996. *Violent Land: Single Men and Social Disorder from the Frontier to the Inner City.* Cambridge, MA: Harvard University Press.

Csikszentmihalyi, Mihaly, and Eugene Rochberg-Halton. 1981. *The Meaning of Things: Domestic Symbols and the Self.* New York: Cambridge University Press. Reprint, 1995.

Cummings, Peter, and Thomas Koepsell. 1998. "Does Owning a Firearm Increase or Decrease the Risk of Death?" *Journal of the American Medical Association* 280(5): 471–473.

Custer, George A. 1874. "Wild Bill Hickok." In *My Life on the Plains, or Personal Experiences with Indians.* New York: Heldon. Reprinted in *In Their Own Words: Warriors and Pioneers.* T. J. Stiles, ed. New York: Perigee, 1996, 130–132.

DeConde, Alexander. 2001. *Gun Violence in America: The Struggle for Control.* Boston: Northeastern University Press.

Diaz, Tom. 1999. *Making a Killing: The Business of Guns in America.* New York: New Press.

Dixon, Jo, and Alan Lizotte. 1987. "Gun Ownership and the 'Southern Subculture of Violence.'" *American Journal of Sociology* 93(2): 383–405.

Dizard, Jan E., Robert Merrill Muth, and Stephen P. Andrews Jr. 1999. Introduction to *Guns in America: A Reader.* J. Dizard, R. M. Muth, and S. P. Andrews, eds. New York: New York University Press, 1–13.

Douglas, Mary, and Aaron Wildavsky. 1982. *Risk and Culture.* Berkeley: University of California Press.

Duncan, Otis Dudley. 2000. "Gun Use Surveys: In Numbers We Trust?" *Criminologist* 25(1): 1–7.

Durkheim, Emile. 1960. *The Division of Labor in Society.* G. Simpson, trans. Glencoe, IL: Free Press.

Erikson, Kai T. 1966. *Wayward Puritans: A Study in the Sociology of Deviance.* New York: Wiley.

Etzioni, Amitai. 2001. "Are Liberal Scholars Acting Irresponsibly on Gun Control?" *Chronicle of Higher Education* (6 April): B14.

Fagan, Jeffery, and Deanna L. Wilkinson. 1998. "Guns, Youth Violence, and Social Identity in the Inner Cities." *Crime and Justice* 24: 105–188.

French, Peter A. 1997. *Cowboy Metaphysics: Ethics and Death in Westerns.* Lanham, MD: Rowman and Littlefield.

Funk, T. Marcus. 1995. "Gun Control in America: A History of Discrimination against the Poor and Minorities." *Journal of Criminal Law and Criminology* 85(3): 794–801. Reprinted in *Guns in America: A Reader.* J. Dizard, R. M. Muth, and S. P. Andrews, eds. New York: New York University Press, 1999, 390–402.

Gibson, William James. 1994. *Warrior Dreams: Violence and Manhood in Post-Vietnam America.* New York: Hill and Wang.

Giddens, Anthony. 1991. *Modernity and Self-Identity: Self and Society in the Late Modern Age.* Stanford: Stanford University Press.

Godwin, Marcia L., and Jean Reith Schroedel. 1998. "Gun Control Politics in California." In *The Changing Politics of Gun Control.* J. M. Bruce and C. Wilcox, eds. Lanham, MD: Rowman and Littlefield, 88–110.

Goldberg, Bernard. 2001. "On Media Bias, Network Stars Are Rather Clueless." *Wall Street Journal* (24 May): A22.

Goode, Erich, and Nachman Ben-Yehuda. 1994. *Moral Panics: The Social Construction of Deviance.* Cambridge, MA: Blackwell.

Grossman, James R. 1994. Introduction to *The Frontier in American Culture: An Exhibition at the Newberry Library, August 26, 1994–January 7, 1995.* J. R. Grossman, ed. Berkeley: University of California Press, 1–5.

Halbrook, Stephen P. 1989. *A Right to Bear Arms.* Westport, CT: Greenwood Press.

Hawley, F. Fred. 1990. "Culture Conflict and the Ideology of Pariah Groups: The Weltanschauung of Gun Owners." In *The Gun Culture and Its Enemies.* William R. Tonso, ed. Bellevue, WA: Second Amendment Foundation, 109–125.

Heller, Thomas C., and David E. Wellbery. 1986. Introduction to *Reconstructing Individualism: Autonomy, Individuality, and the Self in Western Thought.* Stanford: Stanford University Press, 1–15.

Herz, Andrew. 1995. "Gun Crazy: Constitutional False Consciousness and the Dereliction of Dialogic Responsibility." *Boston University Law Review* 75: 57–153.

Homsher, Deborah. 2001. *Women and Guns: Politics and the Culture of Firearms in America.* Armonk, NY: M.E. Sharpe.

Hosley, William. 1996. *Colt: The Making of an American Legend.* Amherst: University of Massachusetts Press.

Jacobs, James B. 2002. *Can Gun Control Work?* New York: Oxford University Press.

Japenga, Ann. 1994. "Would I Be Safer with a Gun?" *Health* 8(2): 52–64.

Kaminer, Wendy. 1995. *It's All the Rage: Crime and Culture.* Reading, MA: Addison-Wesley.

———. 2001. "Politics of Identity." *American Prospect* 12 (September 24): 32.

Kates, Don B., Jr. 1992. "The Second Amendment and the Ideology of Self-Protection." *Constitutional Commentary* 9: 87–104.

———. 2001. "Guns and Public Health: Epidemic of Violence, or Pandemic of

Propaganda?" In *Armed: New Perspectives on Gun Control*. G. Kleck and D. B. Kates Jr., eds. Amherst, NY: Prometheus, 31–106.

———. 2001. Introduction to *Armed: New Perspectives on Gun Control*. G. Kleck and D. B. Kates Jr., eds. Amherst, NY: Prometheus, 13–30.

———. 2001. "'Poisoning the Well' for Gun Control." In *Armed: New Perspectives on Gun Control*. G. Kleck and D. B. Kates Jr., eds. Amherst, NY: Prometheus, 107–128.

Kates, Don B., Jr. and Daniel D. Polsby. 1997. "Of Holocausts and Gun Control." *Washington University Law Quarterly* 75(3): 1237–1275.

Kates, Don. B., Jr., Henry E. Schaffer, John K. Lattimer, George B. Murray, and Edwin H. Cassem. 1995. "Bad Medicine: Doctors and Guns." In *Guns: Who Should Have Them?* D. B. Kopel, ed. Amherst, NY: Prometheus, 233–308.

Kates, Don B., Jr., and Nicole Varzos. 1990. "Aspects of the Priapic Theory of Gun Ownership." In *The Gun Culture and Its Enemies*. W. R. Tonso, ed. Bellevue, WA: Second Amendment Foundation, 93–107.

Katz, Jack. 1990. *Seductions of Crime: A Chilling Exploration of the Criminal Mind—From Juvenile Delinquency to Cold Blooded Murder*. New York: Basic Books.

———. 1997. "Ethnography's Warrants." *Sociological Methods and Research* 25(4): 391–423.

Kellermann, A. L., and D. T. Reay. 1986. "Protection or Peril? An Analysis of Firearms-Related Deaths in the Home." *New England Journal of Medicine* 314: 1557–1560.

Kellermann, A. L., F. P. Rivara, N. B. Rushforth, et al. 1993. "Gun Ownership as a Risk Factor for Homicide in the Home." *New England Journal of Medicine* 329(15): 1084–1091.

Kellermann, A. L., F. P. Rivara, G. Somes, et al. 1992. "Suicide in the Home in Relationship to Gun Ownership." *New England Journal of Medicine* 327: 467–472.

Kennedy, David M. 1994. "Can We Keep Guns Away from Kids?" *American Prospect* 18: 75–80.

Kennedy, David M., Anne M. Piehl, and Anthony A. Braga. 1996. "Youth Violence in Boston: Gun Markets, Serious Youth Offenders, and a Use-Reduction Strategy." *Law and Contemporary Problems* 59: 147–196.

Kennett, Lee, and James LaVerne Anderson. 1975. *The Gun in America: The Origins of a National Dilemma*. Westport, CT: Greenwood Press.

Kerber, Linda K. 1980. *Women of the Republic: Intellect and Ideology in Revolutionary America*. Chapel Hill: University of North Carolina Press.

———. 1998. *No Constitutional Right to Be Ladies: Women and the Obligations of Citizenship*. New York: Hill and Wang.

Kintz, Linda. 1997. *Between Jesus and the Market: The Emotions That Matter in Right-Wing America*. Durham, NC: Duke University Press.

————. 1997. *Targeting Guns: Firearms and Their Control.* Hawthorne, NY: Aldine de Gruyter.

————. 2003. "Absolutist Politics in a Moderate Package: Prohibitionist Intentions of the Gun Control Movement." In *Armed: New Perspectives on Gun Control.* G. Kleck and D. B. Kates Jr., eds. Amherst, NY: Prometheus, 129–172.

————. 2003. "The Frequency of Defensive Gun Use: Evidence and Disinformation." In *Armed: New Perspectives on Gun Control.* G. Kleck and D. B. Kates Jr., eds. Amherst, NY: Prometheus, 213–284.

Kleck, Gary, and Marc Gertz. 1995. "Armed Resistance to Crime: The Prevalence and Nature of Self-defense with a Gun." *Journal of Criminal Law and Criminology* 86: 150–187.

Kleck, Gary, and Don. B. Kates Jr., eds. 1999. *Armed: New Perspectives on Gun Control.* Amherst, NY: Prometheus.

Kohn, Abigail A. 2000. "Cowboy Dreaming: Guns in Fantasy and Role-Playing." In *Gun Women.* M. Z. Stange and C. Oyster, eds. New York: New York University Press, pp. 187–196.

————. 2000. "Shooters: The Moral World of Gun Enthusiasts." Ph.D. diss., University of California, Berkeley and San Francisco.

————. 2001. "Their Aim Is True." *Reason* 33 (May): 26–32.

Kohn, Abigail A., and Jesse A. Dizard. 1999. *Individual versus Social Responsibility for Gun Crime: Shooters Talk Back.* Paper presented at the 1999 annual meeting of the American Society of Criminology, Toronto.

Kohn, Richard H. 1975. *Eagle and Sword: The Federalists and the Creation of the Military Establishment in America, 1783–1802.* New York: Free Press. Reprint, 1985.

Koop, C. Everett, and George D. Lundberg. 1992. "Violence in America: A Public Health Emergency." *Journal of the American Medical Association* 267: 3075–3076.

Kopel, David B. 1992. *The Samurai, the Mountie, and the Cowboy: Should America Adopt the Gun Controls of Other Democracies?* Buffalo, NY: Prometheus.

————. 1995. "Background Checks and Waiting Periods." *In Guns: Who Should Have Them?* D. Kopel, ed. Amherst, NY: Prometheus, 53–126.

————. 1995. "Children and Guns." In *Guns: Who Should Have Them?* D. Kopel, ed. Amherst, NY: Prometheus, 309–406.

————, ed. 1995. *Guns: Who Should Have Them?* Amherst, NY: Prometheus.

Kurz, Demie. 1999. *"Real Knockouts:" The Physical Feminism of Women's Self-Defense,* by Martha McCaughey. Book review. *Gender and Society* 13(1): 145–147.

Landes, Richard. 2003. "The Question of Rationality: A Response to Joel Kovel." *Tikkun* 18(3): 54–57.

Laws, Susan. 1997. "On the Trail with the Single Action Shooting Society." *Gun New Digest* 3(2): 26–32.

Lears, Jackson. 2001. "Guns' Mystique Clouds Debate." *Newsday* (27 March): A36.

Levy, Leonard Williams. 1999. *Origins of the Bill of Rights*. New Haven: Yale University Press.

Lewontin, Richard C. 1993. *Biology as Ideology: The Doctrine of DNA*. New York: HarperPerennial.

Limerick, Patricia Nelson. 1987. *The Legacy of Conquest: The Unbroken Past of the American West*. New York: Norton.

Lingren, James D., and Justin Heather. 2002. "Counting Guns in Early America." *William and Mary Law Review* 43: 1777–1842.

Lipset, Seymour Martin. 1997. *American Exceptionalism: A Double-Edged Sword*. New York: Norton.

Lizotte, Alan J., David J. Bordua, and Carolyn S. White. 1981. "Firearms Ownership for Sport and Protection: Two Not So Divergent Models." *American Sociological Review* 46: 499–503.

Lott, John R., Jr. 1998. *More Guns, Less Crime*. Chicago: University of Chicago Press.

Lorde, Audre. 1983. "The Master's Tools Will Never Dismantle the Master's House." In *This Bridge Called My Back: Writings of Radical Women of Color*. C. Moraga and G. Anzaldúa, eds. Latham, NY: Kitchen Table Press, 98–101.

Lupton, Deborah. 1993. "Risk as Moral Danger: The Social and Political Functions of Risk in Public Health." *International Journal of Health Services* 23(3): 425–435.

Madriz, Esther. 1997. *Nothing Bad Happens to Good Girls: Fear of Crime in Women's Lives*. Berkeley: University of California Press.

Main, Gloria. 2002. "Many Things Forgotten: The Use of Probate Records in Arming America." *William and Mary Quarterly*, 3d ser. 59 (January): 211–216.

Malcolm, Joyce Lee. 1994. *To Keep and Bear Arms: The Origins of an Anglo-American Right*. Cambridge, MA: Harvard University Press.

McCaffrey, Dawn. 1999. "*Real Knockouts: The Physical Feminism of Women's Self-Defense*." Book review. *Violence Against Women* 5(7): 829–833.

McCarthy, Thomas J. 1999. "Whatever I Want: The Freedom to Wield a Gun Symbolizes Our Twisted National Desideratum." *America* 181 (25 September): 6.

McCaughey, Martha. 1997. *Real Knockouts: The Physical Feminism of Women's Self-Defense*. New York: New York University Press.

McIntyre, Thomas. 2000–2001. "Attacking Gun Owners." *Sports Afield* 224 (December/January): 28–29.

Morse, Janice M., and Peggy Ann Field. 1995. "An Overview of Qualitative Methods." In *Qualitative Research Methods for Health Professionals*. Thousand Oaks, CA: Sage, 21–41.

Nelson, Dana D. 1998. *National Manhood: Capitalist Citizenship and the Imagined Fraternity of White Men*. Durham, NC: Duke University Press.

Nisbet, Lee, ed. 1990. *The Gun Debate: You Decide*. Buffalo, NY: Prometheus.

Ortner, Sherry B. 1978. *Sherpas through Their Rituals*. Cambridge, UK: Cambridge University Press. Reprint, 1990.

Patrick, Brian Anse. 2003. *The National Rifle Association and the Media: The Motivating Force of Negative Coverage.* New York: Peter Lang.

Petersen, Alan, and Deborah Lupton. 1996. *The New Public Health: Health and Self in the Age of Risk.* London: Sage.

Pfeil, Fred. 1997. "Sympathy for the Devils: Notes on Some White Guys in the Ridiculous Class War." In *Whiteness: A Critical Reader.* M. Hill, ed. New York: New York University Press, 21–34.

Pocock, J. G. A. 1975. *The Machiavellian Moment: Florentine Political Thought and the Atlantic Republican Tradition.* Princeton, NJ: Princeton University Press.

Pollitt, Katha. 2000. "Moms to NRA: Grow Up!" *The Nation* (12 June): 10.

Polsby, Daniel D., and Don B. Kates Jr. 1997. "Of Holocausts and Gun Control." *Washington University Law Quarterly* 75(3): 1237–1275.

Purdy, Lawrence J. 1992. "Knife and Gun Clubs of America." *Journal of the American Medical Association* 267: 3086.

Quinley, Hal. 1990. *Memorandum Reporting Results from Time/CNN Poll of Gun Owners, February 6.* New York: Yankelovich Clancy Shulman Survey Organization.

Reddin, Paul. 1999. *Wild West Shows.* Champaign: University of Illinois Press.

Reynolds, Glenn Harlan. 1995. "A Critical Guide to the Second Amendment." *Tennessee Law Review* 62(3): 461–512.

Robertson, James Oliver. 1980. *American Myth American Reality.* New York: Hill and Wang.

Rosen, Gary. 2000. "Yes and No to Gun Control." *Commentary* 110 (September): 47–53.

Rosenberg, Mark L., Patrick W. O'Carroll, and Kenneth E. Powell. 1992. "Let's Be Clear: Violence Is a Public Health Problem." *Journal of the American Medical Association* 267(22): 3071–3072.

Rosenblatt, Roger. 1999. "Get Rid of the Damned Things." *Time* 154(6): 38–39.

Rosenblum, Nancy L. 1998. *Membership and Morals: The Personal Uses of Pluralism in America.* Princeton, NJ: Princeton University Press.

Roth, Randolph. 2002. "Guns, Gun Culture, and Homicide: The Relationship between Firearms, the Uses of Firearms, and Interpersonal Violence." *William and Mary Quarterly,* 3d ser. 59 (January): 223–240.

Rotundo, Anthony. 1993. *American Manhood: Transformations in Masculinity from the Revolution to the Modern Era.* New York: Basic Books.

Scarry, Elaine. 1991. "War and the Social Contract: Nuclear Policy, Distribution, and the Right to Bear Arms." *University of Pennsylvania Law Review* 139(5): 1257–1316.

Shalhope, Robert E. 1999. "To Keep and Bear Arms in the Early Republic." *Constitutional Commentary* 16: 269–281.

Sheley, Joseph F., Charles J. Brody, and James D. Wright. 1994. "Women and

Handguns: Evidence from National Surveys, 1973–1991." *Social Science Research* 23: 219–235.

Sheley, Joseph F., and James D. Wright. 1995. *In the Line of Fire: Youth, Guns, and Violence in Urban America.* New York: Aldine de Gruyter.

Shields, Nelson. 1981. *Guns Don't Die, People Do.* New York: Arbor House.

Short, James F., Jr. 1997. *Poverty, Ethnicity, and Violent Crime.* Boulder, CO: Westview.

Slotkin, Richard. 1973. *Regeneration through Violence: The Mythology of the American Frontier, 1600–1860.* Middletown, CT: Wesleyan University Press.

———. 1986. *The Fatal Environment: The Myth of the Frontier in the Age of Industrialization, 1800–1890.* Middletown, CT: Wesleyan University Press.

———. 1992. *Gunfighter Nation: The Myth of the Frontier in Twentieth-Century America.* New York: HarperPerennial.

———. 2000. "The Fall into Guns." *Atlantic Monthly* 286 (November): 114–118.

Smith, Tom W., and Robert J. Smith. 1995. "Changes in Firearms Ownership among Women, 1980–1994." *Journal of Criminal Law and Criminology* 86: 133–149.

Snider, Lauren. 1998. "Toward Safer Societies: Punishment, Masculinities, and Violence against Women." *British Journal of Criminology* 38(1): 1–39.

Snyder, Jeffrey R. 1976. "A Nation of Cowards." *Public Interest*, no. 113. Reprinted in *Guns in America: A Reader.* J. Dizard, R. M. Muth, and S. P. Andrews, eds. New York: New York University Press, 1999, 182–193.

Spradley, J. P. 1979. *The Ethnographic Interview.* New York: Holt, Rinehart & Winston.

Squires, Peter. 2000. *Gun Culture or Gun Control?* London: Routledge.

Stange, Mary Zeiss. 1995. "Arms and the Woman: A Feminist Reappraisal." In *Guns: Who Should Have Them?* D. B. Kopel, ed. Amherst, NY: Prometheus, 15–52.

Stange, Mary Zeiss, and Carol K. Oyster, eds. 2000. *Gun Women: Firearms and Feminism in Contemporary America.* New York: New York University Press.

Stebbins, Robert A., and William Shaffir. 1991. *Experiencing Fieldwork: An Insider View of Qualitative Research.* Thousand Oaks, CA: Sage.

Stenross, Barbara. 1990. "Turning Vices into Virtues: The Dignifying Accounts of Gun Avocationists." In *Marginal Conventions: Popular Culture, Mass Media, and Social Deviance.* C. R. Sanders, ed. Bowling Green, OH: Bowling Green State University Popular Press, 56–64.

Toch, Hans, and Alan J. Lizotte. 1992. "Research and Policy: The Case of Gun Control." In *Psychology and Social Policy.* P. Suedfeld and P. E. Tedlock, eds. New York: Hemisphere Publishing, 223–240.

Tonso, William R. 1982. *Gun and Society: The Social and Existential Roots of the American Attachment to Firearms.* Washington, DC: University Press of America.

———. 1990. Introduction to *The Gun Culture and Its Enemies*. Bellevue, WA: Second Amendment Foundation, 1–24

———, ed. 1990. *The Gun Culture and Its Enemies*. Bellevue, WA: Second Amendment Foundation.

Vizzard, William J. 2000. *Shots in the Dark: The Policy, Politics, and Symbolism of Gun Control*. Lanham, MD: Rowman and Littlefield.

Wagner, David. 1997. *The New Temperance: The American Obsession with Sin and Vice*. Boulder, CO: Westview Press.

Wellman, Carl. 1995. "Rights." In *The Cambridge Dictionary of Philosophy*. R. Audi, ed. Cambridge, UK: Cambridge University Press.

West, Robin. 1999. "Gun Rights." *Tikkun* (1 September): 25.

White, Richard. 1991. *"It's Your Misfortune and None of My Own": A New History of the American West*. Norman: University of Oklahoma Press.

———. 1994. "Frederick Jackson Turner and Buffalo Bill." In *The Frontier in American Culture: An Exhibition at the Newberry Library, August 26, 1994–January 7, 1995*. J. R. Grossman, ed. Berkeley: University of California Press, 7–66.

Wilkinson, Rupert. 1984. *American Tough: The Tough-Guy Tradition and American Character*. Westport, CT: Greenwood Press.

Wills, Garry. 1995. "To Keep and Bear Arms." *New York Review of Books* 42 (21 September): 62–73.

Wood, Gordon S. 1991. *The Radicalism of the American Revolution*. New York: Vintage Books.

Wright, James D. 1990. "Second Thoughts about Gun Control." In *The Gun Control Debate: You Decide*. L. Nisbet, ed. Buffalo, NY: Prometheus, 93–107.

———. 1995. "Ten Essential Observations on Guns in America." *Society* (March/April). Reprinted in *Guns in America: A Reader*. J. E. Dizard, R. M. Muth, and S. P. Andrews, eds. New York: New York University Press, 1999, 500–507.

Wright, James D., and Linda Marston. 1975. "The Ownership of the Means to Destruction: Weapons in the United States." *Social Problems* 23: 93–107.

Wright, James D., and Peter H. Rossi. 1986. *Armed and Considered Dangerous: A Survey of Felons and Their Firearms*. Hawthorne, NY: Aldine de Gruyter.

Wright, James D., Peter H. Rossi, and Kathleen Daly. 1983. *Under the Gun: Weapons, Crime, and Violence in America*. Hawthorne, NY: Aldine de Gruyter.

Zimring, Franklin E. 1996. "Kids, Guns, and Homicide: Policy Notes on an Age-Specific Epidemic." *Law and Contemporary Problems* 59: 25–38.

Zimring, Franklin E., and Gordon Hawkins. 1987. *The Citizen's Guide to Gun Control*. New York: Macmillan.

Index

gun enthusiasts' interest, 10
  home defense, 106
  patriotism, 108–9
Colt, Samuel, 84, 94
community. *See also* civic responsibility
  citizen soldiers, 62, 81
  cowboy action shooting, 40, 47, 52
  cowboy myths, 86
  dependence on, 71
  gun enthusiasts as, 3, 13–15, 18, 28, 35, 38, 166
community safety. *See* public safety
community service. *See* civic responsibility
competitions. *See* shooting competitions
Congress, 148
Congress of Rough Riders, 87
conquest. *See* imperialist conquest (Old West)
conservatism
  gun debate, xi, 66, 156, 167
  gun enthusiasts, 23
  gun ownership and use, ix, 4, 8, 92, 95, 137
  NRA, x
  toughness and, 114
Constitution, 148
  Fourth Amendment, 137
  Second Amendment, viii–x, 74–75, 82, 93, 140, 163
context, 11, 37–38, 145
Cook and Ludwig, 156
core values. *See* American core values
Cortese, Janis, 122
costume (cowboy action shooting), 40–41, 43, 45–47, 52–53, 97
courage (cowboy myths), 83–84, 87
cowboy action shooting, 39–54. *See also* Single Action Shooting Society (SASS)
  description of shoots, 40, 48–53
  fantasies, 38, 43–44, 46, 97–98
  interviews and participant observation, 7, 27–28, 34–35, 109
  modern day cowboy lawmen, 89–99
cowboy aliases, 43, 46–47
cowboy guns, 10–11, 34, 43–46, 98
cowboy lawmen, 83–102
  modern-day, 43, 88–99
cowboys (real and mythic), 42–47, 53, 84–88
Creigh, Harper ("Judge Roy Bean"), 43
crime. *See also* victims of gun violence
  buying guns, 32–34, 164–66
  citizen soldiers and, 68, 71–73
  cowboy shooters and, 89, 91–92, 95–96, 109–10
  cowboys and, 85
  gun control and, 17, 122, 148–50
  gun debate, 138–39, 145, 148–57, 160–62, 164–66, 168
  gun enthusiasts' attitudes, 23, 26
  gun ownership and, ix, x, 8–9
  gun safety, 79
  public health issues, 133, 135–36

subculture, 15–16
  toughness in fighting, 111–12, 126–29
criminal justice system, 132, 148
criminology
  cheap guns, 91
  empirical evidence, 155–57
  good guys and bad guys, 150
  gun licensing and registration, 161, 165
  gun ownership, x, 8, 13, 128, 158
  public health issues, 121, 133, 135
  violence, 168
Crusader Rabbit, 119
cultural change, 139–41
cultural conflicts, 5–6. *See also* gun culture
cultural problems (cowboy action shooting), 53–54
Custer, General George, 104

danger
  children and guns, 105–6
  citizen soldiers, 68, 71–72, 75
  gun culture, viii
  gun debate, 144, 154, 159, 162, 164–67
  gun enthusiasts' attitudes, 12–14, 25
  gun safety, 79
  public health issues, 135
  toughness and, 104–7, 116, 120, 124
Darwin, Charles, 83
Davis, Bette, 112
dealers. *See* gun dealers
defensive use of guns. *See also* home defense; self-defense
  alternatives to, 94
  gun control policies, 164
  public health issues, 135
  purposes of gun ownership, 8
  shooters interviewed, 9
  statistics, 155–57
  toughness and, 108–11, 116–18, 120, 125–27, 129–30
democracy
  citizen soldiers, 62
  cowboy action shooting, 40, 90, 101
Democrats, 6, 8
demography, 8, 137. *See also* geographic differences
deviance, 16
Dirty Harry, 103
disarmament. *See* gun control
dress. *See* costume
duty. *See* civic responsibility

Earp, Wyatt, 52
Easterners, 84, 109
education. *See* gun education; shooting classes
Edward (interviewee), 108
egalitarianism. *See* equality
elites, political, 90–91, 92–97
Ellen (interviewee), 108

geographic differences, 3–4, 8, 13. *See also* demography

German history. *See* Nazis

Gertz, Mark, 155–56

Gibson, Mel, 57

"good guys and bad guys," viii. *See also* heroes
cowboy action shooting, 40, 43, 46
cowboy myths, 86–87, 97–99, 101
gun debate, 144, 168
inherent badness, 150–54
public health issues, 134
shooters as, 15–16, 109

government. *See* state

Great Britain. *See* Britain

Greek and Roman philosophy, 58

Greg (interviewee), vii, 25–26, 71–74, 111, 120

gun control, viii, x, 28, 78, 95, 106, 113. *See also* public health
aims and motives, 14, 18
citizen soldiers and, 63, 67–68, 76
colonial society, 59–60
Emerson decision, 163, 164–69
gun enthusiasts' hostility to, 5, 18, 23, 79–80, 109–10, 151
laws, viii
media attitudes, vii
organizations, vii, 6
political equality, 91–97
politics, 6, 8
supporters' assumptions, 136–47
supporters in gun debate, ix, x, 16, 131, 153, 155–56, 157
toughness and, 119, 122, 128

gun culture
American culture and, 15, 17–19, 38, 108, 137–38, 140
citizen soldiers, 70
criticism of, viii, 15–16
definition, 4
eradication, 14, 31, 136–39
geography, 3
gun debate, 142, 148
interview questions, 171
Northern California, 3, 6
subcultures, 15, 137

gun dealers, 3–4, 30–31, 32–34, 43, 84, 109. *See also* buying guns; gun shops; gun trafficking
licensing and law enforcement, 31, 161, 166, 168

gun debate. *See also* evidence, in gun debate; pro-gun advocates; public health
citizen soldiers and, 65–66, 68
gun control supporters, 157–62
gun control supporters' assumptions, 136–47
gun enthusiasts, 14–18, 162–69
gun enthusiasts' assumptions, 147–57
publications, 5

stereotypes, vii–xi, 15
suggestions for advancing, 131–32

gun education, 78–79, 105–7. *See also* gun safety; shooting classes

gun enthusiasts. *See also* citizen soldiers; cowboy action shooting; interviews
activities, 19–38
definition, vii, 9–11
gun debate, 6, 131–36, 138, 143, 147–57, 158–59
gun ownership and, 9
stereotypes, vii–xi
study of (*see* interviews)
toughness, 130
women, 13, 20, 27–28, 106, 115–20, 123–27

gun industry. *See* gun manufacturers

gun laws. *See* laws

gun licensing and registration, vii, 32–34, 143–44, 161–62

gun manufacturers
cowboy lawmen, 84
government and, 137
interviews, 7
opposition to, ix, 162
women gun owners, 114–15

Gun Owners of America, 164

gun ownership. *See also* gun enthusiasts; gun rights
academic opinion of, viii–ix
American ethos, 15
citizen soldiers, 57, 62–72
colonial society, 58–60
demography, 8
gun culture, 4
gun debate, 17–18, 137–39, 144, 147, 151–53, 155, 157, 161, 164
gun enthusiasts and, 9, 20, 37
ideology, 7, 40
interviews, 3–4, 171
local and neighborhood, 159
media portrayal, vii–viii
motives, x–xi, 7, 137
patriotism and, 108
penalization, 159–62
political equality, 92
psychosexual pathology, 12–13
public health issues, 132, 134
social and political worth, 141–45
social control, 96
statistics, 159
stigmatization of, 6, 15, 38, 54, 158–59
toughness and, 106–8, 110, 113–16, 126, 128
women, 113–16, 118–27

gun rights
citizen soldiers, 63, 68, 74–77, 80–82
cowboy shooters, 96–97
Emerson decision, 163–64
gun debate, 131, 133, 138, 141, 157, 162, 167, 169
scholarship, ix

Kathy (interviewee), 37–38
Kennedy, David, 166
King, B. B., 12
Kleck, Gary, 155–56, 165, 168
Kopel, David, 168
Ku Klux Klan, ix, x

Las Vegas, 105
Latinos. *See* Hispanics
law-abiding citizens
    gun owners as, ix, 40, 109, 122, 131, 149, 151,
        165
    transforming criminals into, 136
law and order
    contemporary ideologies, 92, 154, 165
    cowboys, 85–86, 154
    toughness and, 104, 112
law enforcement officers. *See also* cowboy
        lawmen
    citizen soldiers and, 64, 72
    cowboy shooters, 43, 46, 89–90, 94–95
    gun enthusiasts, 7, 20, 22, 27, 30, 77, 107, 116
    gun ownership, 137, 142
    gun safety and education, 78–79, 159
    powers and programs, 143, 161, 164–67
    public health issues, 136
    shooting sports, 34
    toughness, 107
    women, 114, 116
law journals, ix
laws. *See also* gun control; gun licensing and
        registration
    buying guns, 33
    California, 6, 33, 65–66
    colonial, 59–60
    cowboy shooters, 40, 91–92
    gun debate, 136, 140, 144, 149, 158–59, 163–65
    gun safety and education, 78–79
    interview questions, 171
    responsibility for protection, 95
    shooting ranges, 29
legal rights. *See* rights
lessons. *See* shooting classes
Lewis (interviewee), 91, 93–94
liberal opinions. *See also* public health
    gun control, x, 122
    gun debate, xi, 142, 144, 147–48, 150–55,
        158–59, 167–68
    gun ownership and use, 4, 8, 14, 23, 92, 94
    gun rights, viii
    politicians, 21
    toughness and, 114, 122
libertarians, 8, 68
liberty
    citizen soldiers, 58, 61–62
    cowboy lawmen, 84
licensing. *See* gun dealers; gun licensing and
        registration

lifestyle
    cowboy action shooting, 40, 46, 97, 99–100
    gun debate, 154
    gun enthusiasts, 6, 18, 22
    interview questions, 171
    public health issues, 132, 135
liminal position (women gun users), 114
Lonesome Dove (television program), 86
Lorde, Audre, 114
Los Angeles area, 13
Louise (interviewee), 27, 68–69, 123–25
Louisiana, 163

McCaughey, Martha, 120, 123
machismo. *See* masculinity
"Major Disaster," 47
Malcolm X, 103
male shooters. *See also* masculinity
    citizen soldiers, 66
    colonial society, 59–60, 80
    cowboy action shooting, 39–41, 45–46, 51, 53
    interviews and participant observation, 3, 7,
        9, 20, 26, 27–28, 120, 171
    shooting sports, 34
    toughness, 105–7, 110, 126–27
"Manly, Colonel," 103
Manuel (interviewee), 20, 29, 36, 75, 110, 127
manufacturers. *See* gun manufacturers
Marcus (interviewee), 101–2
Marine Corps, 64
marksmanship. *See* skill
Martin, Benjamin *(The Patriot)*, 57
masculinity. *See also* All-American manhood;
        family responsibility; male shooters;
        misogyny; patriarchy; patriotism;
        personhood
    chauvinism, 115
    citizen soldiers, 57, 70
    cowboy action shooting, 50
    cowboy myths, 84, 87–88
    gun culture, ix, 70
    gun debate, 141–42
    gun enthusiasts, 25–26, 27–28
    gun fetish, 12
    gun owners, 8, 30
    toughness, 103, 104–10, 112–13, 115–16,
        120–21, 123–25, 129
Massachusetts, 59
Masterson, William Barclay "Bat," 85
media reporting and attitudes. *See also* enter-
        tainment and entertainment industry
    antigun, vii–x, 5, 65–66
    defensive gun use, 156
    fear of guns and crime, 26
    gun behavior, 78–79
    gun magazines, 10
    public health issues, 134
    women gun owners, 114–15

socialization, 4
soldiers. *See* citizen soldiers; military
South Carolina, 57
Southern California, 13, 42–43, 66
Southern states, 4, 59
special interest groups, 65–66
sports. *See* shooting sports
Stagecoach (movie), 86
Stange and Oyster, 115
state (government)
    abuse of power, 75, 94–97, 128
    citizen soldiers and, 63–65, 67–68, 71,
        74–75, 80–82
    colonial society, 58–60
    cowboy shooters and, 91–97, 109
    guns and, 123, 133–34, 137, 139–44, 163, 165,
        167
statistics. *See* evidence, in gun debate
status. *See also* personhood
    citizen soldiers, 64–66, 73–74, 76, 80–81
    colonial society, 60
    cowboy myths, 84, 87, 94
    cowboy shooters, 52, 100–101
    gun debate, 142, 144
    gun enthusiasts as rebels, 14
    gun ownership and, 123
stereotypes
    cowboy myths, 101
    crime and poverty, 91–92
    ethnographic research, 5
    of gun culture, 38
    of gun enthusiasts, 19, 70
    gun fetish, 12
    of gun owners, vii–x, 15
    women's self-defense, 120–21
stigmatization of gun owners, 6, 15, 38, 54,
        158–59
stores. *See* gun shops
strength
    cowboy shooters, 40, 49, 84
    patriotism, 108
    toughness and, 104, 113, 118, 129–30
strength of character
    cowboy shooters, 99
    toughness and, 114–15, 118, 130
stress
    citizen soldiers, 71–72
    cowboy shooters, 53–54, 100
    toughness and, 126–27
subcultures. *See also* gun culture
    cowboys, 85
suburban people
    cowboy action shooting, 44
    gun ownership, viii
    Old West mythic history, 53–54
suicide, viii, 29, 132, 135, 160
Switzerland, 139
symbolism of guns. *See also* freedom
    citizen soldiers, 62, 67–69, 71, 77, 80, 109

colonial society, 60
    context, 144–45
    cowboy shooters, 39, 54, 94, 99, 102
    to critics, 26, 96, 106, 141
    Frontier, 84, 88
    gun control, 95
    gun culture, 4, 16, 38
    gun ownership, 128
    Indians, 83
    interview questions, 172
    to minorities, 142
    power, 123–25, 145
    to shooters, 11, 16, 25–26, 96, 106, 111
    threats, 72
    value of, 155–56
    to women shooters, 118, 123–25

target shooting, 4, 7, 10, 15
targets, 20–21, 24–26, 30, 34, 35–37, 48, 51
team shoots (cowboy action shooting), 51–53
television programs. *See* entertainment and
        entertainment industry
Tenth Cavalry, 121
terrorists
    gun owners as potential, vii, 138, 145
    protection against, 128–30
Texas, 163
textbooks, 22–23
Thanksgiving, 39
The Contrast (comedy, 1787), 103
Thea (interviewee), 13–14, 27–28, 108, 118, 121
Third Reich. *See* Nazis
threats of violence
    actual violence and, 135
    citizen soldiers and, 71–72, 75
    defensive gun use, 157
    experienced by interviewees, 9, 89–90, 110
    toughness in face of, 116, 118
Tobias (interviewee), 77
Tombstone, 44, 46
Tombstone (movie), 86
toughness, 103–30. *See also* masculinity; patri-
        otism; victimization; vigilance; women
    cowboy action shooting, 49–53
    cowboy myths, 83, 87
    gun debate, 157
    gun safety and education, 79
    national character, 129–30
training. *See* gun education; shooting classes
transgressive behavior, enjoyment of, 12, 123
Tribe, Lawrence H., 163
Turner, Frederick Jackson, 87, 100
TV. *See* entertainment
Tyler, Royall. *The Contrast* (1787), 103

Union (Civil War), 102
United Kingdom. *See* Britain
United States Practical Shooting Association
        (USPSA), 34

University of California, 3
upper class. *See* class
urban areas, 4, 8, 14, 31, 36
    addressing violent behavior, 167–69
    cowboy action shooting, 46, 52–54
    gun debate, 154
    gun safety and education, 79
    shooting sports, 34
    toughness, 111
USPSA (United States Practical Shooting Association), 34
Uzis, 76

values. *See* moral principles
veterans. *See* military
victimization
    gun debate, 149
    gun enthusiasts' attitudes, 16, 73, 76
    protection against, 95–96, 111–12, 116,
        118–20, 125, 126–29
    public health issues, 133
victims of gun violence
    gun debate, 143
    politics, 6
    respect for, ix
    shooters interviewed, 8–9
Victorian values, 112
Vietnam veterans, 25
Vietnam War, 98
vigilance, 110–12, 114, 118, 120, 125, 127–30, 157
vigilante groups, 52, 86, 99
violence. *See also* suicide; threats of violence;
        victims of gun violence
    citizen soldiers and, 57, 61, 73
    cowboy myths, 84–85, 87, 92
    cowboy shooters, 95, 99, 102
    gun debate, 131–36, 139–41, 143, 145–55,
        157–58, 160–61, 165–69
    gun enthusiasts' attitudes, 12, 16, 26
    gun ownership as cause, vii–viii
    racist, viii–ix
    shooting sports and, 35–36, 38
    toughness and, 106–8, 110–24, 126–28
Virginia, 59
vulnerability
    citizen soldiers, 72
    cowboy shooters, 94, 96
    gun debate, 143–44, 147–48
    gun enthusiasts, 13, 36
    public health issues, 136
    toughness and, 110, 122, 126–27, 129

War of Independence. *See* American Revolutionary War
War on Terrorism, 129–30
wars. *See* citizen soldiers; military
Washington, George, 61
Washington Post, vii, x

Washington's Birthday, 39
Wayne, John, 52
    alias, 46
Weaver, Sigourney, 112
West. *See* Old West
West Coast, vii–viii, 4. *See also* California
Western Action Shootists Association, 42
Western democracies, 139–40, 145, 153
westerns (movies). *See* entertainment and
        entertainment industry
white supremacists, ix, 15, 137
whites, 87, 92, 94, 101
    citizen soldiers, 65–67
    colonial society, 58–60, 80
    cowboy action shooting, 40, 43–44, 53, 89,
        101–2
    cowboy myths, 86, 92–94
    gun debate, 141–43, 151–53
    gun enthusiasts, 7, 11–13, 20
    gun ownership, viii–x, 8
    shooting sports, 34–35, 37
    toughness and, 121, 123
"Wild Phil Hiccup," 41–42
Wild West. *See* Old West
Wild West shows, 87, 112
wilderness. *See* civilization
Wilkinson, Rupert, 108
Wills, Garry, 137
women. *See also* personhood
    buying guns, 32
    citizen soldiers and, 65, 67–69
    colonial society, 59, 80
    cowboy action shooting, 39–41, 43, 45–47,
        49–51, 53
    feelings of safety, 13–14
    gun debate, 142–43, 160
    gun enthusiasts, 13, 20, 27–28, 106, 115–20,
        123–27
    gun ownership, 113–16, 118–27
    gun shops, 30
    guns and power, 13–14, 124–26
    interviews with, 3, 7, 9, 171–72
    misogyny, 12–13
    pro-gun organizations, vii, 121
    protection of, 107
    shooting classes and instructors, 26–27, 30,
        120, 123–26
    shooting sports, 35–38
    toughness, 106, 108, 110, 112–14, 129–30
    toughness and guns, 114–26
    violence against, viii
working class. *See* class
Wyatt Earp (movie), 86

Yale Law Review, ix
Yellow Pages, 20
Yosemite Sam, 48
young people, 153, 166–67. *See also* children

HV 8059 .K65 2004
Kohn, Abigail A.
Shooters